REMEMBERING WOMEN

REMEMBERING WOMEN

Lessons From The Ancient World

CHRISTINE LEHNEN

Published in the UK in 2025 by
Icon Books Ltd, Omnibus Business Centre,
39–41 North Road, London N7 9DP
email: info@iconbooks.com
www.iconbooks.com

ISBN: 978-183773-217-3
eBook: 978-183773-219-7

Text copyright © 2025 Christine Lehnen
The author has asserted her moral rights.

Every effort has been made to contact the copyright holders of the material reproduced in this book. If any have been inadvertently overlooked, the publisher will be pleased to make acknowledgement on future editions if notified.

No part of this book may be reproduced in any form, or by any means, without prior permission in writing from the publisher.

Typeset by SJmagic DESIGN SERVICES, India

Printed and bound in the UK

Appointed GPSR EU Representative: Easy Access System Europe Oü, 16879218
Address: Mustamäe tee 50, 10621, Tallinn, Estonia
Contact Details: gpsr.requests@easproject.com, +358 40 500 3575

For Milla

CONTENTS

Women & Memory ix
Introduction xi

1. Names 1
2. Mirrors 25
3. Play 47
4. Sex 69
5. Power 85
6. Teamwork 105
7. Partnership 125
8. Spotlight 139
9. Pleasure 157
10. Mourning 169

Conclusion – Afterlife 183

Acknowledgements 199
Bibliography 201
Endnotes 217
Index 243

WOMEN & MEMORY

There are women whose names we remember. They are few and far between, but some of them even become mythical. In fact, some of them have always been mythical, coming to life only in the stories we tell ourselves, the stories we invent to talk to each other about what it means to be human.

One of these women is called Helena. You may have heard of her as Helen of Troy. It is said that Troy and Greece went to war over her some three thousand years ago, and fought it out for ten years, and that the most beautiful city in the ancient world was captured and destroyed to win her back.

It is also said that you should not believe everything you hear.

There is another woman. Her name is Penthesilea. She is not remembered as widely as Helena. We have not recovered all the treasure of her story, her myth. It is said that she came to fight on the side of the Trojans in the war over Helen, to defend the city fighting for its survival, besieged by an aggressive enemy. She was born and raised a warrior woman on the southern coast of the Black Sea. The Greeks called her Queen of the Amazons, but she may have been a regular woman: a regular woman who chose to take up riding, hunting and fighting to make a living, who chose to fight in a war on the side of her allies, against an invading army, because that was the right thing to do. Her myth may have been based on historical women living in Ancient Scythia in the first millennium BCE, who spent their lives hunting and fighting, who were buried with their horses and their weapons.

Some things we choose not to believe, even when we should.

There are Helen and Penthesilea, and then there is my grandmother, whose name you have never heard, and my niece, whose name you do not know. There are millions of women alive, or who were once alive, whom we do not remember. This book is about them, and about us. It is about why we do not remember them, and what we are missing out on. It is about the stories no one has told you about, among them the most important story of all: the story of women and memory.

INTRODUCTION

I hesitated for a long time before writing a book on woman. The subject is irritating, especially for women; and it is not new.

These words are not mine, but they could be. This is how Simone de Beauvoir opens her book *The Second Sex*. Published in 1949, it went on to become a classic of modern feminism and can be found on the shelves of any well-stocked bookshop to this day.

When I first read *The Second Sex*, it was the year 2020, I was thirty years old, and I could relate. I had spent my whole life trying to pretend that it did not matter that I was a woman. It did not matter before the law, or so I thought. It did not matter in my career, or so I told myself, naively overlooking the many women who had had to fight for me to get to where I was. It did not matter to me personally, having grown up with two brothers, always a stick in hand pretending to be holding a sword, on a story diet of *The Lord of the Rings*, Greek myths and European fairytales. I was the hero of my own story, and whether I said hero or heroine did not matter, or so I believed. My mother, my aunt, my grandmother: They had suffered the oppression of the patriarchy. Neither my grandmother nor my aunt had been able to work without their husband's permission. My mother had become a surgeon, but it was made clear to her that she would never be promoted over a man, no matter how hard she worked or how well she performed in the operating theatre. These women had been held back, but not me, I thought. I had been given every opportunity, I had thrived, and the patriarchy was a thing of the past.

Then I separated from my boyfriend of seven years, the man I thought I would marry and have children with. I have met many men before him and since who said things that left me shocked: that it would ruin a relationship if I were to make more money than them, if I were to be more successful than them, if I were to become a famous writer, appointed a prestigious chair at a respected university, or win a coveted literary prize. Some said that they would not march for women's rights, because they were not their rights, and that I or any other woman could not contribute to any debate on the subject, because we would be prejudiced. A few of them felt it should be men who decided women's fates. Some felt that men were objective and women irrational.

In hindsight, I wonder why I continued to have friendships or relationships with men who said such things, and whether these relationships and friendships were always doomed to fail. At the time of my separation from my former boyfriend, however, I was heartbroken. He had been my first love, and we had imagined a future together. I was thirty at the time and felt that I had missed my only chance at happiness. I was convinced that I was too old to meet someone else, to have children, to make a meaningful romantic connection with another person.

We split up early in the year 2020. Three months later, the world went into lockdown. Living on my own for the first time

Introduction

in three years, with nothing but heartbreak to keep me company, I pulled the Vintage Feminism edition of *The Second Sex* off my shelf in an effort to distract myself from the dark mood I felt myself sliding into. I had bought the book years ago on a whim at Shakespeare & Company in Paris, promised myself to read it one day, put it on the shelf and promptly forgot about it. Until then, I had mostly devoured the books of more recent feminist and queer thinkers such as Judith Butler, Chimamanda Ngozi Adichie, Margarete Stokowski, Leïla Slimani and bell hooks. In spite of my former boyfriend's conviction, women and non-binary persons had many brilliant things to say about the way we lived our lives. I did not think that I needed de Beauvoir.

It turns out that I had been wrong. Once I started reading *The Second Sex*, I found that I could not stop. De Beauvoir's writing would change the way I looked at the world.

While intersectional and genderqueer feminists in the past fifty years have opened up the gender rights movement to include an ever-growing portion of humanity, moving beyond de Beauvoir's analysis, what she added to my feminist thinking was the long view, the look at the past: she inspired me to take a historical approach to feminist thinking. De Beauvoir did not write only about her own present; instead, she scoured the past for the origins of the inequality she experienced in her everyday life throughout the twentieth century. This opened my eyes to a whole new way of looking at the past, and would eventually lead to my return to university to complete doctoral studies at the University of Manchester on how we remember women from the past, and why we forget so many of them.

At the same time as I was reading de Beauvoir and preparing for a return to research, my grandmother was battling advanced dementia. When I went to visit her, I believe that she knew I was a person who loved her, and whom she had loved, even though she was no longer sure who I was. At this late stage of her dementia, we could not have a conversation in the traditional sense. As her memories vanished – memories of a long life lived in a tumultuous and violent century, I could no longer tell her about the research project that was taking shape in my mind, about how fascinating I found the way we come together as a society to commemorate some events, remember some people, grieve some lives, while forgetting entirely about others. I could not tell her that many of the people we choose to forget are women, particularly women of colour, and women with little power or money. Women like her, who grew up on a farm in rural Germany in the early twentieth century, where families would still go hungry or even starve when crops failed, and where entire families would leave no traces in the records other than a line or two in the parish book. We do not grieve these women as a society. All the women and men my grandmother had known, her brothers and sisters, her mother and father, her grandmothers and grandfathers, lived on only in her memories, and those were fading fast.

I could not tell her about any of these thoughts. What I could do was dress her in her favourite coat and cap, push her wheelchair up into fields, north of her nursing home, to visit the horses and see the wildflowers in bloom. On a rainy day, I could take out the old family photo album, the precious sepia photographs, and look at them with her. I could say to her, this is the house you lived in, this is the church you used to go to, this is your brother as a child, the brother you loved so much, whose funeral we went to five years ago, although the care home suggested we had better not, because it might

Introduction

upset you. It did not upset you. You loved travelling, you loved going somewhere with us, and you wanted to be there with him. You were very clear that day, and saw many members of your family, your sons, your grandchildren, whom you loved. I knew some of these things because my grandmother had noted the names of people and places below the photos, in her spidery handwriting that I sometimes found difficult to decipher. Paling traces of a bygone era. Others I could say to her because they made up part of my own memories. I remembered how much she had loved her brother, how alert she had been on the day of his funeral, how fondly she had spoken of the village where she had grown up. The stories we tell each other are so important, because they keep the candle of remembrance burning: every story we tell prolongs the life of a memory by another day, another year, perhaps another generation. My grandmother had told me about her brother, about her village, about the apples she used to pick from a neighbour's garden so that she would not go hungry while pregnant with my aunt in the middle of a war: because she told me, I was able to guard those memories, to care for them and pass them on, even as they were fading from her mind.

As I sat with my grandmother, stroking her hand or rubbing her neck or brushing her hair, I realised that my memories of her would be lost one day, just as her memories of her grandmother had gone to a place where she could no longer share them with me. No one would remember her pain or her triumphs, her joy at travelling, the diligence with which she would fit her seat belt, always insisting she had to do it herself, even while battling dementia, determined to keep moving, to see even more of the world she loved so much. She would be one of those women that we choose to forget.

My grandmother died on Christmas Eve, just shy of ninety-nine years old, one year after I had begun my research on the way we remember women from history, and what our memory, and memory loss, says about us as a society. I have learned that the way we look at the past is still deeply patriarchal. In fact, we remember the past as a place of the patriarchy. We assume that women of the past were oppressed, that they lived grim and miserable lives, that they were prisoners of men, wherever they found themselves in the world, however far we look back into time.

I discovered this same assumption in de Beauvoir's analysis of women's place in the world, and women's place in history. In *The Second Sex*, she writes that 'there have always been women; they are women by their physiological structure; as far back as history can be traced, they have always been subordinate to men.'[1]

And she wonders: why is that? 'Why is it that this world has always belonged to men and that only today things are beginning to change?'[2]

Sharing a conviction still widely held to today, Simone de Beauvoir believed women had always been, as far as human history goes back, oppressed by men. Much of contemporary feminism focuses on recent gains in the movement. Emancipation and equal rights are still considered a recent invention, a privilege, a gift given to us in the West by modern times.

It is unsurprising that we should think so. The idea that our world has historically belonged to men is deeply entrenched in anglophone Western culture. It is a misconception, but one that props up the patriarchy as powerfully as any institution, code of law, or system of governance. It is a story, a fable, a myth, a collective memory that we believe to be true, even though it is not.

Introduction

This collective memory has grown out of the foundational stories that we are raised on in the West, and in turn pass on to our children: in the creation myths of the Abrahamic religions as they are told today, man is created first, followed by woman.[3] The story of Adam and Eve goes further, once the Christian apostle and missionary Paulus transplants it into patriarchal Ancient Greek and Roman society: he uses it to paint women not only as inferior but also as sexually sinful, as the bringers of evil. The Roman Emperor Augustus completes this unholy alliance of religion and power when he presents sexual urges as demonic and women as eternal seductresses in league with the devil.[4]

This is mirrored in the fate of Pandora in Greek myth, an even older story: Prometheus at first creates only male clay figures, and it is not until Pandora comes along that women join men on Earth. You might remember her jar, later mistranslated as a box by Erasmus of Rotterdam,[5] bringing all evil into the world. But the jar and its evils are inventions that don't appear in older versions of that myth: it is only with Hesiod, living in the second to third centuries BCE, that the jar enters the picture.[6] And he may be biased, as far as we can tell. The way Hesiod writes about women, one can only assume that he was not very lucky in love.

Even today, it is commonly accepted that Western civilisation springs from two sources: the Bible on the one hand, and the cultures of Ancient Greece and Ancient Rome on the other, what we would call the Classics.[7] Their eras are considered the foundational periods to our present, and it is both the Bible and antiquity that we keep turning back to when searching for who we are and where we come from.[8] They make up an important part of our *cultural memory*.[9]

In human societies, cultural memory serves to explain and legitimise our present. This in turn serves our deeply ingrained need to explain the way the world is, a psychological trap we are all born with: we look at the things in the world and believe that they must have a purpose, that they are the way they are for a reason.[10] In order to explain why our world looks the way it does, we look at the past and turn antiquity into a story, a myth, an oftentimes inaccurate memory of a foundational past; reducing it to Archaic Greece and Classical Athens, to male philosophers and male playwrights, to male voters and male democracy, to male power and male domination. And we have made the Bible into a myth as well, into a text that has no precedent and no inheritors, less a rich expression of human thinking and faith than a foundational story that preserves the power of men in the present.

As I continued my research into our memory culture, I realised that too little had changed about the way we look at the past and women's place in it. Memory scholars know that myths are immensely powerful, whether national, religious, ethnic or otherwise. Myths create identities, collective and individual. They are not true stories, but we take them to be. Our cultural memory describes how we conceive of ourselves; it explains our present to us and defines what we consider normal, natural, and good. It even shapes how we envision progress and a better future.[11]

Memory studies is an inter-disciplinary research field that first emerged in the second half of the twentieth century. While all historians look at the past – at what we can know about it – memory scholars look specifically at how we use the past in the present and for the future.

Remembering Women: Lessons from the Ancient World is a book about cultural memory. More specifically, it is a book about the cultural memory of women in the anglophone West. It is also a book about my grandmother, my mother, my aunt, myself, and my niece, a line of women whom cultural memory would consign to the sidelines, the footnotes, the dustbin of the archive. And it is about the women from myth that we remember, such as Helen, and the stories we have lost, such as the tale of Penthesilea. In Greek myth, Penthesilea is a fearsome warrior and Queen of the Amazons, an all-female community of warriors riding into battle on horseback. As the daughter of Ares, the god of war, she fights in the Trojan War against the Greek hero Achilles. He kills her in battle but falls in love with her at the moment of her death, when he removes the helmet of his vanquished foe and sees her face for the first time.

Amazons were long believed to be a figment of the Greek patriarchal imagination: a group of women that possessed all the freedoms that Greek women did not. However, due to advances in bioarchaeological methods and the more reliable sexing of skeletons, evidence is accumulating that these legendary warrior women had historical counterparts in the real world: in antiquity, Scythian women rode into battle, died in combat, and were buried with their weapons and horses. They lived on the outskirts of the Greek world, in the liminal spaces of Asia Minor, where they would have come into contact with citizens of Greek city states on the western coast of Turkey. According to Stanford research scholar Adrienne Mayor, Greek legends of fearsome Amazons may have been based on reports of and encounters with real warrior women from Scythia who rode into battle with bow and arrow or axes.[12] As she explores the mounting evidence for the existence of Amazon-like warrior women in Asia Minor and beyond in her pathbreaking study *The Amazons: Lives and Legends of Warrior Women Across the Ancient World*, she comes to the conclusion that, while the Amazon Queen Penthesilea may be mythical, women like her were very real. They lived, fought, died and thrived in Scythian communities in the first millennium BCE. Yet, in spite of the accumulating evidence, we have not learnt their stories; most of us do not know that they were real; we do not think of their history as our own.

This needs to change. In this book, I argue that if we make their stories part of our history, part of our cultural memory, we will make life better for women in the present. If we fail to do so, we will continue to experience setbacks to achieving gender equality in the future, and it will never seem normal and natural to us.

At its heart, that is what this book is about: the stories we could be telling each other to make a better life for the women around us, and those who come after us, and about what our foremothers have to teach us about how to live a better life, whether we are women, men, or neither. At the end of this book, I want to have shown you how we can use our cultural memory for good, and what we can do to do right by the women of our past. Women such as my grandmother. Women such as Penthesilea or Helen of Troy. Women such as you or I, your sister or your daughter, your friends or your family.

But before we can turn to our foremothers, before we can think about how to retell the story of the past in such a way as to make life better for women and girls in the present, we need to look at what exactly cultural memory is.

The Three Levels of Collective Memory

There are two scholars who have been particularly influential in contemporary memory studies: Jan and Aleida Assmann. Born

Introduction

towards the end of and just after the Second World War respectively, they went on to study Egyptology and, in Aleida's case, English, with stations in Heidelberg, Munich, Tübingen and Paris. They were working on archaeology and memory when the social renewal movements of the 1968 generation swept through German and European institutions, removing former NSDAP officials from positions of authority and striving for a more liberal and fair society. From 1968, the Assmanns would spend their time on archaeological digs in Upper Egypt for the following seven years. Inspired by the way that the Ancient Egyptians conceived of time, history, and memory, and shocked by the way that collective memory had been abused by the Nazis to justify the Holocaust, war, and atrocities committed all over the world, they set out to rethink collective memory after the end of the Second World War. Drawing on the work of many of their colleagues and predecessors, they revolutionised our understanding of memory and the uses we put the past to.

Jan Assmann has proposed to differentiate between three levels of memory: personal memory, communicative memory, and cultural memory.[13]

Personal memory is what an individual remembers. It consists of all the neurological and mental processes involved in individual memory-making and forgetting, and is the primary purview of neurologists, psychologists, and oral historians. It is framed and shaped by communicative and cultural memory. My grandmother had personal memories that were lost as she battled dementia.

Communicative memory is what we remember in conversation with each other and our families. It is a form of collective memory and consists of those events and processes in the past that we talk about with our parents and grandparents, our children and grandchildren. Communicative memory is not fixed. Every family, every intergenerational memory community will have its own. However, communicative memory is shaped by cultural memory; memory communities within the same memory culture are likely to experience significant overlaps in what they remember.

The field of communicative memory is the purview of sociologists and oral historians. In the United States and Europe, memory of the First and Second World Wars is on the threshold of passing out of communicative memory; soon, no one who witnessed these events will be alive. Communicative memory generally stretches across three generations and covers eighty to one hundred years. My grandmother and I shared communicative memories. Through her, I am connected to the decades of the twentieth century in Western Europe that I did not experience, among them the Second World War, the student uprisings in the 1960s, the oil crisis in the 1970s, and the criminalisation of rape in marriage in the 1990s in Germany and elsewhere.

The final category is *cultural memory*. It falls into the purview of cultural and literary critics, classicists, historians of ancient and pre-history, theologians and philosophers. Cultural memory is made up of those events that a collective locates in its distant, foundational, even mythical past. This past is remembered and kept alive through rituals, images, icons, commemorations, sacred and foundational texts, and performances of various kinds.

The story of the Trojan War is a perfect example of an event belonging to cultural memory: Homer's *Iliad*, set during the Trojan War, is routinely referred to as the founding piece of Western literature,[14] and the Trojan War cast as a founding moment of Western civilisation. Famously, medieval poets

Introduction

and scholars believed that Britain had been founded by survivors of the Trojan War and that the legendary King Arthur descended from the ranks of the Trojan refugees.[15] The Trojan War continues to occupy a peculiar place in our collective memory, implicitly remembered as a historical event rather than a fiction, in spite of the evidence. Although an ancient city was discovered in eastern Turkey in Anatolia, which is today considered to have been Troy, and which may have been called Wilusa by those who lived there, it is highly unlikely that a ten-year war was fought on its doorstep. It is more probable that a series of smaller raids and catastrophes beset the ancient city of Wilusa, a vassal state of the Hittite Empire on the coast of the Aegean Sea.[16]

And yet, the Trojan War makes up part of our cultural memory. The Trojan War has recently been updated in countless ways: British novelists have written novels set during or after the Trojan War, global streaming platforms have produced a mini-series adapting the *Iliad*, and in 2019, the British Museum presented a major exhibition called *Troy: myth and reality*. Alongside the Bible, the *Iliad* still shapes our culture and our memory today – our cultural, communicative, and personal memories, the norms we set ourselves in the present, for example with regard to whether a woman should be able to go outside at night without fear for her life, whether consent in sexual relationships is crucial, and what we think makes a 'strong woman' or a 'heroic man'.

This is because the boundaries between personal, communicative and cultural memory are porous. It is better to think of them not as borders but as membranes, which can be permeated from all directions. Cultural memory needs to be constantly updated if it is to remain salient. It is always mediated and comes to us through the hands of experts. According to Jan Assmann, these used to consist of shamans, poets, clerks, priests, rabbis, mullahs. In the West today, significant influence is exerted by historians, researchers, museums and heritage professionals, politicians, civil servants in education ministries, novelists, writers, and journalists.

Together with these people, we can retell the story of the past in a way that benefits women and girls, because all of them retell stories to update our cultural memory for the present. During the course of this update, cultural memory is adapted to present circumstances and changing norms. It shifts, transforms, until it is once more able to fulfil its function: to endow a group in the present with a collective identity and shared norms rooted in the powerful legitimising illusion of a shared foundational past. We must remember the same cultural memories in order to belong to the same group.[17]

Cultural memory creates the past that we need in order for us to think of our lives in the present as normal. We use the past to make sense of our present, even to justify it. Memory is part of a normative order, an 'order of justification', in the terms of German philosopher Rainer Forst.[18] This means that it performs a normalising function, in that it serves as a source of narratives that help us justify our lives in the present.[19] What we want from the past is legitimacy, to rest safe in the knowledge that the present is all right, and that we are part of an enduring tradition, an enduring collective. That is why we are tempted to remember the past as a place of the patriarchy, why we retain the memory of men rather than women: to justify the continued marginalisation of women in the present. Unless we make women a part of our cultural memory, gender equality will always seem strange to us, like a modern invention, an arrangement that is not part of human nature. It means that feminist progress will always remain up for grabs, as we witnessed in the United States when the Supreme Court overturned federal abortion rights in 2022, giving as a reason that a woman's right to choose was 'not deeply rooted in this Nation's history or tradition'.[20]

However, we are lucky: cultural memory can be shaped. It is not only a tool of the powerful, it does not consist only of an archive of oppression. Aleida Assmann points out that the archive is in fact the place where we can go to change the canon of cultural memory.[21] Assmann emphasises that the canon is always in flux, as new and old stories are taken from or returned to the archive, transforming the cultural memory and cultural attitudes of a given collective in the process. As we retell stories, we change our cultural memory.

This is what we are witnessing today: writers, novelists, journalists, and museums are working in new ways with the Trojan War narrative and Greek myth, they are turning to the past, to their collections, their knowledge, our cultural archive, to update the canon, to transform our cultural memory and our attitudes in the present. Some of them wish to make this a feminist transformation: to remember the women from history who have been silenced by poets, prophets, priests, and historians in the past. If we transform our memory in such a way, then we will enable women and men to live better lives in the present, and make it easier for us to work towards gender equality in the future.

The reason why our cultural memory matters is because it is so powerful at changing norms: the rules we live by, the things we think of as normal. Conversely, it is also very good at upholding outdated norms. This is one of the reasons why discriminating norms and sexist behaviours endure long after laws have been changed and punishments meted out for them.

Take the nature of the culture around rape in Western societies: as studies on the endurance of rape myths have shown, one third of the adult population in the UK still believe that women are fully or partly to blame when they are raped.[22] Common rape myths include: if women drink or take drugs on a night out, it is their fault if they are raped; that women lie about being raped to get attention, take revenge on specific men, or when they regret having had sex with someone in hindsight; that women 'are asking for it' if they wear an outfit the perpetrator considers attractive; that a woman was not really raped if she did not scream, run away or fight back; that men cannot 'help themselves' once they get turned on and have to have sex; that women 'play hard to get' and say no when they mean yes; and that women should not go out alone at night if they do not want to get raped.[23]

These myths have been comprehensively debunked.[24] The victim is never responsible for the rape; false accusations of rape are vanishingly rare; it is common for victims to find they cannot move or speak, because this is a normal reaction of our body to danger and fear; there is no scientific evidence that men cannot control their sexual urges; and 86 per cent of women are raped by someone they know rather than a stranger in a dark alleyway, so not going out after dark will not help them.

The facts seem to make little difference to the endurance of rape myths. As a rather exasperated spokesperson from Rape Crisis England and Wales put it in 2021: 'Although we've had, for over 15 years, a clear definition of "consent" in law, and in fact have some of the most progressive sexual violence laws in Europe, we haven't seen a culture shift alongside that's essential to embed change.'²⁵

One of the reasons why we are not seeing this cultural shift is that our norms do not only spring from our laws – they also spring from our history, or rather our cultural memory, and what we choose to remember from our past, what we consider to have been normal throughout history.

This is one of the many reasons why we are experiencing a moment in Western societies where many women wish to challenge the perceived version of history, to decide afresh who our foremothers were, how they ought to be remembered, what this means for how we think of ourselves as women today and what we can imagine for our daughters in the future. They are convinced, as am I, that we need to change our memory of the past if we are to see progress in the present: if we want to see a world where women and girls can go outside at night without fear, where women are not ignored in middle age, and where women of all ages are in control of their bodies and the choices they make about them.

The Story So Far

What is the story that we tell each other about women in the past? We have all been raised on the tales of Adam and Eve, of Pandora and her jar, of witch hunts and women as victims. The story does not change, or so we learn, until the advent of the Enlightenment in eighteenth-century Europe. This is when women such as Olympe de Gouges or Mary Wollstonecraft began to demand equal rights, supported by a few exceptional men, among them the philosopher John Stuart Mill. Their pleas fell on deaf ears until the First World War came around: with millions of young men at the frontlines, women had to step up, work in their jobs, run farms and factories. This was a watershed moment. After the war, women were no longer content with their lot and organised to lobby for equal rights, building on the important work of earlier activists. With republics proclaimed all over Europe and social democratic parties rising to power, women finally received the right to vote in the interwar years, bestowed upon them as a gift by men in power. Sometime in the early twentieth century, give or take a few decades, men were kind enough to allow them to go to universities and to work even in peacetime.

To younger people, this might feel like ancient history. An eighteen-year-old voting in their first council election will take it for granted that there will be women and men in the queue outside the polling station. And yet, things are not so simple: the disenfranchisement of women is not as far behind us as we would like to believe. It still exists on the edges of our living memory, of oral history. My grandmother was born only five years after women won voting rights in the Weimar Republic. She would have heard stories from her mother about the many years in which she had not been allowed to cast her vote. It still makes up part of our communicative memory: the time when women were not allowed to vote. When they were considered too irrational, too hysterical, or too childish.

This is even more true of women's right to choose. My grandmother remembers a time when women had no such right. So does my mother. Consider the persistence of rape myths: my grandmother was seventy-one when parliament finally decided that it was illegal to rape your wife. My mother was already married to my father, she had already given birth to three children. One of them was me. Even within my lifetime, it was still legal for husbands to rape their wives. This is part of our communicative memory. It is part of our personal memory. That consent matters is not deeply embedded in our collective memory. It feels new. And whatever is considered new, can be turned back. Whatever is considered new, we are suspicious of. Will this last? Is this part of our future, or is it just a fad, a phase, a quirky little idea that is going to be outlasted, outgunned, by what we think of as human nature? Through its absence in our cultural memory, gender equality is not an immutable norm; women's rights in the West are still under threat.

All of the progress we have made in the past century for women, girls, and non-binary people is at the risk of being rolled back when it is not considered normal, not part of a collective's history or tradition. This is true even for progress that we take for granted, such as women going to work. It is still the norm for women to take on the majority of childcare duties, domestic labour, and the labour of reproduction, much to their disadvantage. Women who succeed in their professional lives are more common than they used to be, but they are still considered to be an exception to the rule. They make up part of our communicative memory although not of our cultural one. Since the early twentieth century, a few exceptional women have made it to the top, the story goes, such as German Chancellor Angela Merkel, Taiwanese President Tsai Ing-wen, or Christine Lagarde, director of the International Monetary Fund and later the European Central Bank. But these women are not quite normal; they are 'not like other girls', a phrase that any woman enjoying even a modicum of professional success will have heard applied to her at one point or another.

If select women achieve something extraordinary, this implies, it is because they are different from other women. Women in general are not capable of exceptional deeds, the story goes, are only a few exceptional women. That is because women succeeding – all women, not just a select few, like Queen Elizabeth I or Boudicca or Princess Leia or Wonder Woman – is not part of our cultural memory.

Instead, the role reserved for women in our cultural memory is that of oppression. Most women in our cultural memory are cast as either victims or villains, meek and subservient or dangerous and rebellious. The memory of the past that we created during the emergence of the modern European nation state in the 1800s, the myths we invented to explain and justify our patriarchal, colonial present, are still very much alive: they tell us that women are inferior and evil. The new stories, the contemporary myths from communicative memory, allow that there are a few exceptional women who may be heroines, but even these are new inventions, a fruit of male progress, a modern phenomenon without a past, without history, without tradition or precedent.

That is the story we tell ourselves today. As women. As men. As non-binary people. About ourselves, and about each other. This is our cultural memory, our history of women, even in the twenty-first century. This is the history that will gloss over the Amazon warrior woman Penthesilea, vilify Helen of Troy, and consign my grandmother to the dustbin of the past: women are villains, or women are victims. Only a few exceptional women will rise to the top, but these are aberrations: They aren't really women.

However, this is not what the past tells us. It is not what the material world tells us. It is not the stories that our ancestors tell us, their bones, their graves, their tales. That is not what history tells us.

We do not remember the whole story.

We do not remember that there were women in antiquity and beyond who may have led independent lives in egalitarian societies.[26] In these societies, women were not reduced to their roles as mothers, wives, or daughters. They may have been craftspeople, poets, warriors, artists; invented the battle axe and besieged the city of Athens; painted the artworks in the caves of Lascaux; raised an army when their sisters were in peril; ruled a state on Bronze-Age Crete; fought and won; loved and lived; died and left us their bones, their belongings, their legacies.

There is precedent for more egalitarian communities in the past. These communities do not need to have been utopias of perfect gender equality for us to be able to learn from and build on their gender politics in the present. Ancient Scythia was made up of complex and diverse communities and practices, some deeply patriarchal, others not. What their more egalitarian practices show us is that gender equality is not an aberration. Throughout time, humans have been able to find ways to live together as equals. We have done it before. We can do it again.

This is a book about the times and places when this may have been the case. If we are to change the way we think about history, we must remember those times, and the historical and mythological heroines of antiquity and prehistory that we have forgotten; we must understand why they have been forgotten; and how we can use what they have left us to build a better future. Together, we will put heroic women at the heart of our cultural memory, women like my grandmother or the rulers of

Minoan Crete or the warrior women from Scythia, so that we can understand the heroic efforts of women today and create a better future for our daughters, nieces, and all the women who will come after us.

Remembering Women

I invite you to travel back in time with me. I ask you to accompany me on a journey into the unknown depths of our collective memory. Together, we will dive into the deep sea of time. We will recover the treasures from the bottom of the ocean of history that will allow us as women to have a history, to have a memory of our own. A past in which we were not victims but actors, not silenced but outspoken, not locked up inside our homes but out in the world, changing it, living life, having fun, making the world a better place – in short: a past in which each and every one of us was a heroine, and in which we said yes to everything life had to offer.

We will also discover why these treasures have not been salvaged before, and which other treasures have been brought up and put in museum displays in their stead. Since our interest is in cultural memory, we will have to dive to the very bottom of the ocean, to those periods of our past that we think of as foundational, as primordial, in the terms of memory scholars.

We will travel back to and even beyond antiquity, but not to look at parts of the ocean of the past that are already well-known to us: the treasures of Athens; of the male politicians, poets, and philosophers. Instead, we will attempt to discover the treasures of Scythia.

Introduction

Scythia is a term used by Ancient Greek historians to describe lands and nomadic and semi-nomadic cultures living on an area reaching from the Black Sea to the Himalayas and across the Altai mountains, from the country we today call Georgia to the present day's People's Republic of China.

For centuries, researchers assumed that women in Ancient Scythian communities would have been oppressed in the same way as their counterparts in Ancient Greece. Some still think so. However, recent discoveries in archaeology, cultural studies, history, and linguistics paint a very different picture of a woman's life in some communities in Ancient Scythia about three thousand years ago: a life that may have been lived in equality and freedom.[27]

Due to advances in bioarchaeological methods, scholars have discovered that one out of three Scythian woman was an active warrior buried with her weapons.[28] Far from being confined to their homes, these women rode out to hunt, travelled to distance places, or used weapons to fend off their enemies. They were buried with arrows, swords, and the bones of their loyal horses – in significant numbers. If one out of three women in some Ancient Scythian communities was an active warrior, then they were not exceptions to the rule. It must have been normal, seemed natural, for women in these communities to take up arms and act as the equals of men.

Such a choice may have had consequences far beyond the realm of warfare. Stories from Ancient Scythia abound not only with queens and princesses, but also with councils made up of women who were in charge of the affairs of their communities. The Scythians have left behind no writing of their own, but they have left us traces of their lives in their graves. We have their bones, their mirrors and swords, their arrowheads and bows, their hemp seeds and make-up, the skeletons of their horses and children, their stories and legends.

The Ancient Greek historians wrote of Scythian communities as egalitarian, and so did Ancient Greek storytellers. Stanford scholar Adrienne Mayor believes that these women were the historical counterparts of mythical Amazon warrior women such as Penthesilea.[29] It is only later that these heroic women and egalitarian societies were forgotten, and only now that their treasures can once be more salvaged, their lives remembered.

Similar treasures were left to us by women in areas as diverse as Minoan Crete and Stone Age Asia Minor, as well as the more familiar world of Ancient Greece, but in our collective memory of the past, we prioritise the heirlooms of Classical Athens. What we remember – and what we have forgotten – still implicates women and men today, casting us as opposing forces in the struggle for equality. But it does not have to be this way.

If we are to reframe our past, it is important to consider what has been generally remembered and believed, rather than what is known within expert circles. The stories we tell each other about the past matter – memory mystifies and generalises, it turns history into myth. That is why it is so powerful, and why we need to examine it very carefully. As Suzannah Lipscomb has pointed out in *What Is History, Now?*, for feminist historians, it is especially important to look for the gaps in the record, the silences in the archive, for those episodes where the historical narrative does not add up.[30]

Our memory of the ancients provides us with plenty such gaps: we remember Plato, and are taught about Helen of Troy, and sometimes visit the Acropolis – but has anyone ever told

Introduction

you that Plato wrote about our heroic foremothers in Scythia and said it would be better to raise girls and boys as equals?[31]

Have you ever read about the mythical warrior woman Penthesilea, who nearly saved the city of Troy from ruin, and wondered why it is that our great playwrights William Shakespeare and Christopher Marlowe wrote plays performed to this day that prefer to feature Helen of Troy than Penthesilea the warrior queen?

You may even have been to the Acropolis in Athens, and no one may have mentioned that the Athenians believed that an army of Scythian warrior women laid siege to it and nearly took the city of Athens when it was first founded – warrior women that already may have had much more sophisticated democratic processes than what the Athenians liked to think of as the perfect democracy.

If we explore these gaps, recover those treasures, put them into museum displays for all to see, a different story of the past emerges: a past in which it was possible for women to live as the equals of men, providing precedent for gender equal societies and inspiring us to develop new ideas for lived equality in the present. Women and men, living together as equals: that is part of our history, of our tradition as humans.

In ten chapters, beginning at the moment of our birth and taking us all the way to the day we die and are mourned, *Remembering Women* traverses a woman's life in the modern West and uses literary and material evidence from Ancient Scythia and beyond to demonstrate that things do not have to be the way they are today. Focusing on Scythia, we will look at communities from the past where independent women were not the exception to the rule, where they were cherished and able to flourish: as children, teenagers, mothers, political leaders, elders and even in death.

I hesitated for a long time before writing a book on woman. The subject is irritating, especially for women; and it is not new.

But it should be. Because we have not been remembering the whole story.

Time to change that.

So far, the story we have been telling each other about women from the past has been holding us back. Our mnemonic meta-narrative runs like this: in the past, women were either helpless victims or active villains. Some extraordinary women have been allowed to thrive – queens, presidents, heroines – but they are the exception to the rule. They are 'not like other girls'.

That is not what the past looked like for all women. We must change the story we have been telling each other about women in the past to account for the mounting evidence that women have been living as the equals of men in different places and different ways at various historical moments in time. We must understand that it could be normal for us to live like this: egalitarian communities have a tradition, and they have existed before. Otherwise, we will always believe that there is something not quite normal, not quite natural about women and men as equals.

Our foremothers can help us with this. They have left us many traces of their lives, countless objects in their graves that allow us to retell the story of the past, and discover a new and better cultural memory for women and men.

We will begin our discovery with an heirloom that powerfully defines our individual identities. It is something that we all own, each and every one of us. Some of us are asked to give it up. Some do so gladly. Others wish to keep it. Men, more often than not, are not asked to give up theirs.

I am speaking of names.

1. NAMES

Both my grandmothers gave up their last names on their wedding day. They each lost that part of their self forever, but it would have been unthinkable not to take the name of their husbands. In fact, it would have been illegal. They both grew up in Germany, where couples were legally obliged to adopt the husband's surname until 1976. They could not even have chosen to double-barrel their surnames. This only became possible in 1958, long after they were married.

My mother made use of the privilege and double-barrelled her surname. Imagine her surprise when she went to see a solicitor with my father in the year 2022, nearly 30 years after she had married, to find the solicitor rise from his chair, greet my father with his correct name, then turn to my mother and address her with my father's surname, as if she had no name of her own. In one single interaction, he had erased her. She was no more but an extension of my father.

My mother was seething when she told me about this, and so was I. Names are powerful. Our name is the first thing that is given to us, and in contemporary Western culture, it is the only thing we take to our graves with us. Someone puts it onto our headstone, sometimes while we are still alive to see it. They engrave it into stone or carve it into wood.

However, in the case of many women, the name that is given to them at birth is not the name that will go on their headstone. For centuries, women were forced to give up their last names, and it is still expected of them to this day. Significantly more women change their last name upon marriage than men.[1]

This matters for our collective and cultural memory, because women are often forgotten as a consequence, appearing under different names in local, regional, or national archives, in media reports, in government registers, and in the public realm. This contributes to the Gender Data Gap[2] because we learn fewer things about women from the past, but it also makes it more difficult for women in the present: if you are working in a professional career, it is significantly more difficult to make a name for yourself when you have to do it twice. That is why women who work in professional careers, particularly the arts, research, politics, or journalism, are more likely to hold onto their last names than they used to be.

However, even that is not as simple as it may sound. When Australian scientist Kate Robb discovered a new species of dolphin, she was still carrying the last name of her husband, whom she had married at a young age. After a subsequent divorce, she was afraid that reverting back to her maiden name would cost her the reputation and career she had worked so hard to build. It took her years to finally find the courage to let go of her ex-husband's name and go back to being Kate Robb, a name she felt represented who she was.[3]

The tradition of women giving up their name makes up part of our collective memory. It can be traced back to Ancient Greece and beyond, to the ancient empires of the Middle East, often considered one of the cradles of human civilisation. In the Neolithic, communities of hunter-gatherers settled and became farming societies. The transition from relatively egalitarian hunter-gatherer societies to patriarchal farming societies was a complex and centuries-long process which yielded different results in different areas of the world,[4] but one consequence of a certain kind of farming society was that possessions came into existence. In many hunter-gatherer societies, the notion of exclusively owning land or food would have seemed absurd. Game that was hunted, food that was gathered, was shared. Reputation mattered more than anything else in these communities, and the easiest way to gain reputation was to share. In fact, it was a necessity: all had to contribute, otherwise there would not have been enough to go around.[5]

In later farming societies, people owned land and generated surpluses that needed to be stored and defended against those less fortunate. In some farming societies, sons were preferred for the protection of the stores, so they had to be kept nearby. In other words: these societies became patrilocal. From now on, young women went to live with their husband's family after marriage.[6]

They also became patrilineal: it was the father's name and lineage that were passed on to and through the children, most importantly sons, because they needed to retain possession of the land and the food stores.

With the passing on of the male name came the forgetting of the female name. As men's names were recorded and retained, women's disappeared from record and posterity.

This patriarchal practice had been perfected by the heyday of Ancient Greece, in particular in Classical Athens. That is how the story commonly goes, this is the tradition we place ourselves in – with dreadful consequences for the memory of women. We barely retain the memory of any historical women living in Ancient Greece. Unless we have undergone specialist training, we might remember only Greek men such as Plato, Aristotle, and Socrates, the poet Homer, the mathematician Pythagoras.

If we enjoy the theatre, it may also occur to us to name a number of ancient playwrights, most notably Sophocles for his *Antigone*, Euripides and his *Trojan Women*, maybe even Aristophanes and his *Lysistrata*, a play in which Greek women decide to enter into a sex strike to end the Peloponnesian War.

Plenty of women, then, one might argue: Antigone, the women of Troy, among them Hecuba, Helen, Andromache, and all the wives and mistresses of all the men in Athens.

However, all of these are fictional, sometimes even mythical women. This is also the case for the great pantheon of Greek goddesses we would probably immediately be able to name: Athene, goddess of war and wisdom, Aphrodite, goddess of beauty, Hera, wife of Zeus, God of gods.

None of these women were real. I cannot think of them as someone to emulate, because I am not a goddess, or a princess. My life does not consist of a two- or three- or even eight-hour-snapshot in the theatre or an epic poem. Even the Greek audiences themselves would probably not have thought of these women as real, not in the sense of a fellow human being made of flesh and blood. Women were not allowed to perform, and it is unlikely that women were even allowed to attend the theatre. The women we encounter in Greek popular culture and myth never had a body; they never lived.

And yet, in spite of the difficulties faced by the women of Ancient Greece, some of their names have come down to us.

If we look at how and why we have been able to retain their names, how they have been saved for our collective memory, we can understand the deeply sexist nature of our cultural memory as it operates today, before turning to our foremothers in Scythia and finding out how they might help us.

Let us begin by looking at the women from Ancient Greece. If we try to think of *historical* women from that period of human history, who comes to mind?

If you are interested in antiquity, you might think of the poet Sappho. And then maybe the courtesan Aspasia or Phryne. Those are the three historical women from Ancient Greece featuring in the popular radio show *Natalie Haynes Stands Up for the Classics*. How did their names survive, and what does that tell us about the misogyny of our cultural memory today?

Art and Memory

Sappho was a poet who lived on the island of Lesbos from around 630 to 570 BCE. It is from her that we retain the adjective sapphic, and from the island where she lived the word lesbian. Sappho was a lover of women, as her poetry will readily reveal to you. Many of the fragments we retain of her poetry deal with 'her girls'. One is a fragment on jealousy surrounding a former lover called Atthis, a Greek female name and the name of the region where Athens was to be founded, Attica:

> I loved thee Atthis, once long ago
> In doubt I am, I have two minds,
> I know not what to do.
> With my two arms, I do not aspire to touch the sky.

> So, like a child after its mother, I flutter.
> The messenger of Spring, the sweet-voiced night-
>   ingale.
> Now Love, the ineluctable, with bitter sweetness
> Fills me, overwhelms me, and shakes my being.
> But to thee, Atthis, the thought of me is hateful;
>   thou fliest to
> Andromeda.[7]

Sappho, incidentally, wrote about the Trojan War and its women, although her focus is on the desirability of a woman named Anactoria in the present rather than the victimhood of women in the past:

> A troop of horse, the serried ranks of marchers,
> A noble fleet, some think these of all on earth
> Most beautiful. For me naught else regarding
> Is my beloved.
>
> To understand this is for all most simple,
> For thus gazing much on mortal perfection
> And knowing already what life could give her,
> Him chose fair Helen,
>
> Him the betrayer of Ilium's honour.
> Then recked she not of adored child or parent,
> But yielded to love, and forced by her passion,
> Dared Fate in exile.
>
> Thus quickly is bent the will of that woman
> To whom things near and dear seem to be nothing.

> So mightest thou fail, My Anactoria,
> If she were with you.
> She whose gentle footfall and radiant face
> Hold the power to charm more than a vision
> Of chariots and the mail-clad battalions
> of Lydia's army.[8]

It is her explicit desire for women which has enormously supported Sappho's recovery in modern cultural memory. Since she wrote openly about loving women, her memory was reinvigorated by lesbian and queer communities throughout the ages, and inspired twentieth-century feminist and lesbian poets such as Stephania Byrd or H. D.'s 'Fragment Thirty-Six'. Her poetry, in other words, has held a particular mnemonic affordance: Sappho could be mobilised in the memory efforts of a particular community.

In a patrilinear society, art is one of very few ways for a woman to ensure that her name is remembered. It will not be through her children, her goods, her houses, her land, her inventions. Under Athenian law, all of these would have belonged, like the woman herself, to her husband.[9]

It was no easy feat, however, to make your way as a female artist in Ancient Greece. Although all the muses, the patron goddesses of the arts, were female, women were not allowed to practice the arts. The most prominent Greek art form was the theatre, which women in all likelihood were not even permitted to attend,[10] and were certainly not permitted to create for. No women could perform on stage or write plays and enter them into the Great Dionysia, the famous dramatic competitions that made the names of the Greek playwrights we remember today: Aeschylus, Sophocles, Euripides.

This tradition of excluding women from the theatre remained intact until well into the eighteenth century, including throughout the Elizabethan Age, the time when Shakespeare wrote his plays. That is why so many of the young women in his plays end up masquerading as men. Since all the female parts were performed by men, Shakespeare's costume departments never had to worry about how to pull that off.

Female artists in antiquity could not expect to receive applause or payment for their own work. Still, they strove for economic independence despite not legally being granted any. They worked from the periphery, pretending to be men or taking up isolated positions outside of conventional social arrangements, forced to choose their career over marriage or family life. Limiting conditions, and the attempt to get around them, would continue to structure female authorship over the ensuing centuries. We see it in the life and work of Jane Austen, who lived from 1775 to 1817 and wrote eloquently about marriage yet never married herself; and that of George Eliot (1819–1880), who was one of the leading writers of the Victorian era but remained unmarried until the final year of her life; and of Colette, Parisian author and the first woman to be given a state burial in France after her death in 1954. Born in 1876, Colette married and rose to fame as a writer under her husband's name, but he would end up stealing her work from her.

Virginia Woolf famously wrote in 1929 that a woman needed a room of her own and a secure disposable income to write in. The room is often remembered, the income less frequently so, although it may be even more important. Virginia Woolf was writing her essay *A Room of One's Own* at a time when wives still required their husbands' permission to be allowed to work. In addition to a lack of income and a difficult choice between the security of marriage and the expression of one's artistic impulse, it was also more difficult for women to find critical recognition. This lack of recognition has lasted into the twenty-first century. Until the early 2010s, female writers were continually underrepresented on literary prize lists, and books that focus solely on a female character still seem less likely to win literary accolades.[11]

Art has been one way to preserve one's name as a woman in the patriarchy, from Ancient Greece to this day, but it is important to remember how many names we have forgotten throughout history. The names of the women who came up with our most beloved fairytales in the eighteenth and nineteenth century, for example, such as *Little Red Riding Hood, Beauty and the Beast,* and *Snow White and the Seven Dwarves*, are not commonly remembered. Their names were Gabrielle-Suzanne Barbot de Villeneuve, Henriette Dorothea 'Dortchen' Wild, Marie Hassenpflug and Dorothea Viehmann.

Instead, we remember the names of the men who wrote down some of their stories, two brothers and scholars from Kassel in Germany, which was occupied by the Napoleonic army at the time. Tellingly, named characters in fairytales are few and far between. Names were not something that women could get attached to in the past, so perhaps they did not consider them to be very important in the stories they told.

Recently, significant efforts have been made to recover the names of the female storytellers of the past, ranging from the inventors of the Grimm fairytales to the Old Babylonian poet Enheduana, but what about the women from Greek antiquity who did not work as artists? Rare as they are, there are some we remember, for example Aspasia and Phryne. How did they ensure that their names would go down in history?

Memory and Sex

Aspasia came to live in Athens as a young woman, originally from a city in Asia Minor. In other words: she was not a citizen and could not become one. Had she married an Athenian man, their children would not have been citizens either.

Ironically, the law decreeing that children of mixed marriages would not be citizens of Athens was passed by the very man who would choose Aspasia as a lifelong partner: the Athenian general Pericles, famous to this day, immortalised among other places in a rarely performed drama by William Shakespeare.

Pericles and Aspasia were partners in more ways than one. It has been suggested that she may even have written one of his most famous speeches, the Funeral Oration.[12] Classicist Armand D'Angour has proposed that it was Aspasia who trained Socrates, one of the most famous philosophers in history.[13] Equally notable, Aspasia is the only historical woman who gets to speak in Plato's entire works, which consists exclusively of dialogues.[14]

What is so interesting about Aspasia is that she was not only, from all that we know, fiercely intelligent, a master at rhetoric, and very beautiful: she was also a courtesan.

Here we have another prominent way for a woman under patriarchy to be remembered: by being sexually interesting to famous men. Pericles, Plato and Sophocles each would have met Aspasia in the context of erotic possibility. Tellingly, Armand D'Angour's book about Aspasia is called *Socrates in Love* (2019). The men who remembered her, and who passed her name down to us, did so out of desire.

Phryne too was a powerful courtesan and possibly one of the wealthiest women in Greece. Her name has been retained in cultural memory because male artists throughout the ages have enjoyed painting a mythical scene from her life: accused of impiety, she is said to have bared her breasts for the court in order to escape a death sentence. To be exact, it is her male lawyer who is credited with bearing her breasts and protecting her from the sentence. European painters have immortalised the pornographic moment for us, especially in the latter half of the nineteenth century, the period where many of the institutions of the modern European nation-state were created. During her lifetime Phryne also served as the model for the world-renowned sculpture called *Aphrodite of Knidos*, a statue which has apparently received the sexual attentions of many a visitor throughout the ages.[15]

The Gender Data Gap

Our cultural memory, then, operates in a fundamentally sexist manner: we largely only remember those women who were renowned for their sexual appeal to men, and the few women who managed to carve out an artistic career for themselves, against all odds. Since women were not allowed to participate in public life, and their names not passed on to their children, they were essentially struck from record and left very little data for historians to investigate today.

Caroline Criado Perez calls this the Gender Data Gap, in reference to the Gender Pay Gap. Even when historians increasingly turn their attention to, and go looking for, historical heroines from Greek antiquity, they sometimes simply cannot find them.[16]

Women under Western colonial rule suffered a similar fate. As late as 1897, an army made up entirely of women who were sometimes called Amazons fought in Dahomey, a kingdom in West Africa that was often compared to Sparta. After invading the kingdom, French colonial rulers ensured that nothing was remembered of these women warriors as part of their 'civilising mission': they disbanded the army of women, drew up new school curricula, and made sure that the Amazons of Dahomey were not mentioned to the new generation of children learning about the history of the country they lived in.[17] As monuments were left to fall into disrepair, the Amazons survived only in the memory of a few elders, who continued to tell their stories.

Outside of oral history, the memory of these women has largely been lost today,[18] making this another case where the names of women have simply been forgotten – not the names of a few outstanding exceptions, but the names of all the women who fought in that army.

The past has more to offer us than that, however. Our cultural memory does not have to be sexist in this way, retaining only the memory of those women who knew how to please a man. If we dive to the depths of the deep sea, if we turn to our foremothers in Scythia, we find a treasure trove of the names of normal women.

Names are a crucial part of our identity, both in formal and informal settings. Authorities identify us by our name, and so do our loved ones. Names can be changed, but it is not always easy, particularly if the changes are supposed to be made to the official record.

Names may have mattered just as much to our foremothers in Scythia. In their myths, passed down to us through the oral storytelling traditions compiled in the Nart sagas,[19] the Narts say that:

> If our lives are to be short,
> Then let our fame be great!

Making a name for themselves during their lifetime was important to the Narts. Interestingly, they add

> Let us not depart from truth!
> Let fairness be our path!
> Let us not know grief!
> Let us live in freedom!

It wasn't all about fame, then. They also valued truth, fairness, happiness and freedom.

The Nart sagas were passed down orally by male and female bards and only written down in the eighteenth century. Every century in which they were told must have left its mark on the stories, a process referred to as historical layering.[20] Due to historical layering, the Nart sagas are not identical with the stories our foremothers in Scythia may have told each other over the fire or on a hunt. But it is likely that they contain traces of those same stories.[21] The importance of names, concurrent with similar themes in Greek myth and culture of the same period, may very well be captured in these traces.

Other than these sagas, the Nomad and semi-nomadic cultures of Scythia have not left us any written records, at least none that we can understand.[22] However, there is some contemporary textual evidence about the Scythians and their names. It has come to us from Ancient Greece.

Men in Ancient Greece, while happy to leave behind daughters, sisters, and wives in the house, were equally happy to collect, tell, and relish stories and accounts about independent warrior women from Scythia. This means that a surprisingly large number of names of these women has been preserved – although it took us more than two thousand years to figure out just how many.

The majority of Scythian and Amazonian names has been recovered from vase inscriptions in Greek. We know of one hundred and thirty such names in total, seventy of which have come down to us through vases.[23] Vase painting, alongside theatre, was another popular artform in Classical Athens, and there is a great number of vases depicting legendary Amazon women as well as historical female Scythian archers.

Many of these vases carry the Amazonian names that are familiar to us from Greek myth: Hippolyte, for instance, who is well known all over the world, not least of all because she features as Hippolyta in William Shakespeare's widely performed comedy *A Midsummer Night's Dream*.

Most of these names, however, are Greek or 'grecified' names: while some of them may have been inspired by the languages spoken by the Scythians, Hippolyte is clearly a grecified name, as indicated by the prominent position of the word *hippo*, which means *horse* in Greek.

Since the Scythians left us no written records that we have discovered or can understand, we have mostly had no way of learning their names as they would have styled them. Even the term used throughout this book to describe them, 'Scythian,' is a Greek umbrella term.

This knowledge gap, however, began to close in the 2010s. In 2014, an ingenious linguistic discovery suggested that we may be able to recover the original names of our Scythian foremothers after all – and that they have been right under our noses for over two thousand years.

When three scholars came together to decipher mysterious writings on Ancient Greek vases, they did not know that they were on the verge of making a spectacular archaeological discovery, although one of them had an inkling: Adrienne Mayor, historian and folklorist at Stanford University.

She had been examining Ancient Greek vases collected all over the Western world which portrayed female warriors, mounted archers, or legendary Amazons. Above some of the images of these warriors, words had been written in Greek letters, but they seemed to be gibberish. No meaning could be construed from them in Greek.

Such inscriptions were routinely referred to as 'nonsense 'descriptions', and it was believed that the vase painter, working in a widely illiterate society, had simply added a few nonsense words for decorative purposes.

Mayor was less certain. She and her colleague David Saunders of the Getty Museum took twelve of those nonsense inscriptions to John Colarusso in Canada, a leading expert on Circassian and one of the few linguists worldwide specialising in Caucasian languages.

Together, Mayor, Saunders, and Colarusso took another look at twelve Ancient Greek vases – and at what researchers had considered to be gibberish for centuries. In the process, they discovered the names that our foremothers may have given their daughters, or the names that our foremothers may have made for themselves.

It turned out that the words on the vases had not been meaningless at all. The Greek vase painters had, in fact, tried their hands at a spell of phonetic transcription: when spoken aloud, Colarusso recognised the supposed nonsense as phonetic renditions of words and names from ancient languages spoken in the Caucasus. Here were the names the Scythians may have given their daughters, or that these daughters may have made for themselves over a lifetime. In her 2014 book *The Amazons: Lives and Legends of Warrior Women Across the Ancient World*, Adrienne Mayor provides a list of names given to female warriors of Scythia, none of which are anything short of wonderful. They range from *Alkaia*, which means 'mighty', over *Kheuke,* 'one of the heroes/heroines', to *Pantariste*, meaning 'best of all' – surely a name many freshly minted parents would be tempted to bestow on their newborn.

It is striking how powerful these names are. Three millennia ago, mothers and fathers in egalitarian communities on the outskirts of Ancient Greek influence named their daughters:

> Khasa, 'one who heads a council', clearly wishing for their little girl to go far in politics.
>
> or Euryale, 'far roaming', confident their daughter would explore the world and do the very opposite of staying at home and minding the hearth.
>
> or even Molpadia, 'Death or Divine Song'.

The latter probably implies a certain flair for the dramatic, and we must remember that actors, poets, and prophets living three thousand years ago also had to name their children something.

Certain qualities are conspicuously absent from that list: modesty, passivity, submissiveness. Even beauty or elegance, to this day associated with traditional femininity, are mentioned only very rarely. There is Chichak, which means 'flower', although we should remember that some flowers are poisonous, and Kallie, which translates as 'beautiful'.

Instead, what these names emphasise are action and assertiveness. Three thousand years ago on the steppes of Scythia and beyond, parents did not want for their daughters merely to be beautiful. They wished for them to be leaders (*Hegeso*), to have a forceful nature (*Iphinome*), to be famous (*Klymene*), or to have a mighty spirit (*Oas oas*). These are the names the Scythian women made for themselves: Khasa headed a council, Laodoke received the army, and Peisianassa persuaded the Queen. These are actions, not passive qualities. This is the stuff of myth, of history, and of memory.

And these actions, these activities, were remembered. Even all the way across the Aegean Sea, in Classical Athens, the names of these women were painted onto vases and so retained for posterity. While Phryne, Aspasia and Sappho had to work incredibly hard to commit their names to posterity – three Greek women and no more – more than five dozen Scythian women were remembered on Greek vases for their deeds, their actions as warriors, leaders, and adventurers.

In mnemonic terms, this suggests a path to revolution. Here we have a human tradition, a history of giving women heroic names and remembering them for their deeds, that could inform our own efforts to reshape our cultural memory.

There is precedent for remembering women not for their sexual appeal but for their acts of leadership, acts of heroism, acts of courage.

Our Scythian foremothers have revealed a central mechanism in the sexism of our cultural memory: if we are remembered, it is through our actions, and prohibiting action prohibits being remembered. If women are not expected to act upon the world, they will be forgotten; we will not consider their stories worth retelling or their memories worth conserving.

Our cultural memory is structured in this way because it is patriarchal; it supports the rule of men. That is why it is considered normal and natural, even safe and good, for a woman to spend her life primarily in the house. The norms that structure our memory and society still seek to keep women in their place – which is to say, to keep them passive, away from activity and away from taking action.

This patriarchal dynamic also explains why we have such a hard time changing our mnemonic norms, even today. It constrains, for example, our ambitions as women, the limitations we set for ourselves and others. Names contribute to how we think of the people around us, but more importantly, they contribute to how we think of ourselves. While we are not necessarily conscious of what other people's names mean, we may well have looked up the meaning of our own name when we were growing up. I was given a card by my late godfather which told me the meaning of my name. Christine is derived from the Latin expression for (female) follower of Christ.

That is not the reason why my parents picked it, and I am happy with my name, but as a young woman growing up I would have found it slightly more inspiring if Christine meant 'one of the heroines' rather than a woman who follows the religious teachings of a man. I wonder whether I would call a daughter I may one day have Kheuke, clearly an unusual name, because I would love for my daughter to look up the meaning of her name as a teenage girl who is struggling to find her sense of self and discover that it meant she was a heroine.

While Kheuke is an unusual name today, according to Greek vase painters and the inscriptions they left us, there may well have been a Scythian warrior woman called Kheuke. Unlike the Amazon Queen Penthesilea, unlike Helen of Troy, Kheuke would have been a real woman, like you and me, like your mother or your daughter, like my nan and my niece. She may have lived in an egalitarian Scythian community on the south coast of the Black Sea in the first millennium BCE. She may have been born in the Pontic Alps. At the age of five, she would already have been shooting arrows from horseback, riding at speed across the steppes. Her parents would have had no reason to prefer a boy over a girl and would already have been teaching her all the skills required to survive: riding, hunting, fighting. When she asked them what her name meant, they would have told her, and it would have made sense to her, surrounded by women like her mother, who also would have ridden and hunted; women who took care of her, who taught and nurtured her; women who were heroines to her.

In this book, we will follow Kheuke through her life. We will imagine what her days may have been like. We will do so to fill the silences in our story of the past, because we must begin to make women like Kheuke part of our cultural memory. They have always been there. We know this, because we have always known women like her: strong women, happy women, independent women, ambitious women, who pushed against the limitations of their times, who did what they could to leave their mark on the world with the cards they had been dealt. These are real women like my nan, like my mother, full of willpower and strength; and mythical women like Penthesilea, who nearly beat Achilles at Troy, or Helen, who fled a violent husband to make a new life for herself. It is time we made these women part of our history, and of our tradition.

What have the names of our foremothers taught us about how memory works? To this day, the great majority of heterosexual women give up their last name upon marriage, taking on their husband's name and passing his on to their children. Norms put into place thousands of years ago still work on us in the present, ensuring that the male name is retained while women's names are forgotten.

The names of some historical women have been painstakingly retrieved from traces and gaps in the archive by historians. However, the names of most have simply been forgotten.

This is not the case for names used in parts of Ancient Scythia. The names of countless women who lived and acted in Asia Minor in the first millennium BCE were remembered and have been passed down to us by their male contemporaries, vase painters in Classical Athens.

These names have something to teach us about memory: emphasising activity and memorable actions, such as heading a council, receiving an army, or defending one's village, they point to the fact that memory is story. We remember stories that we tell about ourselves (personal memory), or have been told by others that we know (communicative memory), or about the communities that we live in, work for, move through or were born in (cultural memory).

In other words: our cultural memory consists of stories describing actions, and our collective identity is defined by acts in the past we hold to be true, having been committed by people that we consider our ancestors.

In the United Kingdom, this recalls the importance of the Second World War to collective identity, remembered as a time where our ancestors showed great heroism by carrying on at home or going into battle abroad. In the United States, the War of Independence and the writing of the constitution come to mind.

Both recall moments of what we remember and consider to be heroic deeds, deeds defined by committing and enduring acts of violence, usually along gendered lines: men were supposed to fight, women supposed to endure. The truth, of course, looked very different, and there are alternative to these heroic narratives of the past. In modern Germany, for example, a different story has been told: the atrocities that our ancestors committed in the Second World War are the thread from which collective identity in Germany is spun today, where villains instead of heroes remember a past of unspeakable crimes.

In many countries of the West and other patriarchal societies, especially in heroic memory cultures, one thread has consistently been spun: the thread that remembers women only as active villains or immobile victims, that uses cultural memory to keep women in a place of passivity.

Our foremothers in parts of Scythia provide us with a different kind of thread, a better treasure: their names suggest that in a more egalitarian society, women were respected and remembered for their actions and were not expected or pressured to live passive lives in which their defining quality was their beauty or their ability to bear and raise children. They suggest that women who stood up for themselves were not considered to be villains, but heroines.

In the next chapter, we will turn our attention away from names and towards another set of norms harnessed to this day to keep women in a state of passivity: beauty standards. Vanity is a sin, we are told, yet only pretty women succeed in life. Greek myth teaches this, and so do our fairytales, as well as countless social media success stories. They warn us not to look too deeply into the mirror, yet also rehearse the idea that only the beautiful among us will ever get to enjoy a happily-ever-after.

Yet not all is what it seems when it comes to beauty and vanity. The myth of Narcissus also involves a woman, European fairytales are much more ambivalent than we may think, and our foremothers in Scythia have left us another heirloom that they may have viewed very differently from us: another object found in their graves that most of us still use in our everyday lives, every morning and every evening, in our cars or on the tube, at work or at home, and which may tell us something about how they raised their children.

Mirrors.

2. MIRRORS

When I was a child, I put up postcards on my bedroom walls. Wisely, my parents suggested that I use push pins rather than adhesives, and quite typically, I ignored them. I used tape to put up a photo I had taken of a lake on holiday in Sweden, a postcard of my favourite television couple (Brian Kinney and Justin Taylor from *Queer as Folk*), and a drawing a friend had made for me depicting a drag queen and the words out and proud, although I had no idea at that age that being bisexual was something one had to come out about, or that I was in fact bisexual. It seems that she knew, and maybe so did a part of me.

Over the years, I added many postcards and photos to this wall, but when I returned to my childhood bedroom during the preparations for this book, I realised something extraordinary: there was only one picture of a woman on my wall. Even more astonishingly, she was doing something that I cannot recall ever having done as a child. This beautiful young woman was looking at herself in a large mirror, with a sorrowful expression on her face, holding up her hair with one hand and the hem of her long white dress with the other, clearly unhappy with the way she looked. I do not remember where I bought the card, but wherever it was, a part of me must have understood even at quite a young age that women were supposed to look pretty, and always to find themselves wanting in this regard.

I took the postcard with me and placed it on the shelf above my desk. It sits beside a photo of my astonishing niece, who I hope will grow up in a different world, a world that does not tell girls that they always need to be beautiful, and can never be beautiful enough.

Sadly, the data tells us that we have not created that world yet. Half of the girls in the UK aged seven already feel boxed in by stereotypes about what girls can and cannot do, when it comes to exercising, playing video games, studying STEM subjects, and caring about looking pretty.[1] It may be tempting to compliment little girls on their looks, but studies have shown that even well-intentioned positive comments about their appearance encourages girls to think of themselves as objects of the male gaze.[2] Our girls are already growing up to be the young woman in my postcard, who is the picture of beauty yet still gazes longingly into the mirror, imagining all the ways in which she is found wanting.

Our damaging beauty standards are related to our cultural memory: we find similar depictions of these standards' effects in artefacts from Classical Greece. In the iconography of the period, mirrors are associated with women. Only women are depicted with mirrors, and mirrors have been recovered from the graves of women, not men, up until the fifth century BCE.[3] Mirrors were presented as a particularly important tool in women's love lives.

The Metropolitan Museum in New York City counts among its collection a sumptuous example of a Classical Greece mirror: a reflective bronze disk is mounted on top of the head of a woman in Greek robes. She is surrounded by two figures that we might identify as angels, but they are *erotes*, winged figures who make up part of the retinue of the goddess Aphrodite and symbolise love and desire. *If you want any of that, you better be looking the part*, the mirror seems to say, and to women rather than men.

We can imagine a woman such as Helen of Troy holding such a mirror, staring at her own reflection. She may have kept it on her dressing table, always at hand to gaze lovingly at her face, described by Christopher Marlowe as the face that launched a thousand ships.

Or perhaps her interactions with the mirror would have been businesslike, perfunctory. She would have picked it up, put rouge on her cheeks, dabbed her lips with colour, run a hand through her hair, then put it back down on the dresser, turned around and left, got on with her day.

Or perhaps her gaze would not have been loving, her gestures not perfunctory. Perhaps her glances would have been furtive, her observations critical, her every interaction with the mirror led by fear. Would today be the day when she would lose what everyone was praising her for? Perhaps she was living in fear of spotting a wrinkle, a spot, a blemish that the men who praised her beauty would not be able to overlook.

Does that mean that mirrors in Ancient Greece were simply a misogynist tool, telling women to look beautiful at any cost? Things may not be so simple. In contrast with Greek iconography, mirrors in Greek myth are sometimes the prerogatives of men rather than women. Famously, Narcissus falls in love with his own reflection, and it is from him that we retain the term 'narcissist' for someone who is too much in love with themselves.

In the Roman poet Ovid's telling of the myth, which builds on the Greek version and is widely known today, there are both men and women who desire Narcissus, who is born as a child of rape and grows into a beautiful man. A young man called Ameinias begs him for his love, but Narcissus refuses. A young woman likewise desires him, a nymph by the name of Echo. Echo is no longer able to use her voice after a punishment by the Greek goddess Hera, who should have taken out her anger on her cheating husband Zeus but decided instead to revenge herself on Echo, who now is only capable of repeating the words spoken by someone else. Echo seeks out Narcissus, hoping to hear words of love and desire so that she may repeat them back to him, but he rejects her, too.

Both Ameinias and Echo kill themselves. Narcissus, too, will die for love of a sort: when he chances upon a pond, he falls in love with his own reflection, and dies of sorrow because he can never be united with his lover.

As I have said, it is from this story that we take the term of 'narcissism', a psychological disorder reported to have painful consequences for those who are close to the narcissist. A 2023 comprehensive study of 250,000 participants found that men are more likely than women to suffer from and inflict their narcissism on others.[4]

The tale of Narcissus is not kind to the male narcissist, but it is equally unkind to mirrors. When I reread this story, I thought about what it must have been like for girls and boys to hear this story told in Ancient Greece.

As a girl, you might have seen your mother with her mirror and felt desire for this lush and valuable object, belonging to the world of the grown-ups. Helen might have been such a girl. At the same time, you might have heard this story, and every gaze into the mirror would turn into a repetition of Narcissus's sin, loading with guilt what was considered a feminine activity. *Look into the mirror to please men, but do not look too hard.*

As a boy, it might have put you off mirrors for good, and allowed you to resent the object your wife was using to remain desirable to your gaze, or the object you yourself were using to please the gaze of another man. *I look down on you for wanting to please me, but please, please me.* If this is the attitude engendered in boys, using a mirror spells trouble for girls, and later, for women.

In the tale of Narcissus, the mirror is cast as an object of danger, to gaze into it as a guilty pleasure. Here begins the dilemma of women that endures to this day, a dilemma Helen may well have experienced herself had she been a real woman, handling the mirror sometimes with love, sometimes with trepidation. If you spend too much time looking into the mirror, you are considered vain, but if you do not use it to be pleasing to the male gaze, you are hardly considered a woman at all.

In fact, the refusal to please the male gaze and fulfil male desires may well turn you into a monster. There is another mirror in Greek myth, a polished surface that features prominently in one of its most famous tales, that of Perseus and Medusa. Mirrors serve men well in the case of Perseus, a violent man routinely considered one of Ancient Greek's most revered heroes.[5]

I never much cared for the tale of Perseus as a little girl, and neither did my parents, I believe, because they never read it to us. Rereading it as a grown woman, I see why. It is not a story I would read to my children.

As a young man, Perseus agrees to kill Medusa, a woman who has been raped. Her rapist escapes unscathed, but Medusa is punished for the crime committed against her by Athena, goddess of wisdom, who turns her beautiful hair into snakes.

From that moment, Medusa is considered a monster, and her gaze will turn anyone who looks at her to stone. Perseus is the only one, or so the Roman poet will have us believe, who is clever enough to figure out that he may use his shield as a mirror and reflect Medusa's deadly gaze back at her, thus turning her to stone.

I read the tale with astonishment. The woman looks into the mirror of the man, and it is this gaze that turns her to stone. If there is one thing to be said for Greek myth, it's that it does not beat around the bush; this myth explains the effects of the 'male gaze' – how it immobilises women – two thousand years before Laura Mulvey coined the phrase.[6] When Medusa sees her face reflected in Perseus's shield and turns to stone, it serves as a powerful metaphor how debilitating it can be to focus all your attention on how others see you, and how it will keep you small and afraid. When I first encountered this myth, I wondered what women in Ancient Greece would have made of it, and how it made them feel when they handled the reflective bronze surface on their dressing table. I wondered if they did what I did when I was younger: look in the mirror and find myself compelled to imagine, just for a second or two, what I would look like with snakes for hair. Look and imagine myself as Medusa, and feel the horror of realising that something as normal as looking in the mirror could kill you, turn you to stone.

I later learned that the tale of Medusa may have its origins in Berber culture, that there are many versions of this myth, some kinder to the women than others. Medusa does not turn into a beautiful young woman until the fifth century BCE, in the period known to us as Classical antiquity, so real women alive at the time of Helen would not have known this version. It is likely that rival versions of the tale were in circulation even then, as they still are today.[7] For the purposes of cultural memory, however, there is only one version: the one where Medusa is raped, turned into a monster, and finally killed by looking in a mirror. Perseus gets to keep her head, in this version. He cuts it off and uses it as a weapon, as it can still turn his foes to stone. He ends up giving it to Athena, the very goddess who turned Medusa into a monster.

As the story of Medusa shows us, women during this time were caught in a cruel double-bind. On the one hand, archaeology and iconography indicate that mirrors made up a foundational part of what it meant to be a woman, to grow up from girlhood and enter into womanhood. On the other hand, the stories told to girls and boys at a young age made mirrors out to be evil: if you looked at them for too long, you would lose yourself in them. If you looked into them and your reflection was considered monstrous, you would turn to stone. Already, those holding the mirror could only go wrong – look too little, or look too much. The mirror comes to symbolise vanity and evil. If beauty is all you have to secure your income – through marriage or prostitution – then your small amount of economic currency has just become a sin (although the Christian idea of sin is, of course, still five hundred years away at this point).

This tradition of the mirror as a source of evil and female vanity is alive and well in cultural memory. Not every child today may learn about Greek myth, but many will hear the fairytale of *Snow White*, first told by Marie Hassenpflug to Wilhelm and Jacob Grimm, who published it in 1812 without crediting her as the author, and significantly reworking it over multiple editions.⁸ The tale was popularised by Walt Disney's animated 1937 feature film *Snow White and the Seven Dwarves*.

In *Snow White*, the Evil Queen famously asks her magic mirror, *Mirror mirror on the wall, who is the fairest of them all?* When she finds out it is not her but her step-daughter Snow White, she hatches a plan to murder the child. Here, the mirror continues to stand for female vanity and evil. In Ancient Greece, mirrors killed female monsters; today, they create them. We cannot live without them if we seek to sleep with men, but we are made to feel guilty for needing them.

Beauty standards from the past are fundamental in structuring collective memory, and therefore beauty standards, today. Male artists have done their part to keep this mnemonic dynamic alive. As John Berger points out in his 1972 book *Ways of Seeing*, the mirror has come to signify the essential vanity of all women through the concerted effort of male artists. The hypocrisy is not lost on him: 'You painted a naked woman because you enjoyed looking at her, you put a mirror in her hand and you called the painting "Vanity", thus morally condemning the woman whose nakedness you had depicted for your own pleasure.'⁹

That is what the waters of our cultural memory of beauty and mirrors look like: Our cultural memory tells us that we do not have a choice about the double bind we are in as women, that it has always been thus. Archaeology is enlisted to corroborate what we seem to remember, and hold to be true: that women have always used mirrors rather than men, that women have always been vain.

Archaeology was the ideal helpmate to this story for two centuries. As a discipline, it was born in the nineteenth century, and archaeologists were often wealthy male members of patriarchal and imperial societies. It made sense for them to project their present onto the past. For the first two hundred years of archaeological enquiry, if a mirror was present in a grave, the (usually male) archaeologists would take this as proof that the buried person must have been a woman. If a sword was present, it was assumed they were looking at a man.[10] Mirrors were associated with the spiritual and the feminine.

This is, however, a fallacy. The past, and our history, knows another tradition of beauty and mirrors, one of equality, power and pleasure. And we know about it because of the advent of feminist archaeology. According to Marylène Patou-Mathis, director of the department of ancient and prehistory at the Museum of Natural History in Paris, all prehistorians working at Western universities up until the 1950s were men.[11] This began to change in the 1970s, when a number of women entered the discipline, bringing with them the potential to challenge its nineteenth-century misogyny. In the 1980s, the term 'feminist archaeology' began to emerge. The archaeologist Liv Helga Dommasnes, working and living in Norway, founded the journal K. A. N., (Kvinner i Arkeologi i Norge, or Women in Archaeology in Norway) in 1985. Together with several other women, she provided a crucial platform for research in this field, enabling feminist archaeology to gain momentum.[12] Norwegian archaeologists were building on the revolutionary thinking and courageous work of the US archaeologists Margaret Conkey, Janet Spector and Joan Gero, who had criticised the way modern Western norms were being applied to the past.[13] The past, according to these thinkers, had been made to perform in accordance with the social norms of the men who were it in the present.

It took the work of these women to uncover the phantasm of the vain and passive woman, always staring into a mirror, for what it was: a carefully constructed cultural memory, a version of the past made up by men who needed it to prop up their present. Archaeologists such as Sir Arthur Evans or Sir Leonard Wolley were well-established men whose wives were given every legal incentive to please them. This cultural memory allowed such men to say, and think: women have always been vain, and this is just the way things are, the natural, the God-given order of being.

The wives of these archaeologists, Margaret Freeman and Katherine Menke respectively, were independent and strong-minded women, literate and educated, with Katherine Woolley an archaeologist in her own right. However, even women like them may have had little choice but to hand mirrors to their daughters, to tell them from their youngest age that they would have to please a man if they wanted even a small measure of comfort and independence. Perhaps that is how real noblewomen like the mythical Helen came into possession of their first mirror, a bronze disc sitting on her dressing table, given to them by their mother. The first archaeologists created a fantasy of the past, but they lacked imagination. It looked exactly like their present.

This was no accident. It is cultural memory in action. We shape the past to our needs, and often we cast it in our image. That is why it matters who does the shaping, who has the right to cast an image. Male archaeologists saw what they wanted to see. Female archaeologists took another look, and saw something quite different.

And they saw it in Scythia. This is where we come across a different tradition around beauty and mirrors, women and men.

In Scythian cemeteries, women, men and children alike are buried with mirrors.[14] Adrienne Mayor proposes that, far from implying a certain gender, vanity, or a passive lifestyle, these mirrors are so widespread as to suggest they must have had a much more practical use: they may have been used for communication – to exchange light signals between hunting or travelling parties on the steppes[15] Signal mirrors are a standard feature of military kits and life rafts to this day, used for exactly this purpose.

The first time I saw a signal mirror on a life raft, I remember it brought me up short. It was the moment I realised that I had misconceived of mirrors all my life, thinking of them in the same way as generations of women before me. I had absorbed the cultural memories I had been raised with and thought of mirrors as something I hated.

Spotting the signal mirror on the life raft, I realised that I, too, had bought into the Western cultural memory of mirrors as something women use so that they may please men. I had thought of myself as a confident child and teenager, but I had not been confident, merely resigned: I had spent my teenage years thinking of myself as lacking, and at the age of eighteen, after a long period of trying and failing to find a boyfriend and lose my virginity, I had decided that I was not pretty enough to find a man. They would have to desire me for my brains or not at all. The hateful mirror had become a part of the way I thought of myself, of women and men.

By that time, I had internalised the norms supported by our cultural memory of beauty, but in order to protect myself from their harmful consequences, I did not think about this cultural memory in terms of women. Instead, I thought about men. I told myself that men were vain and superficial, that they only wanted me to please them. This was a lie that I told myself to protect myself, and in order to make it sound true, I told myself that it had always been like this, since the dawn of time.

My encounter with the mirror on the life raft, the mirror that challenged my ideas about these objects, happened when I was navigating a difficult break-up. I wanted to prove to myself that I was still a whole person, and had decided to learn to sail and cross the Flensborg Fjord between Germany and Denmark. I was going through the safety procedures when it first caught my eye.

It was small. I could cup it in one hand. In fact, it was of a similar size to the pocket mirror in my handbag, the handbag I had left at home, the mirror that my mother had given to me as a gift, bought at a fair she had visited with a friend, from a local craftswoman near the town where I had grown up.

This mirror, we were told, could save our lives if we found ourselves adrift at sea in a lifeboat. With a little light, we could use it to send light signals that would be picked up by anyone turned towards us, as far away as sixty kilometres or thirty-three nautical miles: flashes on the horizon. Three short flashes, three long flashes, three short flashes. SOS, spelled out in letters of light with the help of what the instructors referred to as our survival mirror.

A survival mirror. That is what I had been keeping in my pocket all this time. Not an object to hold and gaze into, not a reflective surface that kills or creates monsters. This is what my mother, her friend, and the local craftswoman had given me: a way of communicating. A mirror that could send signals. A way of saying, help me, a way of saying, I want out. A tool to save myself, to leave a bad situation when I found myself in it, to ask for help and receive it.

I loved the signal mirror, and I was glad to realise that I had one in my handbag. As I began writing this book, and researching mirrors in the graves of our foremothers and forefathers in Scythia, mirrors at French courts of the twelfth century, mirrors on life rafts and the mirror endlessly held up to women and girls on social media, I always kept in mind the survival mirror in my pocket.

The mirrors in the graves of the Scythian cemeteries captured my imagination. On the steppes, they could have been put to even more uses than signalling for help. They would allow women and men, girls and boys alike to tell each other when they had tracked game, when they had found fresh water, when they had come across a shady place to rest or a patch of hazelnut bushes laden with fruit. When they wanted to go home, when they wanted to stay out for a little longer. Remember the girl called Kheuke who we imagined may have grown up in Ancient Scythia on the southern coast of the Black Sea? She was five when we last imagined her, already learning how to ride and shoot a bow and arrow. She must have grown older in the meantime: perhaps she is eight, ten, twelve. She may have been given a mirror by her mother, or her aunt, or a family friend. It is a mirror that fits in the palm of her hand. She carries it wherever she goes. She is learning how to track game, how to find water, how to lay traps. She loves her mirror, and she particularly likes to tease her parents, riding further and further away, always sending light signals in response to theirs, asking her to come home, saying not yet, not quite yet, just one more hill, one more ride across the plain. As she grows older, she may start signalling to a friend, to a boy or girl she likes. Pretending to be at risk only to see her beloved come rushing towards her, or to be tricked by them in turn. The equal distribution of mirrors in Scythian cemeteries suggests something to me about how these people raised their children, perhaps as equals.

Famously, Plato advised educating girls in the same way as boys in Ancient Greece,[16] but his proposal did not come to fruition. I find it staggering to think of a Greek girl holding her mirror in Greece, the shining bronze disc, asking the equivalent of *Mirror mirror on the wall*, and then of Kheuke, across the Aegean Sea, slipping it into her pocket before she rode out in the morning, signalling to her crush. No matter who it was that Kheuke liked, their mirrors would have put them on equal footing. You cannot see who is sending a light signal: woman or man, girl or boy, or anyone in between? If you see a light signal asking you to come, asking for help, promising a shady patch of grass or a merry river or a bounteous hazelnut bush, then you come to them not because they are pretty, or smart, or someone you can control. You come because of the grass, or the river, or the hazelnuts that you want to share with them.

In Ancient Scythia, all children may have been equipped with what they needed to stay alive, well and active. They may also have used mirrors to look at their own reflections – for example when they had just been gifted a pair of new earrings, another object found both in male and female Scythian graves – but perhaps in a manner less gripped by gender roles. It is not unlikely to think that Scythian children would have been able to take pleasure both in looking at the world, and in looking at themselves. The mirror in this scenario is no longer a static object, fixed to a wall or held firmly in our hand. It becomes a tool, even a plaything. Women do not need to be vain. Men do not need to be shallow.

If we use the way the Scythians used mirrors as our starting point, if we think of the past as a place where mirrors were used as a tool of communication and as an object for play and cooperation, in a universal language spoken by all, something extraordinary happens: new memories take shape, a new tradition comes to light. These memories resurface out of the strange and unfathomable waters we call history, from the queer and beautiful sea we call the past.

Crucially, this tradition is already ours. It already has a role to play in cultural memory, albeit not the dominant one. Mirrors have been used in a playful and empowering way in our history. In her 2023 book *A History of Women in 101 Objects*, the feminist writer Annabelle Hirsch discusses a French mirror from about the year 1300. The reverse side of the mirror is engraved with a scene that depicts an episode of courtship between a nobleman and noblewoman in the court of Eleonore of Aquitaine. Eleonore is famous as a French queen who spread the Lancelot legend, and fostered all that is pleasant and makes us happy: art, music, song, love.[17] The scene depicts the lovers, but they are not staring into a mirror, not worrying about the way they look. They are playing a game of chess.

Here is a mirror, but it is not telling you to worry about the way you look, or that men want you to. It is saying, *your look in the mirror is part of a game, a joyful, intellectually thrilling, but peaceful pas-de-deux*. Or, in the case of Hirsch's mirror, de-quatre: there are two observers, standing behind the players, watching the game. Neither love nor desire have always had to be monogamous.

The mirror is a thing of beauty. Since the scene, carved into ivory, can be found on the back of the mirror, you would have felt it as you held the mirror in your hand and looked at yourself. You could have traced the outline of the scene with your fingers, felt it pressing gently into the palm of your hand, a reminder that love is flirtation, that beauty is found in the relationship between two people and how they treat each other, and not in the one glance, every morning, every evening, into the mirror. Beauty is not an attribute, it is a relationship, even a game, and it can be fun to play!

It would not be right to romanticise the court of Eleanor of Aquitaine: there was no gender equality in France at the time, and the only women to be courted with love and respect were noblewomen.[18] However, at least these noblewomen were having a bit of fun. The tale of Lancelot is, most of all, a tale of reciprocal love and lust, even if it ends in tragedy. And the tradition of mirrors as items of power stretches further than the objects used at the court of Eleanor of Aquitaine: traces of it can be found in the stories we tell each other, and our children, today.

The fairytale as we know it, *le conte de fées*, was invented by French noblewomen, and it includes countless stories about violent suitors and husbands. Consider *La Belle et la Bête* or *Beauty and the Beast*, best known across the world as another Disney classic. The Disney adaptation makes the courtship of Belle and the Beast appear romantic, but the fact remains that the Beast imprisons Belle, shouts at her, and threatens her. Fairytales are full of monstrous husbands, and so was life when they were written. Happy endings are much easier to make up than to bring about in real life, and the mirror in *Snow White* is the epitome of the male gaze staring back at us.

This is not, however, the only kind of mirror in Western storytelling: the Beast possesses a mirror of a different kind to that in *Snow White*. It is a mirror that allows any woman or man to see whatever they wish. It allows Belle to see when her father is in danger, the Beast to see when Belle is, and the angry mob to discover where the Beast is. For better or for worse, the mirror in this tale is a tool that allows women and men to garner information, to look far beyond their own reflection, to make decisions and become actors in their own lives.

These are our two fairytale mirrors, then: the mirror on the wall in *Snow White*, that tells you are lacking. And then there is the handheld mirror used by Belle and the Beast, which reveals so much more.

There are two traditions in Western culture around mirrors, around looking, and around beauty. One of them is dominant: it equates mirrors with vanity and vanity with women, it forces women to please the male gaze and allows men to despise and belittle them for it, it casts men as shallow and spiteful.

The other is waiting just beneath the surface of the ocean of history, a memory ready to resurface. There is a different story we could be telling ourselves about mirrors, about looking at ourselves and looking at others, a memory waiting to be recollected. This story does not equate women with vanity, mirrors with passivity, men with shallowness. It is a story of equality between women and men, of beauty as a game, of flirtations as fun.

It is a memory we can only recollect, a story we can only tell, if we use a different starting point for our history, our traditions: not Ancient Greece, but Ancient Scythia. This is where mirrors may have been used by girls and boys, by women and men on the steppes, to communicate with one another, to form bonds of solidarity, to meet each other as equals.

This perspective helps us look more closely at the mirrors of the Middle Ages and the Renaissance, at the playful courtship in the court of Eleanore of Aquitaine, at the mirror given to the Beast by an enchantress, used by Belle to save her father, by the villagers to hunt down the Beast.

It also allows us to look differently at the ubiquity of reflective surfaces today: the way we all have a phone in our pocket with a camera in it, and at any given moment we can and do turn this camera on ourselves. If we remember the Ancient Scythians, we are able to realise that not every selfie is an act of submission to tyrannical beauty standards. Selfies posted on social media may be an act of communication. They are inviting other people into a conversation. Some of these conversations may be harmful, but others are important, and cannot take place anywhere else. Selfies can be a way for us to say: I am here, and I am human, and I deserve to be listened to. The myth of Medusa is so cruel precisely because Perseus turns her from a human into an object as he continues to carry around her head, to use it as a weapon. It is this act that finalises the transformation from woman into monster.

We do not have to be like Perseus. Instead, we can choose to be more like the Scythians: to remember the way they used mirrors, to give credence to their tradition. We can teach our children, girls and boys, trans and non-binary, that they do not have to look into mirrors to please others, or please themselves; that they do not have to post selfies on group chats or social media to find approval, and that they are not lacking if this approval does not come their way.

We can teach them that mirrors are tools, that they can be used to communicate with others, as the Scythians may have done; that a face is an expression of our full humanity, of our vulnerability, not so much of our beauty. Beauty is a game we play, with another person, or more than one person; it is neither shallow or vain. 'On s'amuse mieux à deux', said Holocaust survivor and French philosopher Emmanuel Lévinas, there is more fun to be had when there is two of you.[19] Beauty is made in the relationships we have with other people, not through a look in the mirror. Mirrors are how we shape the world around us. They do not shape us.

Of course, for us to reclaim all this as memory, we need to think about where we come from, where we begin our story. Where is the foundational past our cultural memory refers to? So far, we have tended to begin with Ancient Greece, Ancient Rome, with disastrous consequences for women and girls everywhere.

We ought to start earlier than that. We ought to start elsewhere. It is time to widen our focus on the Classics, and cast our net wider as we fish for treasure at the bottom of the ocean of history.

The mirrors found in the graves of Scythian women, men, and children indicate that they did not think of mirrors as gendered objects. They may have raised their children as equals, as Plato suggested the Ancient Greeks should do. This did not come to pass – in Ancient Greece. But it may have come to pass elsewhere. If others have done it before, we can do it anew. We can teach our children that mirrors are tools for action, not passive surfaces, as our foremothers in Scythia did. That women are not inherently vain and men not inherently shallow. We can change the starting point of our cultural memory. In this case, look a little further to the East, a little further back, and the whole story changes. It is a story that is much more fun – and a story in which children were allowed to have fun, girls and boys alike.

Let us look even further back, then. As girls and boys grow into adolescents, as their bodies change, what do we teach them about how to use their bodies? And what does that have to do with memory, or indeed, the ancient Minoans?

3. PLAY

I grew up playing video games. It was an unusual hobby for a girl in the 1990s and 2000s, but I loved it from the moment I first held the gamepad of a Nintendo SNES in my hands. My brothers and I often played together. Donkey Kong Country, Secret of Mana, Asterix, Power Rangers: you name it, we played it. I also played solo adventures, and did on the screen what I liked best to do in the real world: pretend I was going on an adventure, sword in hand, bow at the ready.

My brothers and I used to joke that as children we always wanted it to rain, so that we could stay inside and play video games. This tells you what we did when it was not raining. We spent every available minute outside, playing in the streets, the churchyard, the school playground, or in the garden. We lived in what would today be called a low traffic neighbourhood, but back then was just known as a nice place to live. I learned how to ride a bike in the streets of our neighbourhood, and how to rollerblade, and in the evenings we cycled to fencing and dancing lessons in the local schools.

Fencing, too, was considered an unusual sport for a girl. I always knew this, although I found it difficult to pinpoint how. My parents did not make us feel this way. Perhaps it was the way we were separated at the fencing school, the girls and the boys. I spent all day fighting and competing with my brothers. In the evenings, I was suddenly supposed to be no longer fit for that competition.

I am not the only girl to have this instinct. If others tell you that you are not fit to compete, no wonder you think about taking yourself out of the competition. According to research compiled by Women in Sport, more than a quarter of the parents of school-aged girls surveyed have heard their daughters say that 'sport isn't for them'. Their daughters, and more than three-quarters of girls, have themselves heard negative comments about girls in sports from fellow students and friends, members of their family, or coaches.[1] When we consider these findings, it is unsurprising that 65 per cent of women in a survey conducted by a sports insurance company said that they were not exercising because 'sport isn't their thing'.[2]

The persistence of negative attitudes towards women and girls in sport is particularly surprising in light of the recent growth in popularity of women's sports, most notably women's football.[3] Why this reticence to rethink the relationship between women and sport?

You will not be surprised to hear that there may be a further cultural memory at play here; that in fact it is time that we began to conceive of our cultural memory as play: that in fact our cultural memory does not contain many playful stories for women. It is not playful, not fun, not enjoyable or full of pleasure in ways that it could be. Cultural memory could be filled with better stories; ones that worked better for women and girls. We will come across some of these stories as we consider the role that exercise, or the pleasurable moving of our bodies, played for our foremothers in Greece, Scythia, and even further back in history.

Although the role of women's physical fitness, and fitness to fight, varies across the different city states of Classical Greece (famously, the city state of Sparta, a deeply militarised society, trained up girls as well as boys, although only the boys went off to fight), in Classical Athens, boys went to the arena to train in a variety of sports while girls remained at home. The Greek myths as we remember them today are certainly clear on this point: women do not fight; in general, they do not use their bodies to single-mindedly pursue a goal.

In Greek myth, the only women allowed to do so are non-Greeks. Atalanta, for example, the most famous hunter of Greek mythology, and a figure in one of the few happy stories from the Greek canon. Left to die by her father, presumably because he wanted a son, she was found and raised by hunters. She became such a proficient hunter that she later joined the hunt for the Calydonian boar – a hunt from Greek myth featuring countless heroes living one generation before the Trojan War – and was the one to strike the beast first. When she was offered its pelt as a reward, some male members of the company protested. She got the pelt anyway.

This is not the only way in which Atalanta's story is an unusually happy one: she finds a man to love her and respect her, and the gods eventually transform them into lions. We are maybe meant to understand this as a punishment, but I wonder whether two passionate hunters would actually have minded the transformation into fearsome lioness and lion. Perhaps their single-minded pursuit was rewarded: they became the perfect hunters of the animal kingdom.

Happy as her story may be, Atalanta is considered a relative exception. She is the only woman in the hunting party of the Caledonian boar; something the men comment upon.

She is not held up as a shining example to girls and young women in Classical Greece. That said, there are other women in Greek myth who are allowed to be hunters, even warriors: the Amazons for example. Warriors like Hippolyta, Orithyia, or Penthesilea, the Amazon queen who fought Achilles at Troy. They, too, however are outsiders, 'barbarians', as the Greeks used to put it.

Barbarians they may have been, and yet (or perhaps because of this) they clearly held a great fascination for the Greek mind. Amazons are an extraordinarily popular motif in Classical Athenian vase painting.[4] They make up a foundational building block of all the ancient epics we retain, from the Trojan War cycle to Virgil's *Aeneid*.[5] They are the subjects of numerous erotic vases that we have uncovered in Ancient Greece. One of them may have been used to give expression to a more egalitarian form of love between women and men, portraying a woman dressed as a Thracian hunter on the one side and a young man on the other, and another may have been a coded message for women who loved other women.[6] Some of these depictions have a darker twist: a carved gemstone from Ancient Rome shows a violent erotic scene, of a Greek warrior pulling an Amazon off her horse by her hair, both of them naked. These stones were set in golden rings and worn to be enjoyed either privately or with intimate acquaintances.[7]

Representing everything Athenian women were not allowed to be, Amazon women were considered capable warriors and desirable matches, both for Greek heroes and barbarian men. Quintus of Smyrna narrates how Achilles kills the Amazon warrior Penthesilea at Troy, only to fall in love with her at the moment of her death and belatedly bemoan that he cannot marry her[8,9,10] No barbarian made up these stories.

Again, the Greek stories do not beat around the bush. All the encounters between Amazon women and Greek men end in violence, and most of the women are kidnapped, raped, and killed rather than courted.

However, the Greeks were aware that this was not the only way to court an independent and single-minded young woman. Consider one of my favourite stories told by Herodotus in his *Histories*, best translated as 'enquiries': the episode of the Pirate Amazons. The *Histories* are part documentary, part fabulation: Herodotus reports on stories he has heard, some of which are entirely fictional, while others reflect historical events and practices with accuracy.

In Book 4 of the *Histories*, Herodotus tells us a myth, a story he heard. It is said to have taken place during the mythical 'war between the Greeks and the Amazons': after the Greeks, led by the Heracles, won a battle against the Amazons at the mouth of the river Thermodon, they sailed away in three ships, taking the surviving Amazons with them to serve as their slaves.

However, the Amazon women did not want to live a life of slavery and concubinage. While the ships were out at sea, they started a mutiny. Rising up against their Greeks captors, they 'hacked them down'[11] and took control of the ships. Unfortunately, there was one thing the Amazons had not considered: only after they had killed all their captors did they realise that they had no idea how to steer a ship. They were horse-archers, not sailors.

There they were, stranded out on the Black Sea, imprisoned on a ship that they had no clue how to control. They were, in Herodotus's words, at the 'mercy of the waves and the wind'.[12] How terrifying to be stuck out at sea, adrift, with the endless

Remembering Women

expanse of water stretching out on all sides, making sure you realise that you will die of thirst before any help comes.

Now, you might remember what happens when another fleet of ships in Greek myth finds itself at the mercy of the waves, winds, and weather gods. When the Greek warrior Odysseus tries to return home to Ithaca after the Trojan War, the sea gods make sure it takes him ten years to reach the safety of his home, in spite of his mastery of the art of sailing.

Interestingly, the gods and elements who chose to be so disruptive to Odysseus decided they would be much kinder to the Amazon women aboard their captors' ships. The Amazons may have used their mirrors to signal for help, but if they found assistance that way, Herodotus does not tell us so. Instead, wind and waves brought them directly to a friendly coast. Even better, they immediately found a mode of transport: 'The first thing they came across was a herd of horses, which they promptly seized, saddled up and used to plunder all they could from the Scythians.'[13]

At this stage, surely, it would be time for the story to punish these women, who kill Greek slavers, then steal horses and food from Scythian men? All of these women could be turned into swans, or reeds, or perhaps some animal that Zeus could have his way with without his wife noticing.

Not in Herodotus, though. Herodotus describes a surprising reaction among the Scythian men to the appearance of these Pirate Amazons: they decide to offer themselves up as sexual partners.

The Amazons turn out to be very enthusiastic about this idea, telling all of their friends about it, and returning for regular sexual encounters. Quite soon the two camps merge into one, and the Scythian men suggest they should marry the Amazon women, return them to their settlements and have children together: 'we have parents, and we have our own belongings'.[14]

Pirate Amazons, living as Scythian housewives? 'We would never be able to settle down with your women [...]. We shoot arrows, throw javelins, ride horses. But what do your women do?'[15] The women make an alternative suggestion: 'If you really want us as your wives, and to be seen to behave with complete honour as well, go to your parents and take the due share of your possessions. Then, on your return, we can go and set up a home together of our own.'[16]

The young men agree, go and get their things, then settle in a new place with their brides, together founding the new tribe of the Sauromatians. And so, Herodotus tells us, the Pirate Amazons live happily ever after. 'And from that time to this, the Sauromatin women have kept to their primal way of life: they go out hunting, whether their husband are with them or not, they go to war and they dress exactly like the men.'[17]

Note that Herodotus – in this modern English translation – calls this a primal way of life. To my ear, primal is a word that is not too far removed from primordial, the technical term used in memory studies for our foundational past. What a great story this is, full of suspense and romance, and how well it could serve us and our adolescents who are trying to make sense of their changing bodies, and their changing relationships with people of the same and other genders. It could help young women conceive of themselves as free and independent, as people who take life into their own hands and who only enter into relationships when they can live as the equal of their partner.

However, it is not found in collections of myths and legends, certainly not for young people. If you take a look at the bookshelf of the online shop of the British Museum, the stories typically adapted and retold for children of different ages are those of male adventurers, for example the tale of Jason and the Argonauts, of Hercules and his labours, or the tale of the Theseus killing the minotaur.[18] Adults also get their fair share: a Hercules musical in the West End, a second part of Ridley Scott's *Gladiator*, a blockbuster retelling of the Odyssey by director Christopher Nolan. The story of the Pirate Amazons, however, remains an unpopular source for adaptation, as do countless other stories about Amazons.

It is important to take this in. The story of the Pirate Amazons is right there in Herodotus's *Histories*. It has been there since the fifth century BCE. This is one of the most comprehensively studied texts of antiquity. Classicists all over the world have read it, know of it, could tell you about it. And yet, no one seems to have thought to adapt it into a multimillion-dollar Disney blockbuster, or write a novel about it, or even include it as one tale among many into a children's book. There are graphic novels and bestselling books on the Persian war as it is told by Herodotus, but nothing about the Amazons. Our culture does not consider this a story worth telling.

Why do we struggle to tell stories of the past where women are adventurers, warriors, and heroines who live their own lives, in service to nothing but their own happiness and freedom? What is it that makes us read that passage in Herodotus and simply glide over it, pretend it isn't there, that this isn't prime storytelling material? Why do we not want to tell stories about women in the past that are fun, enjoyable, pleasurable?

The issue has to do with how storytelling and memory relate to one another.

Stories are a magical thing. They have been around for as long as we have, and though it might be hard to articulate why, telling and listening to stories is a fundamental part of human life. Stories are also imbued with the potential for great longevity. In other words: they can grow very old. Older than humans. Older than trees. Older than some mountains.

This is partly possible because we keep on adapting them. Stories last because we change them to make sense in a new time and place, a new context. We give them new life, and we can do so because stories share some of the properties of life. They survive if we continue to remember them, changing and adapting them for new generations.

The reverse, however, is also true: stories die. If we do not retell them, do not adapt them, they vanish. Some may still be retained as vestiges in libraries, archives or museums, in a text such as Herodotus's *Histories*, but because they have not been updated, adapted, transformed, we no longer consider them worthwhile, important, or relevant. Often, we do not even think of them. Humans are creatures of habit. If we are not used to doing something, we are unlikely to suddenly start doing it. We are not used to retelling the story of the Pirate Amazons, so we do not. When we publish a new version of Greek myths for children or adults, no one asks, 'but where is the legend of the Pirate Amazons?'

Changing our cultural memory is all about breaking with old habits. It is looking at the past – in our museum collections, libraries and archives – for memories and stories that are worth telling, that are worth adapting and changing so that we breathe new life into them. It is about finding the right memories, the right stories, for our moment in time, for the world we live in and the future we want to see.

For Herodotus, the story of the Pirate Amazons may still have been a communicative memory – a report he heard on his travels, of a mythic event set as far away from us as the end of the First World War, or women winning the vote, or perhaps the French revolution. He chose to run with this story and reproduce it, adapt it for the readers of his *Histories*. He has given us this gift, but we have fallen out of the habit of telling the fun stories of women adventurers, who reach with both hands for happiness. Fun, play, and pleasure seem inappropriate for women and girls today, and for the memories of our foremothers from the past. Their lives, we believe, must have been grim and full of responsibilities. While Herodotus certainly made up many of the stories he tells, he displays great accuracy in his descriptions of Scythian customs, burial rites and material culture, and many of his accounts have been widely confirmed by modern-day archaeologists.

Indeed, perhaps this story throws some light on a curious doll found in the grave of a girl from Ancient Greece. Greek girls were given puppets of Amazons, those man-slaying barbarian women from the East.[19] These puppets were nude, like male Greek heroes; they were warriors and independent women who rode out to hunt and fight and were not made to stay in the *gunaikon*, the place in the Greek home where the women lived separated from the men.

It may seem odd that Athenian parents would give their girls such toys to play with, as no Athenian girl could ever hope to grow into an adult warrior or even an adolescent athlete. Looking at it from 2,500 years in the future, the gift seems almost cruel, but I cannot help but think that I, too, would have given my daughter such a gift, if I had been a mother in Classical Athens. My daughter may never have the same freedoms as the Amazons from Herodotus's story, but at least she would know what to strive for, she would know to be proud, to say what she wanted, and that equal partnerships were possible.

Thankfully, many girls growing up today no longer find themselves in the same situation as their Ancient Greek counterparts. When they grow up today, they can play with the toys they want, they are free to do any exercise they choose, they can strive to become a professional boxer, or simply enjoy fencing. They can have fun.

And yet, simply enjoying fencing does not seem to be so simple for all, and neither does the freedom that girls and young women now have. Memory, tradition, and history come together to make it seem strange when girls have fun, when they move their bodies in a playful way. Today, we still encounter a stereotype that should have vanished decades ago: that women are not great athletes, that sport 'isn't for them'. Women have been competing and achieving great feats at the International Olympic Games for 124 years (22 women first competed in the 1900 Olympic games in Paris), and still there is a prejudice against girls, adolescents and young women who wish to compete in combat sports, or who have great athletic ambitions. We continue to indulge in the stereotype that women are less competitive than men, and in the process, we make women less competitive than men. We do this not least because we have chosen Classical Athens as the site of our origin myth – a place women were not meant to use their bodies for any activity other than reproduction. This is not the fault of the Greeks, but rather of how we have enshrined them in memory. And what we have enshrined is the ideal of a culture in which, when women did compete with men, they were subjects of both horror and fascination, of love and violent erotic desire. Whatever these Barbarian women were to the Greeks, they had to remain outsiders. History has more to offer us. If we shift our gaze just a little to the East once more, we find a different place to begin our recollections. In Ancient Scythia, some of the graveyards contain the remains of warrior women as young as sixteen.[20] As tragic as it is to think of the death of so young a woman, female adolescents in Greece were as likely to die from childbirth at that age, or even earlier.[21] In fact, the term 'adolescence' as we understand it is misplaced in the context of the ancients, where women as young as twelve were considered of a marriageable age, and often married to men twice their age. They had many children, and had them early, and this was what their bodies were busy with.[22]

Adolescents in Ancient Scythia had no set marriageable age that we know of.[23] Ancient commentators such as Herodotus suggest that young women did not marry until they had won their first battle. Both girls and boys were taught how to ride a horse, hunt, fight, and provide for the nomadic and semi-nomadic communities that they were a part of.[24] If young women were dying in combat at sixteen, then buried with their horses and weapons, they must have already spent a great part of their adolescence learning how to ride, and how to fight. They are also likely to have spent less time on childbearing and consequently suffered fewer of its damaging physical consequences. In studies conducted in the 1970s and 1990s, sedentary lifestyles were associated with higher fertility rates. In some nomadic communities cited in the studies, women have fewer children than in settled communities, perhaps only two or three rather than four to six,[25] as in Classical Athens,[26] so much closer to our current birth rate in the Anglophone West.

From these facts emerges the picture of a very different adolescence to that of women and girls in Athens in the first millennium BCE. Female teenagers in Scythian communities were trained to use their growing bodies in ways that would have enabled them to live relatively free and independent lives. If it is true that female adolescents were not considered of a marriageable age until they had won a first battle, whether actual or symbolic, then courtship (or dating, as we might say) may not have consumed their days. Meeting other young men, and other young women, finding someone to grow old or have children with, may not have been the first and foremost priority, particularly as young women and men were already engaging in sexual contact, if the Ancient commentators such as Strabo and Herodotus are to be believed.[27] They were certainly believed to have had sex before marriage, and plenty of it. It is difficult to imagine how learning how to box or wrestle would have been considered a strange thing to do for an adolescent girl in those ancient communities. By the time Kheuke is a teenager, she may have developed a passion for wrestling and footraces. She loves to compete with her peers, and she loves most of all to impress them. She wants to be the best wrestler in the world, and the best archer, better even than Penthesilea, her favourite superhero.

Today, feminists want girls and women, boys and men to enjoy their bodies instead of dedicating them to the prescriptions of gender. We want to encourage women and girls to love their bodies, to exercise in a way that is fun and rewarding for them, to become top athletes if they want to, or cycle to work, or go on long walks, whatever it is that best suits them. Most of all, we want girls and boys to be equals in the way that they are encouraged to love and use their bodies.

There is precedent for this practice in the Mediterranean. There is a tradition of peaceful exercise, and of adolescent girls and boys growing up as equals. Young women in Scythia were trained in battle so that they would be able to fight, and as the bones found in the grave of a sixteen-year-old warrior woman indicate, some of them did, but that is not the only reason adolescent girls have been taught to use and enjoy their body in humanity's past. If we cast our gaze a little further back, reach deeper into the evidence, then we find a peaceful exercise tradition very close to Athens and Scythia: we come across it in the civilisation of Minoan Crete.

Minoan Crete is a civilisation that survived and thrived from 3000 to 1100 BCE, at which point it vanished quite suddenly, along with most other major civilisations of the Mediterranean, such as the Hittite Empire or Greek Mycenae, famously the home of Agamemnon and Menelaus, the kings who started the Trojan War. We still do not have a satisfying explanation for this sudden decline, although there are some hypotheses, such as the sudden invasion of seafaring warriors called the Sea People. Recently, scholars have argued for a combination of various causes, among them climate change, destructive earthquakes, droughts, the cutting of international trade routes, and the powerful rise of societies that revered warfare and violence, setting the Mediterranean, including their peaceful neighbours, on a course of debilitating and ultimately self-destructive conflict.[28]

Before they disappeared, the Minoans built an extraordinary culture. Extraordinary because of its beautiful architecture, its outstanding art, its cosmopolitan trade – and the power of its women. The iconography of Minoan art suggests that women held important positions of power. It also suggests that girls indulged in a particularly thrilling athletic pastime: bull-leaping.

Yes, bull-leaping. Six hundred years before girls in Classical Athens were given Amazon puppets to play with, and as Scythian women were learning how to hunt and fight, young teenagers on Crete were leaping over the heads of bulls. The Bull-Leaping Fresco is one of the most famous frescoes ever found. It was discovered at the Palace of Knossos on Crete by Sir Arthur Evans, who excavated Knossos from 1901 to 1930. It portrays three young persons, presumably two young women and one young man if we wish to fix their gender identities, engaged in the exhilarating and no doubt quite dangerous pastime of grabbing a bull by the horns and flipping one's body across it. And here I was, thinking that fencing was exciting.

I can only imagine that some strutting and preening and showing-off was involved in bull-leaping. However, like fencing, I imagine this as a sport that is, first and foremost, about quick instincts, about strength, about mastering your fears as you prepare to leap across the bull. In the moment that you undertake it, it is all about you, and not about the ones who are watching, the people you might be trying to impress.

I realise you probably have to be between the ages of thirteen and eighteen to want to do such a thing as stare down a bull and leap across its back at no inconsiderable risk of grave injury. This was the brief period of my own life when I enjoyed leapfrogging from a springboard in the school gym over a bock, a cushioned obstacle vaguely shaped like the back of a buck or ram (or, indeed, a bull), landing on a pad positioned behind it.

Sometimes I hit the mat, sometimes I missed. At fourteen, I did not mind. I was an adolescent, someone who is discovering who they are growing into, what they can achieve with their taller bodies, their changed shapes, all that they can strive for and accomplish as they become adults. Perhaps bull-leaping will not be the foremost challenge that awaits them in adulthood, just as I do not routinely jump over rams in my day-to-day life. But what a way to test, and discover, one's limits.

What is important to us is that Minoan Crete is not known as a particularly war-like society. It must have encouraged its young women and men to share in this pursuit for pleasure rather than to help them grow into warriors. Bodily exercise, physical pursuits, were not necessarily linked with warfare. They were playful, competitive, fun. What a difference from the lives led by women in Classical Athens, whose bodies were considered passive even as they gave birth, in spite of the contractions witnessed by (male) doctors.[29] We may know very little about bull-leaping in Minoan Crete with any certainty, but the point of taking it seriously is as much about we don't know as it is about what we do know. It is about what we have chosen to forget, what we continue to choose to forget even as it leaps up before our very eyes.

The Bull-Leaping Fresco is one of the most famous archaeological discoveries ever made. It is an astounding piece of art, a testament to human artistry and craftmanship throughout the ages. It is on display in the Heraklion Archaeological Museum on Crete, where it is one of the most popular pieces on exhibition.

And yet, we do not think of the Minoan culture as part of our culture, as part of our memory. Just like Herodotus looked on the Scythians as strangers, albeit strangers he may have admired, so we look at the civilisation of Minoan Crete as something we may admire, but decide not to make part of our own heritage. It is the strangest arrangement we have made for ourselves. We make memories out of so many Greek myths, and we make them so thoroughly our own that we pass them on to our children, but we do not tell them about the girls bull-leaping on Crete. Instead, we scare them with tales of the Minotaur, half-bull, half-man, slaughtered by the Greek hero Theseus with the help of the Cretan princess Ariadne. Guess what Theseus does to her? At first he takes her with him, only to then leave her to die on a remote island. Greek heroes continue not to be very likable.

As we uphold the Greek storytelling tradition, as we keep re-telling our children the stories of Theseus, Perseus, and Hercules and the women they killed and abandoned, it is as if we were giving dolls to our girls. And not puppets of heroic Amazons, but of Ancient Greek adolescents; of teenagers who might who might have had six children before the age of twenty against her will.

And in some ways, that is exactly what we do. Girls are still routinely given dolls as toys, either baby dolls or Barbie dolls. I had both. I enjoyed playing with both, but I also believe that we sometimes cling to old memories through a Barbie doll, memories of an era where women were dedicated predominantly to beauty, instead of imagining a different time, and a different place; one that would allow us to tell different stories to our children.

Instead, we send mixed messages to our daughters. Exercise is important, we tell them, but the dolls you get to play with are either so thin as to not have a functioning body at all (Barbie), or they are babies, which may one day grow in your womb.

Here are the two things you can do with your body. These are your options.

Influencers, advertising professionals, and a section of professional reporters and entertainers corroborate this stereotype. As Laura Bates has pointed out in *Fix the System, Not the Women* (2022), 'trends in the portrayal of women in our media both reflect and worsen sexist attitudes', with 'endless headlines about women "flaunting", "showcasing" and simply owning body parts'.[30] Women are not supposed to own body parts, much less use them in the way they want them to, rather than what other people (often men) think of as proper. This is sometimes compounded by governments, such as the UK government in the early 2020s, which ran advertisements showing women engaged in childcare and household chores while men in the same picture were lounging on the sofa, according to Bates.[31] There is an acceptable way to use your (thin, able) body, these adverts are saying, but it is certainly not for pleasure, exhilaration, or reaching for the stars.

There are no depictions of women at Knossos doing household chores. There are plenty of them exercising power, leading rituals, or indeed just having a good time together. Women of all ages are shown interacting with others, dancing, talking, or engaging in communal rituals.[32]

In more egalitarian societies, all this suggests, girls and women have been taught how to love their bodies; how to use them not for someone else's, but entirely their own, fun and pleasure: for dancing, bull-leaping, chatting, and making art. If we choose to cast our minds back to Scythia and Minoan Crete, we can imagine societies that taught young women to use their bodies for independence, and for freedom, with children or without. That is what a body is: not a thing to be controlled, not even to be owned. It is what sets us free. If you can ride, if you can run, you will always be able to remove yourself from a dangerous situation, or stand up to it, as did our foremothers in Scythia.

Throughout my adolescence, and indeed all my life, I have used my body to cycle places: to school, to see a friend, home from a night out at the Manchester Student Union bar, where I was given a 'date rape' drug as a doctoral student in my thirties. I enjoy cycling, and it is very quick and convenient, reliable and fun, but the reason why I took it up and will continue to teach it to any woman who wants to learn is a different one: I knew, even as a teenager, that no rapist would be able to catch me at night if they were on foot and I was on a bike. Living an embodied life comes with risks, but our bodies allow us to stand up to those risks.

My story about bicycles, and the graves of our foremothers in Scythia, show us that using your body for yourself, as you want to, is not without risk, but that the reward is precious: it is independence. Which is another term for the privilege to do what you want with your own body, not what anyone else asks you to do, or tries to make you do. It is the privilege of knowing that your body is not there to be used, not by anyone but yourself. And this knowledge is something we must impart on our children, girls and boys, trans and non-binary. Perhaps with some help from our Scythian foremothers. I recommend Herodotus and his pirate story for some nighttime reading. It really is very good, and has a good lesson to teach us all, adolescent or not: that our cultural memory can be fun, and that our bodies are our own – and so is our freedom.

Memory shapes how we see ourselves and what we believe we are capable of achieving. This is true for each of us personally, but it is also true collectively. If we remember a past where women were not allowed to achieve, were not even allowed to strive for achievement, then any sign of this in our daughters will seem odd, strange, unnatural, at least atypical. This is true for career ambitions, but it is also true for something much more basic: the things we believe we are allowed to aim for, that we are allowed to achieve with our bodies.

Adolescence is a time in which our bodies change, but as a teenager, I felt that it was first and foremost a time in which others changed around me: it was their perception of my body that changed, rather than my own. I remember noticing how, after my first period, other people looked at me differently, most of them men. I had become part of, in Rebecca Solnit's words, the group of 'women-as-bodies'. Sex waiting to happen.

Around the same time, I stopped the exercise I enjoyed, cowed by the stereotypes surrounding me, where women's bodies were viewed as something odd, as something not suited to sports. As I contemplate returning to these pursuits, I realise my personal memory is holding me back, just as our collective memory is holding us back as a society. But memories, both personal and collective, can change.

Memory has the power to hold us back but also to enable us. When we remember something we did in the past and did well, or remember enjoying it, these memories may lead us back to the thing we excelled at, or that we found pleasure in. Cultural memory can box us in, but it can also enable us to live freer, better, more enjoyable lives, and it can do the same for our children, nieces, nephews, and all those that will follow in our footsteps, as we are following in the footsteps of the ancients.

Harnessing the power of cultural memory is a powerful thing, but it is not without complications. So far, I have been making it out to be simple: as though all would be solved if only we picked a different time from which to begin our stories of the past; if only we remembered a different place as the site of our primordial past. However, changing cultural memory is more complicated than that. In the following chapter, I will show how and why it is more complicated. I will do so through a subject that still inspires debates about how it is best represented, and that becomes urgently important as adolescents grow into young women and men, and as they navigate one of the greatest but also most fickle pleasures of all: sex.

4. SEX

Memory is complicated, and so are attempts to shape it, and change it, no matter how pure our intentions. This is particularly true when we try to reshape the memory of taboo subjects. One such subject is sex, and how it relates to history, and our memory of the Ancients.

Let us look at how tricky it can be to shape cultural memory afresh. When we think about sex in the past, there is often little sense of taboo around the subject of male desire. Helen of Troy in particular has been a projection for the desires of heterosexual men for centuries. In Christopher Marlowe's 1605 play *Doctor Faustus*, the titular hero makes a deal with the devil in order to meet Helen of Troy. When he meets the spirit the devil has conjured, he is bewitched by the manifestation of his own desires: 'Was this the face that launched a thousand ships, \ And burnt the topless towers of Ilium? \ Sweet Helen, make me immortal with a kiss: \ Her lips sucks forth my soul, see where it flies!'[1]

He does not in fact want Helen herself, it seems – not a woman of flesh and blood, but rather wants, through kissing her, to himself become immortal. Those who sleep with Helen, he knows, are bound to be remembered. He lists their names, as if already fancying himself as famous as them, as if he were writing himself into a future cultural memory of male desire: 'I will be Paris, and for love of thee, \ Instead of Troy shall Wittenberg be sacked; \ And I will combat with weak Menelaus, \ And wear thy colours on my plumed crest: \ Yea, I will wound Achilles in the heel, \ And then return to Helen for a kiss.'[2]

Paris, Menelaus, Achilles, Faustus: men who are remembered, whose names we recall to this day, who moved through the world and claimed it as their own. Faustus splashes his desires across the stage for all to see. In Elizabethan England, the fictive sexual desires of the men of Ancient Greece were very much a cultural presence, a myth transformed into reality, a fantasy becoming a memory. When the play is performed today, memory is layered upon memory, history upon history, and the desires of Elizabethan men and men from Ancient Greece become the desires performed by men in the present day, forced upon the body of a woman from the present day, standing in for Helen, a Helen who is not asked for consent before Faustus kisses her. When Faustus says to the vision he has conjured up, 'none but thou shalt be my paramour',[3] it sounds like a threat. There were other men before him who wanted Helen to themselves. They were willing to kill for it. Faustus may be seeking immortality, but he sacrifices his mortal soul for the opportunity to express this desire.

Helen does not get to speak on stage. Her silence betrays a taboo in our cultural memory: female desire is not part of our spokn history. We simply pretend that it never existed.

This is a difficult situation to be in when you are a young woman developing a sex drive,[4] when desires are strange and sex might seem a great mystery. For the longest time, it seemed to me that I was the only one not having sex. As my female friends and I grew into young adults, as they turned fifteen, sixteen, seventeen, they started dating, entered into relationships with boys their age, and started having sex. I was less successful in my aim to do the same, but I did not turn to the women in my family for advice, or to anyone else, other than teenage magazine columnists. At the time, those were mostly filled with tips on how a teenage woman could change herself in order to appeal to her male peers. None of those tips appealed to me. I did not fancy make-up, or wanted to straighten my hair, or to pretend I was not into video games.

But I still wanted to have sex. In fact, I wanted it quite badly. Perhaps unusually, I did not want sex just to get it over with, or to be like my friends, or not to be left behind. No, I wanted to have sex because I was sure that I would enjoy it.

This certainty had probably grown out of my pleasurable experiences with solo sex. From the first moments I had experienced sexual desire, I had practiced solo sex and enjoyed it immensely, but at the time I never thought of this activity as 'real sex'. The term 'solo sex' was not common currency then, and all representations of sex that I saw in films, books, or on the telly involved two people, usually a man and a woman.

Although it was my number one priority for much of my adolescence, I did not succeed in my endeavour to find a boyfriend and sleep with him before leaving school. Sitting A-levels as a virgin (this is how I thought of myself then: as if the amount of sex I was having, or not having, was a defining part of my identity), as well as attending prom without a romantic partner, did not make me perennially unhappy, but it did make me think I might never have sex in my life.

After sitting my A-levels, I considered different options – apprenticeships, university degrees – but eventually decided

I wanted to go and see the world and work some proper jobs before deciding what I was going to do with what I thought of then, rather dramatically, as *the rest of my life*. I cleaned hostel rooms and communal bathrooms in Newcastle, Australia, I sold upmarket souvenirs and paraphernalia down a sidestreet from Montréal's Notre Dame cathedral, and I tried getting work as a journalist in New Zealand.

I also went out, and met many young men, and some young women, and I finally had some partnered sex. One year after leaving school, I was no longer worried about dying a virgin. My first experience of penetrative sex came with my first boyfriend, a colleague at the first newspaper I worked at. I was twenty-two at the time, and until writing these very lines, I thought of that day as the day when I lost my virginity.

Looking back on it, that is of course not at all what happened that day. It may have been my first experience of penetrative sex with a man, but it was by no means my first time experiencing an orgasm. Looking back at it now, I had already been having solo sex for many years, and had enjoyed many other forms of partnered sex with different people. And it showed: I knew what I liked and what I wanted from the start. Throughout our relationship, my first boyfriend and I had excellent sex, which continued even as our relationship began to fall apart. Some of my female friends at university struggled with having sex they enjoyed. I did not.

If you happen to have been thinking that this is all rather frank and too much information, and perhaps also beside the point, you may be proving a point I am about to make: female pleasure is still a taboo in our society, especially when it is experienced solo, and I would argue that this taboo is deeply connected to the way we look at the past, the way we do history. Outside of reality TV and anonymous online posts, it may still be unusual to talk frankly about one's sex life, but I believe it is important that we do, particularly as women, and particularly when we think about how we look at the past; what stories we tell each other about it, and what great sex lives our foremothers may have had. Just think of the Pirate Amazons and their paramours on the coast of the Black Sea. Just think of Atalanta, who was turned into a lion along with her beloved.

Any of these tales are more pleasant than what we know of the mythical fate of Helen and historical women like her, long married by eighteen to men twice their age. According to Greek myth, as a girl as young as seven or ten, Helen was kidnapped by the Greek hero Theseus. Due to his divine pedigree, Theseus felt that a bride born of the gods was his due. Helen fit the bill, because she had been fathered by Zeus. Her brothers retrieved her, but the rescue operation led only to a brief respite rather than Helen's freedom. She was married a few years later. Her father chose Menelaus for her, who became king of Sparta when he married her. They had at least one child together.

Then she met Paris, the Trojan prince, who came to stay with them in Sparta. Even though we have numerous accounts of Helen's life, we have none about her desires, but there is plenty of speculation. Did she fall in love with Paris? Did she desire him? Did he want and kidnap her, or did he want and court her, or did she simply want an out, a shot at a different life, away from the man who had married her when she was still a child?

The absence of desire and pleasure in our memory of Helen is curious. This is a mythical woman, but she is not permitted any fantasies of her own. All the fantasies and desires we remember are the desires of the men around her.

This is one of the reasons why female sexual pleasure is still taboo, even today: it seems not to exist in the stories we tell each other about our past. It does not exist in our cultural memory. Sex is a true taboo, a blind spot of our collective memory, but this taboo is today selectively applied to women and gay, bisexual and trans men rather than heterosexual men. Everyone knows the name of Casanova, but who recalls the names of his female loves? Meanwhile, male masturbation is a staple of coming-of-age films, and male sexual desire remains the driving force of many bestselling narratives in film, books, television and video games. Few heroes are not 'rewarded' for their troubles by 'winning' the beautiful woman, from Iron Man going off with Pepper Potts to *The Lord of the Ring*'s Aragorn winning the hand of his beloved Arwen.

We suffer the consequences of this blind spot in our present, where we struggle to cast consent as key, and female sexual pleasure is still regarded as something that may not matter, or even exist. While modern-day cinema represents male pursuits of their female love interests as something wanted by these women, this narrative arc commodifies the women in question and corroborates the worldview of an 'incel culture' in which female pleasure is always subordinate to male pleasure, and sex a service that women provide to men.[5]

Incel stands for 'involuntarily celibate'. The incel community unites boys and men online who get together to blame women for their problems, all of which, according to the dominant narrative of this ideology, can be traced back to women not wanting to sleep with them. As a result, they insult and denigrate women and have gone on to injure and kill them.⁶ 'The incel community is the most violent corner of the so-called manosphere,' writes journalist and activist Laura Bates in *Men Who Hate Women* (2020). In incel culture, women 'are constantly hungry for sex, but they only choose to sleep with the most attractive cohort of men'.⁷ Incels believe that the 'top crop', so twenty per cent of men, have eighty per cent of all the sex.⁸ Odd as this view of the world may seem, it harks back to a time and economic system when women were literally 'won' as prizes in battle and made into the slaves of men, where a powerful man might in fact have a wife and multiple female slaves, such as the Greek Kings Agamemnon or Menelaus.

An early example of such a narratives comes from the *Iliad*, Homer's epic portrayal of the final year of the Trojan War. In the *Iliad*, women are treated as any other spoil of war: their fate is to be raped and turned into sex slaves, which has remained a weapon of male warfare throughout the ages.⁹ The American literary scholar Jonathan Gottschall has argued that the *Iliad* is in fact a testament to a wider raiding economy prevalent among Ancient Greek city states. The cities did not survive and thrive merely because of trade or production or the mining of resources but because they stole and enslaved the greatest number of people.¹⁰ No one summarises this lens on the *Iliad* better than Rebecca Solnit, in her essay 'The Problem with Sex is Capitalism':

> It goes back before capitalism, really, this dehumanization that makes sex an activity men exact from women who have no say in the situation. The Trojan War begins when Trojan Paris kidnaps Helen and keeps her as a sex slave. During the war

to get Helen back, Achilles captures Queen Briseis and keeps her as a sex slave, after slaying her husband and brothers (and slaying someone's whole family is generally pretty anti-aphrodisiac). His comrade in arms Agamemnon has some sex slaves of his own, including the prophetess Cassandra, cursed by Apollo with the gift of prophesies no one believes for refusing to have sex with him. Read from the point of view of the women, the Trojan War resembles ISIS among the Yazidi.[11]

We do not need to read the *Iliad* entirely in this light to agree that its primary conflict is between two men, Achilles and Agamemnon, who are fighting over a woman they have enslaved. Her name is Briseis. Needless to say, her opinion or her desires play no part in this epic poem. Even Helen gets to speak only very little relative to the male characters, while her face is still invoked as that which launched a thousand ships, as if it had not been the men on those ships that literally launched them into the sea. We owe thanks to Christopher Marlowe for demonstrating that a good metaphor will quickly morph into memory, and then into myth, outlasting every fact, no matter how certain. Unfortunately, this tradition gives incel worldviews an unwelcome legitimacy, in that it depicts and normalises women as a sexual resource.

In other instances of Greek myth, female sexual pleasure is often subordinate to male sexual pleasure. Very often, men and male gods pursue women to have sex with them while women run from them. When they do not manage to escape, they are cruelly punished, frequently by female goddesses. We have already met Echo – just one of many rape victims in Greek myth. In Classical Athens, rape was not a crime against the victim but against the man who legally owned her, usually her father or husband.[12]

The profusion of rape in Greek mythology is something which has often been pointed out, but it is sometimes treated as something we need not worry about any more, such as when it is glossed over in in contemporary retellings of Greek myth.[13] This glossing over has serious repercussions for our cultural memory of female sexual pleasure. Consensual sex and female pleasure are still implicitly believed to be a recent invention, fads of modernity, something not quite natural, rather than desirable – worthy of being normal. This lack of consensual sex and female sexual pleasure in our cultural memory plays a part in the persistence of the myths of rape culture, including the myth that a woman means yes when she says no.[14]

Much as I wish that rape culture was a thing of the past, it is alive and well, as I learnt when I encountered a man who wanted to incapacitate and rape me in the Student Union bar in Manchester. This was in the year after my grandmother had died, and before my niece was born.

I believe that this man would have succeeded, had I not been able to rely on my body, its muscle memory. As soon as I noticed that something was wrong, that I was blacking out, that I no longer had control over my limbs, my body took me out of the emergency exit and onto my bike. It cycled me home without any conscious effort or intervention on my part. The man who tried to rape me was never caught.

If we are to end the trivialisation of sexual violence against women, we must take immediate steps to change our cultural memory so that it includes consensual and pleasurable sex for women, trans, queer and non-binary people. And yet, as I have mentioned, changing our cultural memory is more complicated than we might expect. Women have begun to seriously write back against rape culture, with countless novels retelling the stories of women from Greek myth, speaking out for rape survivors past and imagined. This is to be applauded, and it has been welcomed by countless readers, but I am afraid that on mnemonic terms, it may not be as helpful as we think. We retell the old stories, we call a rapist by his name, but it is still the man who rapes and the woman who suffers. The past is cast as a regressive place that is defined, even becomes recognisable through the degree of suffering experienced by the women that inhabit it. Female suffering becomes a marker of authenticity when we think about the past; an account of the past only seems realistic when women suffer and men commit violence against them. We continue to think of women as victims, while men are agents of change. We continue to think of sex in the past as rape, or not think of it at all. There continues to be little female pleasure, little consensual sex, in our cultural memory.

We are aware of this dilemma but seem unable to tell a different story. In *The Silence of the Girls* (2018), the novelist Pat Barker gives a voice to Briseis, who has been enslaved by Achilles. Throughout the novel, she attempts to escape the encampment of the Greek army and reshape our memory of the Trojan War. She attempts to tell her own story, but realises at the end of the book that she has failed to escape both her enslavement and the memory of Achilles:

> Looking back, it seemed to me I'd been trying to escape not just from the camp, but from Achilles' story; and I'd failed. Because, make no mistake, this

was his story – *his* anger, *his* grief, *his* story. *I* was angry, *I* was grieving, but somehow that didn't matter. Here I was, again, waiting for Achilles to decide when it was time for bed, still trapped, still stuck inside his story, and yet with no real part to play in it.[15]

As we retell stories of the past, we run the risk of remaining trapped in the memories we have already made for ourselves, or that others have made for us. Briseis realises that she has remained a passive girl throughout her narrative, a footnote of literary history. This mirrors the place she has held in literary history to this day: an unnamed girl who only matters to the story as someone who men want to enslave and rape. This attitude is crystallised by a character in US author Philip Roth's 1999 novel *The Human Stain*, where a male teacher suggests that the *Iliad* amounts to a mere 'barroom brawl', with Agamemnon and Achilles 'quarrelling over a woman. A girl, really. A girl stolen from her father. A girl abducted in a war.'[16]

Female authors have given a voice to the unnamed girls of the past, making a contribution to the contest of collective memory, seeking to modify, correct and revise the canon, to give women a place in it. But all too often, that place is the same one that has already been carved out: a place for women without desires, without options, those who are always suffering, whose lives are grim, who do not act but are acted upon. There is a reason why we stick to the familiar script, why we do not want to recover unknown treasure. The treasure is strange. The memory is familiar. We are human. We like what we know.

However, if we wish to change our cultural memory, we must turn to what is strange to us. We must recover some unfamiliar treasure. Fortunately, our foremothers are here to help us out.

Our Scythian foremothers may well have had more fun than we do. All traces in the records indicate that they put female sexual pleasure, and the autonomy of every woman to seek it, front and centre. Herodotus reports that Scythian women were happy to express and fulfil their desires. If you remember, in the legendary story of how the Sauromatian tribe was founded, Herodotus describes how enthusiastic the Amazons were to become the Scythian men's sexual partners. They even told their friends about the sexual opportunity. Of one woman, Herodotus writes that: 'Unable to communicate with [the Scythian man] verbally, since neither could understand the other, she gestured instead with her hands that he should come to the same spot the following day, and bring another with him. "Make it two of you," she said, using sign language. "And I will bring a friend of my own."'[17]

While this story belongs to the realm of myth rather than fact, it may contain a kernel of truth. It tells us that it was at least plausible to people contemporary with Herodotus that Scythian women were free to enjoy a healthy sex life, that they were happy for other women to do the same, and that they had full autonomy in their choice of partners.

The Greek historian Strabo wrote in his *Geography* about the ways that Scythian women used quivers, hung above the entrances to their huts or tents, to signal to their community that they were entertaining a guest and would rather not be disturbed.[18] Not only women of high status, or sex workers, or priestesses: according to Ancient commentators, all women among the Scythians were free to enjoy sex and its many pleasures.[19] They used their bodies. They used them to run, to sail, to ride, to dance, and for their own pleasure. There are Greek vases that depict a woman wearing the coat of Thracian hunters, offering a rabbit to another woman. The rabbit is a sign of same-sex flirtation, a romantic or erotic overture.[20] In ancient myth and art, Amazons are portrayed as sexually active, as desiring women and men with no compunctions about expressing their attraction.

Anthropologists and evolutionary biologists suggest that this pattern of attraction and expression of desire may be indicative of a period of human history predating the ancients. In semi-nomadic and nomadic communities, women would have had multiple partners, many of whom would pitch in to help with childcare. While the male partners could not be sure that they were the father of a child, they would still offer their support – after all, they could not be sure that the offspring was not theirs, either.[21]

If reshaping our cultural memory of sex involves the telling of different stories, some of these stories will have to be imagined. I like to imagine that one of the women on the vase is Kheuke. She has grown into a young woman who thinks signal mirrors are silly and that her parents don't have a clue. She is in Thrace, where she meets a woman she likes. Perhaps she has never courted a woman before, but she likes this one. She likes her Thracian cloak, she likes that she is a hunter, she likes that she is confident enough to come up to her, to offer her the rabbit pelt, to ask, are you cold?

Penthesilea is not cold. It is not a cold evening. The evenings are not cold in the summer in Thrace. She still accepts the pelt. She looks the other woman in the eye as she slings it around her shoulders, then runs a hand down her pelt. The other woman is not looking at her face. She is looking at her hand. Then at her lips.

They kiss in the harbour that night before the woman takes Penthesilea back to her room. This is where she finally gets her hands on that Thracian coat. Gets to slide it off the shoulders of the woman who keeps looking at her lips. Gets to run her knuckles over her bare shoulders, the naked skin, then puts her hand on her cheek, leans in, and kisses her.

*Shaping cultural memories is complicated. We may feel that we are writing back against a harmful tradition, that we are giving a voice to the silenced, but in so doing repeat the violence committed against them,*²² *corroborate the story of the past as a place where women were victims, where they would be safest at home, locked up, saying no to life instead of yes. Yes, this is what I want to do. Yes, this is where I want to go.*

*Our archives favour stories of violence. It is 'encoded in the way we know about many women's lives' from the past, writes Suzannah Lipscomb.*²³ *We often encounter women in historical documents when they are standing trial for witchcraft, when they have been raped by slavers or sold into marriage. By retelling these stories, no matter how subversively, we retell the same tale about our past, over and over again. This is what the past was like. This is where we come from. This is who we are. This is who we will always be. In this context, a woman's right to say no comes to feel exceptional, and so does her desire to say yes. Yes to solo sex, to partnered sex, to casual or committed sex. Yes to pleasure, and to her body, as well as the pleasure of partners, men, women, or non-binary, who do not force themselves on her. In forgetting about the yes of the women from the past, we also forget about the men who wished for them to say yes, who courted them, who lived in happy consensual companionship with them.*

As we challenge rape culture by reshaping cultural memory, we must take care not to elevate the rapists. If we do not find better stories to tell of the past, we find ourselves in a double-bind: not only do we silence the pleasures and joys of women, not only do we tell a story where their consent does not matter, we also sideline the men who would never commit sexual violence against them. They too come to look like an aberration, an oddity, perhaps even frauds. Those who do appear strange, certainly not representing what it meant to be a man, what it means to be one today, and what it will mean in the future.

It is crucial that we change these stories, both for women and men, as well as for queer and non-binary people. Boys and men in our societies are still raised with a picture of the past where men were men because they committed acts of violence, and because they did not have to ask a woman's consent. When Achilles quarrels with Agamemnon over Briseis, he is not concerned for her welfare, although modern adaptations sometimes cast the story in this light. He does not ask Briseis what she wants.

There is a hero in the Nart sagas, the tales that may have been told among some of our Scythian foremothers. His name is Warzameg. He wins the heart of Psatina, but when her parents offer him her hand in marriage, he turns to her and asks her what it is that she wants. I will tell you more about this tale. It is not widely known and does not feature in picture books for boys, but I remember reading it and thinking: consent is sexy, after all. And finding new stories, reading new stories, telling new stories, can fundamentally change our perceptions.

5. POWER

I rarely feel powerful. I do not mean to say that I feel powerless, only that I rarely have a visceral sense of engaging in acts of power. There is one occasion, however, where I reliably feel in power, and empowered: when I am inside the voting booth.

Not everyone enjoys voting rights, or feels that their vote makes a significant difference, but there are myriad ways in which we are citizens and take part in the political contest, including voting, protest, volunteering, research, and activism. I am in awe of all these democratic processes, and of the structures we have come up with to mediate our differences and find grounds for common action. I believe it is my mother who first awakened this in me. Whenever there was an election, whether European, local, regional or federal, she would throw election parties. We would sit around the telly, drink orange juice or prosecco, eat muffins with frosting in the colours of all available democratic parties, and wait for the announcement of the exit polls. I cannot thank her enough for doing this for us; it instilled a lifelong love for democracy in me. Polling day was a fun day.

One of the most basic forms of power held by ordinary people in democracies is the right to vote. When you cast your vote, you might be electing a member of parliament who will represent your concerns and those of your fellow citizens, or a president who will lead your country, or a fellow citizen who will be tasked with supervising the police in your district. As they spend time in office, as they represent, lead, and supervise, it is up to you to keep an eye on them: are the candidates you have chosen doing well? Have they done what they have promised to do, what you wanted them to do? If they have not, you can choose to give your vote to someone else at the next election. It never fails to amaze me, and is vastly preferable to forms of government based on the power of one (these could be tyrants, monarchs, or dictators) or the few (such as oligarchs, technocrats, or religious leaders). It is also the form of government that enables protest and grassroots activism, even as the right to protest has come under threat in the UK in recent years. And, most importantly, democracy is also a form of governance that allows women to thrive, to grow up emboldened, to realise their dreams. Successive studies have shown that women are doing best in democracies, leading researchers to assert that democracy is intrinsically linked to gender equality and vice versa.[1] This in fact works both ways. As the United Nations Development Programme proclaimed in 2024, there is no democracy without gender equality.[2]

Where does it begin, this form of governance that is so well suited to women? In our established narratives of the past, we remember that the basic form of democracy was invented in Classical Athens. However, what was invented in Classical Athens was a type of democracy that enfranchised property-owning, and that disenfranchised (propertyless) women as well as non-citizens and the enslaved. Had Helen been real, she would certainly not have found herself in a voting booth not even as queen. My grandmother was born a mere three years after women were enfranchised in the Weimar Republic. Her mother may not have had an opportunity to cast a vote yet.

As we will see, the Scythians favoured a different mode of democracy and style of governance. Do you remember Khasa, 'the one who heads the council'? We will meet her again in this chapter. And our bull-leaper from Minoan Crete will also make a re-appearance. Mythical Helen may not have enjoyed voting rights, even as wife of the king, but the Amazon warrior woman Penthesilea may well have. Greek women did not share in their husbands' and fathers' voting rights, but the historical women of Scythia may have participated in the political decisions of their time, even leading the councils tasked with making decisions for the community.

Before we delve into their stories, let us look at the history of democracy as it is usually told today. In Athens, men over thirty who owned property were allowed to come together in the agora, a central public space, to debate decisions that needed to be taken, and then to vote on the outcome. Women did not have the right to vote. History then becomes hazy about what happens next to democracy: some suggest that it ends when Julius Caesar declares himself dictator of Rome, or it may have been some time during the Middle Ages. After the Middle Ages, which are remembered incorrectly as dark and grim, Ancient Greek thought experiences a rebirth during the Renaissance. It inspires Enlightenment thinkers to topple kings and demand democratic rule, for example during the French Revolution, or in the form of the Declaration of Independence in the United States in the eighteenth century. Britain has a

'Glorious Revolution' in the seventeenth century which confirms the primacy of parliament over the monarch, but there are still mostly men involved in this, and no one without property. It isn't until the twentieth century that women in Britain – the suffragettes – become increasingly concerned with political participation. When they do win the vote, it is not least – we are told – because so many men have died in the First World War, and due to the increasing strength of the Labour party.

In mnemonic terms, it is significant that women have not had the vote for very long. The enfranchisement of women makes up part of our communicative, but not our cultural memory. Famously, one Swiss canton only expanded the franchise to women in 1991, and only because they were forced to by Switzerland's constitutional court.[3] Britain was well ahead of them, in that case, when parliament enfranchised women in 1928, yet voting women do not make up a part of our foundational past.

There is also a grubby little detail we like to overlook about British voting rights: Although Britain celebrated the centenary of the women's vote in 2018 as though it were universal, the truth is that it was only a selection of women who was given the vote in 1918 – and they had to meet higher standards of property ownership than British men. The 1918 Representation of the People Act only enfranchised two-thirds of women in the UK.[4] And this only after decades of massive, often violent protests by the suffragettes – a conflict that protest leader Emmeline Pankhurst called a 'civil war' in 1913, on a visit to Hartford, Connecticut.[5]

The same Act abolished property restrictions for men, extending universal voting rights to all men over 21 (over 19 if they were in the military). Women, who in addition to property criteria had to be at least 32 to vote, continued to lose out to men until the Equal Franchise Act of 1928, when they finally won the same voting rights as men.[6]

The continued disenfranchisement of women has repercussions to this day. We may have achieved universal voting rights for women, but the proportion of female representatives and lawmakers is still very low all over the West. In 2021, only a quarter of all lawmakers in the US congress were women.[7] In European parliaments, it is around 30 per cent.[8] In 2022, the UK congratulated itself on having 35 per cent female MPs in the House of Commons.[9] While this is progress, that is only because the bar is so low: until 1997, there had never been more than 10 per cent of seats held by women in the House of Commons. According to the United Nations, at the current rate of progress, we will not have achieved gender parity in national parliaments until 2063.[10] While more and more high-profile political leadership positions are filled by women – think of Germany's Angela Merkel, Tawain's Tsai Ing-wen, and Finland's Sana Marinn, who relatively successfully steered their countries through the COVID-19 pandemic – some still seem out of reach for women and non-binary persons.

For some, this lack of representation may mean the difference between life and death. When the British government introduced lockdown policies during the pandemic, no one stopped to think what this might mean for victims of domestic abuse, as Laura Bates points out:

> After imposing [lockdown] restrictions, it took the Westminster government nineteen days to announce a social media campaign to encourage people to report domestic abuse, as well as an extra £2 million

for domestic abuse helplines. In that nearly three-week period, eleven women, two children and one man had already been killed in suspected domestic abuse cases.[11]

Lockdowns were necessary and widely supported; the point is that, had more women been in the room, someone might have pointed out that victims and survivors of domestic abuse required immediate protection. Bates is right to highlight how serious the blind spots of overwhelmingly male bodies of representatives can be. It does not have be to a matter of life and death in order to be nerve-wrackingly absurd. When the British parliament decided in 2021 to make it illegal to take photos of women breastfeeding in public without their consent, the hereditary (unelected) peer Lord Wolfson of Redegar opposed the law because it would 'unfairly criminalise a man, photographing his wife on the beach for his own sexual gratification, if he accidentally caught a breastfeeding woman in the background.'[12] No, really.

Laura Bates is right to point out that this is 'what happens when we have unelected men inheriting the power to influence our laws because of ancient sexist and classist rules'. This is why voting rights matter, and what's more, it matters that we organise our elections in such a way that every vote counts – that *all* members of parliament are elected, and that at least fifty per cent of them are women. Some political parties have introduced quotas to ensure that an equal number of women and men run for office, but such measures are sometimes met with distrust. A secure place for women in politics, women shaping our lives and government policy, still does not seem natural to us, normal. As far as our cultural memory is concerned, voting rights and political power have traditionally been male, and the privilege of those who owned property.

This may be the foundational story we believe we have inherited from Ancient Greece, and yet this is a misconception. There is of course no Ancient Greek who has left us a will and bequeathed us with their type of democracy. It is we who turn to the past to justify the status quo in the present. For as long as the powerful have wanted to organise voting rights around property ownership and gender, excluding women and the economically marginalised, the Ancient Greeks have been useful forefathers to refer to, useful points of origin to choose.

Those in power have chosen these forefathers at crucial historical points, when democratic rights could have been extended to women and those without property, for example during the period of the French Revolution. When men such as Enlightenment philosopher Jean-Jacques Rousseau had to entertain the idea that women might also be humans, equals of men, and should have voting rights and be able to stand for office, they concluded that women could not become participants in the public sphere, that they could not hold power, because that would distract them from the task that they had been ordained to fulfil.[13] Rousseau stands for a whole group of men who thought it was a woman's job:

> '[t]o please [men], to be useful to them, to make themselves loved and honoured by them, to educate them when young, to care for them when grown, to council them, to console them, and to make life agreeable and sweet to them – these are the duties of women at all times, and should be taught them from their infancy.[14]

It is not difficult to understand why Rousseau and his fellow Enlightenment men did not want to give that up.

When these men cast about for an example of democracy in the past to build upon in their revolutionary and Enlightenment present, they came upon Classical Athens; usefully, this democracy had no women in it, so they could claim precedent for a male-only democratic system.

We still, however, have the opportunity to look back at the past afresh. When I look at the institutions that took shape in Classical Athens, I do not recognise it as the progenitor of the democracies I am familiar with. In fact, in some ways, it seems to me the opposite of all that I value about our democracies: the protection of human rights, of minorities, freedom of speech, religion, and movement. Our democracies are far from perfect – many of its values are ideals we strive for rather than realities – but Athenians only extended political power to a much more select group of people: wealthy, landowning, older men. Ironically, the introduction of democracy in Classical Athens may have disenfranchised women twice over, because it led to a dwindling importance of the household, run by women, in comparison with the city or *polis*, as Angela Saini has argued.[15] Our democracies have many faults, but with regard to voting, women and non-binary persons take part as the equals of men. They have power, as I do, every time they enter a voting booth.

This, too, is not without precedent. There are other, earlier forms of democracy in human history. Many of these included women. In some of them, women may even have held more power than anyone else.

This takes us back to Khasa. Her name suggests that in Scythian communities, adult women may have very naturally taken part in political councils – and even have led them. As we have seen earlier, this word was identified by classicist Henry Rudolph Immerwahr on the a red-figure vase, discovered in Italy in 1958 and attributed to Euthymides, a Greek painter and potter active around 500 BCE. While Immerwahr discounted the word as nonsense, language expert John Colarusso suggests that it means 'one who heads a council' in Circassian.[16] Remember Kheuke, who we last imagined to have met a beautiful stranger in Thrace? Perhaps she is on her way back to Thermodon by now, where she has gone back to live. Perhaps she has been called up to serve on the council of the settlement, under the leadership of an elderly woman called Khasa.

Councils such as these – public forums for communal decision-making at the local or regional level – are present both in the prehistoric and modern record of hunter-gatherer societies,[17] as well as among semi-nomadic and nomadic communities such as the Touareg in Northern Africa today. Ordinary women held considerable sway over these councils, especially as they grew older.[18] Sometimes councils consist entirely of women, sometimes they are led by women, and sometimes they are of made up equally of women and men. These councils were not meetings of noble and monarch. The women who participated in them were not queens or princesses, but ordinary members of the community that they had to govern.

Neither the name Khasa nor the existence of female council leaders would have come as a surprise to the ancients. While the Amazons are mythical, Herodotus draws on their mythic image in his *Histories* to account for the lineage of those who were real, in this case presenting them as the founding mothers of the historical community of the egalitarian Sauromatians. Greek myth, in turn, routinely centres on Amazons who are political leaders. Penthesilea, who fights at Troy, is described as a queen. Hippolyta, who resists the slaughtering Hercules, is the leader of a full band of women warriors. Orithyia, who comes to the rescue of Antiope once she has been abducted by Theseus, is described as the leader of the Amazons. While the Greeks may have thought of these women as queens or princesses, these were not terms that these Scythian would likely have applied to themselves. As Adrienne Mayor points out, '[s]ome famous Amazon leaders were said to have inherited their role from their mothers, but they usually achieve acclaim and leadership because of personal qualities, then declared wars and established laws'.[19] In nomadic groups throughout the ages, leadership may have been inherited, or candidates arisen by popular agreement and consensus group decisions.[20] Most importantly, the Nart saga, which was as foundational to the Scythians as the *Iliad* is to us, refers to a council of women in ancient times.

The Scythian memory of 'olden days' was, then, a time not of male dominance, male democracy and female oppression, but rather a time when women made the laws of the community through discussion, debate, consensus, and majority decisions. Our history is much more interesting than we think, and we can be much more inventive than we have been.

Scythian women are not the only ones in history who have wielded political power. If we fast forward by one thousand years and travel to Seneca Falls in today's United States of America, we come across another group of powerful women: by the 1600s, the Haudenosaunee women had secured veto powers with regards to matters of defence and security. '[F]ull democracy', writes Angela Saini, 'was already an everyday part of Haudenosaunee life',[21] when voting rights were still a long way away for American and British women. If we travel forward by another three hundred years, and to the African continent, we find that the Asanta people in Ghana divided leadership between a queen, a position she held in her own right, and a male leader. As Saini points out, it was the queen who led her army in the rebellion against British colonial rule in 1900.[22]

Historical evidence increasingly suggests that humanity has always known how to share power equally between women and men. The Scythians, the Haudenosaunne and the Asanta people are not historical aberrations, rather – they *are* history. It does not stop at power sharing, either. If we return to the ancients, we may also have found a society back then that was ruled entirely by women. In Minoan Crete (3000 BCE to 1100 BCE), we find depictions of women sitting on a council together,[23] but that is only the start: in the art of Minoan Crete, women are consistently depicted as much taller than male figures. When observed in men, this has routinely been interpreted as a sign of political authority and power in other Mediterranean Bronze Age societies, such as Ancient Egypt.[24] When it is women, however, who are depicted in such a way, (male) archaeologists seem to lose their nerve. According to David Graeber and David Wengrow, many archaeologists have interpreted these depictions to mean that women were not the political rulers of Minoan Crete, but that they were a separate caste of priestesses entirely disconnected from political authority.[25] Sir Arthur Evans, who discovered the ruins of Minoan Crete, was a pathbreaking archaeologist, but his insistence that it was men, not women, who held power on Bronze Age Crete, makes me think he had more to prove about the way he was living his life in the present than he did about the past. As Graeber and Wengrow have pointed out in *The Dawn of*

Everything (2021), the simplest explanation for the depiction of women as rulers in Minoan Crete is that they were, in fact, rulers, an interpretation which earlier (often male) scholars had always rejected.[26]

Living long before the Scythians, the women of Minoan Crete clearly held positions of great power, and there is little iconographic evidence to suggest that their power was shared with men. Even if Minoan Crete was not a matriarchy, women were clearly of vital importance to the political process. In Minoan art, women hold symbols of command, perform rites, sit on thrones, meet together in all-female assemblies, and are never depicted as naked. Men, on the other hand, often turn up scantily dressed. This iconography suggests that Minoan Crete may have been a prosperous cosmopolitan society in the past run by women, where all women may have been valued, respected, and able to rise to positions of political and spiritual power. In any case, it has left us some of the most beautiful, intriguing and vibrant works of art, culture and architecture in human history.

When I first saw the frescoes and art of Minoan Crete, it struck me that I recognised the women depicted here. The way they held themselves, the way they sat together, the way they commanded a space and attention reminded me of my mother, and her mother. My grandmother in particular was the matriarch of the family, for better and for worse. She was not always an easy woman, and she thought it was very important that a lady behaves in the proper way. 'Eine Dame verlässt das Haus niemals ohne Handschuhe,' she would often say to me when I was a child: 'A lady never leaves the house without her gloves.' Never mind that we were not ladies, and I certainly did not want to be one. She still insisted on this, and as a child I found it terribly annoying, even hurtful, and hated the way she singled me out when I was sitting at the table for lunch with her and my brothers. My brothers, apparently, did not have to worry about wearing gloves outside the house.

As I have grown older, I understand her rather better. She grew up during the Second World War and raised five children under immense difficulties. For a long time, she did not have a husband, and raised my aunt on her own, at a time when children born out of wedlock were still referred to as bastards and divorce almost impossible. She later married my grandfather, who returned from the Second World War only after years of imprisonment in a Siberian prison. While I hope that they were happy together, the experiences he underwent during the war and his imprisonment will have left their mark. When he became temporarily unemployed, she went to work in a department store to feed the family, and never looked back. She worked until pension age, and her eyes used to shine when she told us stories about her time selling skiing equipment to the wealthy citizens of Hamburg. I believe that this is where she felt powerful: in the glamorous department store in central Hamburg, helping people choose shirts and skis, underwear and socks, making her own money, providing for herself and the ones she loved. The work gave her money, and it gave her dignity, and that gave her power.

When I look back on our conversations, I believe she was trying to teach me something when she told me to wear gloves outside the house – to think of myself as a lady. She wanted to pass on a sense of dignity that she had fought for tooth and nail throughout her life. No matter how difficult, no matter what life throws at you, you are a lady; you wear your gloves.

You are a woman, and you have dignity. You have power, she tried to tell me.

This is a subtle kind of power. I am not trying to say that a woman's sense of self-worth should be tied up in the gloves she wears, and this is not a lesson I intend to pass on to my niece. The worlds that my grandmother and I grew up in were very different, and she did not understand this, or did not want to understand this, or felt perhaps that not as much had changed for women as I believed they had as a child. She must, in fact, have been much more aware of all that can happen to a woman, and had happened to women such as her in the past. When she spoke of gloves, she spoke of a personal power.

And some of it did in fact stick. In spite of my resistance to my grandmother's advice (they were orders, really), I dress up when I go to vote. I put on what would have been called my Sunday best in her days: a dress, a nice shirt, my good coat. I make sure my shoes are clean. I celebrate when I come home, with a glass of fizz in the garden in summer or a warm meal and a whisky in winter. I agree with my grandmother: we must be aware that we have dignity. Even more, I believe that we must be aware that we have power. We, as women. There is political power: voting, campaigning, standing for office. And there is also personal power.

The private, as we all know, is political, and as women we can make choices about how we act, what we do, and most importantly, who we give our time to, every hour of every day. Have you heard that an increasing number of women are choosing to be single? A recent study predicted that 45 per cent of women aged 25–44 will live single, or perhaps we should call them self-partnered, lives,[27] by 2030. In 2018, the number was already 41 per cent.[28] Women are delaying marriage, divorcing, or not getting married at all. They are also having fewer children.[29] In the US, a third of adults are already neither married nor living with a partner or in committed relationship.[30] The psychologist Gregory Matos predicts a 'rough road ahead' for heterosexual men in a widely read article from 2022, because 'relationship standards' are on the rise in a society where 63 per cent of young adult men are single.[31] He explains that women are looking for men who 'are emotionally available, who are good communicators, and who share their values'.[32]

In other words: women are choosing no longer to date jerks.

When I first read about these studies, I remember feeling a sense of immense, visceral empowerment. I had managed to extricate myself from the controlling man that I had been in a relationship with and decided to go at life solo for a while (months, years, maybe forever, I thought at the time). However long it would take, I was determined never to date anyone again who would be harmful to me, who would not be a good fit for me and my life, who wanted to change me.

Reading that so many other women were already making that same choice made me feel that we had true power. Wherever we turn, popular culture is still telling women that they must look for love, that love will make them happy. Love with a heterosexual man, in most cases. I had not found this to be true, and clearly, many other women shared my assessment. I felt that we were an unwitting network of power, change-makers-by-accident: We were redefining what a good partner was, and we were doing it by choosing not to date anyone who wasn't.

This may sound simple, but it is anything but. We love a hero narrative, one person changing everything for the better, but according to Rebecca Solnit:

> [W]e are not very good at telling stories about a hundred people doing things or considering that the qualities that matter in saving a valley or changing the world are mostly not physical courage and athletic violence but the ability to coordinate and inspire and connect with lots of other people and create stories about what could be and how we get there.[33]

This is one such story, about thousands, hundreds of thousands of women connecting and inspiring each other to change the world. These women are using the power of personal choice to change the way heterosexual men must think of love and connection. Some of them may have looked to history for inspiration, even to the ancients. In the Greek comedian Aristophanes' play *Lysistrata*, the women of Sparta, Athens, and various other Greek city states famously go on a sex strike to end the war between their armies.

For a long time, a sex strike was a matter for storytellers alone, a joke that Ancient Greek playwrights could crack, tongue-in-cheek. Women were not allowed to deny their husbands sex, as rape in marriage did not become a crime throughout the Western world until the late twentieth century. At the same time, women were still forced to marry if they wanted to have a family. I am a member of the first generation of women in the West among whom many do not need to be partnered to survive and thrive: we can often work without asking anyone's permission, we can legally say no, even it still costs us something, and we do not have to get married.

Inspiring as these first step may be, I hope we can look to the past to imagine even better things than simply the right to be single. Consider the Haudenosaunee women: they got a political veto. Or the Pirate Amazons, who met young men on the shores of a strange sea, and said to them, yes, we can be together, but only if you come and live with us, in our way, as equals. The men might have seemed pretty keen, but if they had not been, do you think the Amazons would have stayed? The Pirate Amazons, who had led a mutiny against their Greek enslavers, steered a boat across the Black sea, found safety on its shores, and raided the first group of horses they laid their eyes on? I think not. I think they would have gotten onto their horses and ridden away. Khasa, destined to lead a council, would not have accepted to lead a family instead.

The power is in the no. More precisely, power lies in the ability to walk away. In political terms, this is one of the three elements of freedom described by David Graeber and David Wengrow: the ability to leave.[34] Certainly, governments all over the world are trying to make this notably more difficult as border regimes grow stricter and stricter. No voting with your feet if there is no freedom of movement. We, as women, trans and non-binary people, must be particularly aware of the many attempts to restrict our freedom of movement. Do not go out at night, do not visit your friends for a drink or the local pub in the winter, do not travel or move to this or that country where women are not safe. Politicians, police, even well-meaning friends and relatives are keen to restrict our freedom of movement. They claim this is to keep us safe, but what it does is take away our power.

This is also true in the private sphere. I learned this after breaking up with my controlling partner, who wanted to dictate where I went (ideally, nowhere, unless he was also there), always under the guise of worrying for my safety. After breaking up with him, after learning how to be self-partnered and happy, I experienced a sense of immense freedom, grounded in power: the power to leave. I no longer have to be married; I no longer have to be partnered; I do not have to sit through a dreadful date, or bear the presence of a harmful partner, to have children. As women, we have never been so free to live our lives as we choose them. We have never had so much power to say no.

And with the power to say no comes the power to say yes: Yes to the fulfilled self-partnered life, or the relationship with a man or woman who truly makes you happy, who you want to build a future with. Yes to the career in politics, yes to shaping the fate of entire countries, yes to power.

This yes might also include the decision to have children. Parenthood is the subject of the following chapter. It begins with a mother, fleeing her home, leaving her husband and her daughter, to begin a new life in a faraway land. Her name is Helen of Troy, and this is her story.

Our histories of democracy must be rewritten. It is time we included new memories of bygone eras, of faraway places, into our cultural ideas of political power. Whatever was going on in Minoan Crete, it involved women in positions of power. Some Scythian communities were ruled by firmly patriarchal kings, but there are reports of those that were guided by council, perhaps even by councils made up of older women. Haudenosaunee women also participated in the political arena. There is no reason to remember the past as a place of male authoritarian power, with some female monarchs sprinkled in as consolation prizes. We would again be doing a disservice not only to women, but to men: those who wanted their political lives to be organised around fairness, equality, and justice, long before Western nation states thought that this might be a good idea. We are also doing a disservice to the women and men who have fought for women's rights throughout history. If we remember the story of democracy as a story of men, these revolutionaries are made to look like oddballs, or worse, heretics, when all they were doing was continuing a different tradition of democracy – the very tradition many of us benefit from today.

6. TEAMWORK

Helen of Troy leaves her husband in the dead of night. I imagine her hastily packing her things, casting about her room, wondering what she can part with and what she cannot live without. Will she bring her precious bronze mirror? The warrior Amazon puppet her mother gave her when she was a child? Her brush? (Of course she will bring her brush, and hair pins or bands, anything to hold it in place. It is windy out there on the Aegean Sea.) It must have been daunting to pack her things, to even entertain the idea of running off with Paris, Prince of Troy. This palace in Sparta is all she has ever known. Famously, her husband came to live with her after he won her hand, not the other way around, as would have been more common. She has grown up in this palace, she has barely ever left this city. This is where her family is, where she gave birth to her daughter, where she has made a life for herself. It must have been a hard thing to leave that night. Anyone who is an immigrant, who has had to leave the place they know to go to a strange place, will know how difficult it is. Anyone who has had to leave a lifelong partner, no matter how abusive, will testify to the courage it requires.

Helen is a legendary figure, but women like her existed, and they have existed throughout time: women who left their houses, the men they were with and who owned them, the families they had raised, to go and discover an unknown future, no matter the risks. There is the woman in Ancient Assyria who left her male 'owner' and sought refuge with another woman, a female lover or friend.[1] We do not retain her name, but let us imagine we do. Let us say her name was Atalia, this woman who left her husband knowing it would almost certainly end in her death. Think how courageous she must have been still to leave in the middle of the night, to choose hope over despair, to make a life for herself, no matter how brief. Then there is Neaera, the Corinthian woman sold into prostitution, who left her owners and ran from the pimp Phrynion to live a free life in Athens. She raised her daughter Phanos in the same spirit, a girl who would refuse to become a demure wife once wedded, resulting in legal challenges to the family.[2] More recently, there is my friend R, who had to get a job as a cleaner, hide her wages away from her partner, save up, learn how to drive, pack her suitcases and hide them at the back of the wardrobe, all so that she would be able to up and go one night, vanish within seconds. Atalia, Neaera, R: women who have had the courage to say no to the lives they were living, and yes to the uncertain futures ahead of them.

I have always admired these women, just as I have always admired Helen of Troy. I read her myth as representing something many Greek men could not accommodate, that they could not face up to: that women might want to leave them. That a woman might have a will of her own, unbreakable, even when everything is done to break it. Helen stands in for all the women who have had the courage to make a change. She may have been mythical, but women like her were not. My friend R is not.

Yet the story of Helen has still always struck me as a story told by a man, a man who needed an explanation for why his wife left him. To this man, there could only be two reasons: either she was kidnapped by another man, or she was a whore for leaving willingly with him, a popular narrative for shunned men to this day.[3] I can picture a man like Menelaus – a warlord whose power was based on fear, intimidation, and violence – telling the tale of Paris kidnapping his wife to his family and friends, his allies and warriors, so that he would not have to be embarrassed. A man like Menelaus would not have to admit that his wife preferred a man like Paris over him, and the men he told his story to would not have needed to sit back and think, how am I treating my wife? Might she want to leave me?

It is the Greek version of the myth that we keep telling to each other. It is the Greek version that we pass on to our children, but there may be better versions of that myth to retell. I wonder which versions of the myth the Trojans told each other, if they had one. The historical Trojans were living in a wealthy city, whose riches sprang from the merchant ships that came past Troy on their way to and from the Black Sea. This was not the sort of city that needed to rape or abduct. People came here willingly, as people today flock in their thousands to cities such as Paris, London, and New York. And so might have a woman like Helen of Troy, a woman who was wealthy and privileged and brave enough to say yes to an uncertain future over marriage to a man she abhorred.

In Ancient Greece, the relationship between wife and husband, however happy it may have been in individual cases, was marked by a clear segregation, the repercussions of which we still experience today: women stayed in the home; men went out in the world. As countless studies on care work have shown, women are saddled with most of the mental and physical labour at home and in the family to this day.[4] We remember the past as a place where care work belonged only to women; however, this is not because of some natural order of the world, but rather because they were by law excluded from leaving that sphere.

This exclusion was more intense in some parts of Ancient Greece than in others. Women were slightly more empowered in Sparta than Athens, but on the level of cultural memory, the differences are marginal. Lacking all political rights, women were responsible for the household, while men concerned themselves with public activities. Women raised children, men went out to work. Women and men did not raise their children as a team, and there was no equal distribution of care work.

Encounters with Greek myths drive home the idea that neither women nor men would have been entirely happy with this arrangement, and that it would have been to the detriment of their children. There is a curious proliferation of stories in Greek myth where parents kill their children, or children their parents. It keeps the men particularly busy: Heracles, Theseus and Agamemnon all kill their daughters and sons for one reason or another.

The most famous story is that of a woman, however, immortalised by the Ancient Greek playwright Euripides. It is the tale of Medea, a princess from Colchis in today's Georgia, not far away from Scythian territory on the Black Sea. When the Greek hero Jason travels to Colchis, she helps him steal the Golden Fleece from her father, killing a bronze giant and a hydra in the process, then returning to Greece with Jason to become his wife.

When Jason decides to leave her for another woman, Medea takes revenge on him: she kills their children.

In Classical Athens, an independent, powerful, foreign woman such as Medea could only end up the villain of the story, but I believe her myth, told by a man to other men, betrays a deep unease about the parenting arrangements in Classical Athens. What does the dead child stand for, the child killed by their father, their mother? Whose ghosts are these stories raising? Like fairytales, myths express our fears, the fears we do not dare talk about, do not like to see exposed, out in the open, in the broad daylight. As the novelist Daniel Kehlmann once pointed out to me and an assembled audience of academics, why do we think that there are so many step-mothers and stepfathers in fairytales? Fairytales speak a truth we do not wish to hear.

If we look at fairytales in this way, we realise that plenty of mothers and fathers throughout human history did leave their children in the woods because they could not feed them (Hansel and Gretel), and that some mothers must have been jealous of their daughters because their husbands began preferring them to their wives (Snow White). Other parents would have abused their daughters as servants and treated them as domestic labour (Cinderella). Since we find the notion unbearable that a mother or father might abandon their child in the woods, we make step-parents stand in for these figures. If we are parents, we do then have to look ourselves in the eyes and recognise the truth of what we are capable of; what we would do if pushed to the brink of destitution and height of desperation.

Mothers and fathers past, as well as children, may have been unable to bear these thoughts, but the trauma of these realities needed out, the ghosts of abandoned children haunting their parents. So, they made up fairytales: stories of incest and abuse, murder and neglect, all of it committed by step-parents. This mechanism has survived and is alive and well in the more patriarchal section of today's porn industry, where pretend stepsisters and stepmothers are made to perform all sorts of taboo fantasies about family members.

These are stories that allow us to lie to ourselves: violence has been done to someone else, by someone else, not to me, not by me, not by the person who was supposed to protect me. I did not leave my child in the woods, I do not feel sexual desire for a woman in my family.

Greek myths betray a similar unease. How many Greek fathers would not have been able to tell their children from any other man's, considering how little time they spent with them, how little love they gave them? How many could have injured or killed them as they meted out corporal punishment with a violence unthinkable to us today, or indeed unknowingly broken the incest taboo? How many mothers had nothing but their children, making these children the only people (other than servants or slaves) these women could exert some power over? What acts might that have led them to commit?

To this day, Euripides's play asks us to understand why Medea did what she did. She had no recourse, no power, saw no alternative. The only way she could find of saying no to the patriarchy was murdering her children. Men, too, must have felt the strain of the archaic division of labour. Stories of raging fathers killing their families are so widespread in Greek myth that they must have been something of an outlet – for the frustration of fathers being strangers to their children, and the mothers of their children, a strangeness brought about by the social division of labour that kept women indoors and men outside.

Let us take a moment to appreciate just how odd this arrangement is. No human being from 10,000 BCE to around 300,000 BCE would have recognised it as 'normal'. While the patriarchal division of labour may have been prominent for the last four thousand years in the West, if we look at human history as a whole, the model is a definitive outlier. In hunter-gatherer societies, women as well as men gathered *and* hunted, and they both raised their children together.[5] In fact, cooperative breeding is one of the keys to the immense evolutionary success of the human species, and a habit that sets us apart from our fellow apes. As homo sapiens, fathers began to care for their children, and this behaviour turned into a game-changer. The German historian Kai Michel and Dutch evolutionary biologist Carel van Schaik claim that such care 'made such a difference [to survival of their offspring] that natural selection produced men who became more and more caring'.[6] It is this kind of cooperation that secures optimal survival rates for our offspring. In other words: what sustains the human species is parenting as teamwork.

This has by no means only been the case in our earliest evolutionary history. Women and men continued to share the labour of raising children and procuring food, both as hunters and gatherers, throughout the Stone Age. The Stone Age consists of the Palaeolithic, Mesolithic, and Neolithic eras, and lasted from some 3.3 million years ago to around about 4,000 BCE, covering well over ninety-five per cent of human history. There is no archaeological evidence that women of the Stone Age stayed at home while the men went out to hunt. In fact, the opposite is the case. If the skeletons of our ancestors are telling us anything, it is that that women and men both participated in hunting. Among the skeletons we have of Neanderthals, women and men show signs of regular weapon use, most notably throwing spears to hunt large game.[7] A change in weapons use, according to these skeletons, can only be diagnosed towards the end of the Palaeolithic era, as we approach what has been traditionally cast as the patriarchal world of the Ancient Middle-East.[8] While we retain very few visual representations from the Stone Age, and they are difficult to interpret, some of them portray female and male figurines surrounding a large animal such as a bison, perhaps depicting a hunting scene.[9] There are also depictions of rituals, with figures appearing as half-human, half-animal. Here, too, many of the figures cannot be identified as either female or male, and it is certain that not all are male.[10] Women certainly created art in the Stone Age, leaving their handprints and paintings in prehistoric caves that capture our imagination to this day, for example in the caves of Lascaux in Southern France. In fact, the majority of handprints in the pre-historic caves of today's France are believed to have come from women. This is all the more important, as pre-historian Marylène Patou-Mathis points out, because handprints beside pre-historic paintings are considered signatures of the artists who made them.[11] As early as the Stone Age, female artists wanted their names – their identities, their personhood, their artistry – to endure.

Mounting evidence points to an equality of genders in the Stone Age, writes Patou-Mathis, as well as matrilinear way of life. There is no evidence for a patriarchal or indeed matriarchal style of dominance of one gender over the other.[12] It is not until the Neolithic period, the very end of the Stone Age, on the cusp to the Bronze Age, that we see evidence of the birth of the patriarchy.[13] Only in hindsight was pre-history cast in the patriarchal mode: illustrations of the Stone Age in textbooks typically feature a tall muscular man with a spear, heading out to hunt a mammoth, while a woman stands in the entrance of a cave, carrying two to three babies.[14] Think *The Flintstones* minus the humour.

Momentous as the transition to the patriarchal mode of dominance may have been, it did not take root everywhere, or all at the same time. There were still women (and men!) who said no to patriarchal domination, and yes to a life where women and men were equals, including as partners raising children.

The graves of our Scythian foremothers and forefathers from the first millennium BCE tell a very different story to that of patriarchal domination and sexist child-rearing. In fact, the evidence suggests that cooperative breeding was alive and well in these more egalitarian communities. Not only do these graves leave us in no doubt that warrior women were a historical reality,[15] they also indicate that women's emancipation extended into family life. This contrasts somewhat with the state of affairs today, when the relatively equal distribution of care work among heterosexual couples tends to be upset when children come along.[16] Warrior women were buried with both children and weapons, indicating that they did not give up their identities as hunters and warriors when they had children.[17]

In fact, it seems they did not give up their work even as they grew into grandmothers or older women well past the menopause. In the Dnieper Don region in today's Ukraine, an archaeologist discovered twelve graves of women warriors between the ages of sixteen and sixty. The age when women became mothers may also have been much more closely aligned to the average age in the West today: Four of the women discovered in Ukraine were buried with infant children, with the adults aged between twenty-five and thirty-five.[18]

Not only did women apparently stay in public life as they became mothers, men also seemed to have felt a deep bond with their children. We have found graves of women, men and children laid to rest together,[19] but even more intriguingly, there are Scythian graves at Pokrova in today's Kazakhstan where children were buried with single adult men, which Adrienne Mayor interprets as indicating that at least some men associated with warrior women helped to raise children.[20] It may have been far more than some men: in some graveyards, Mayor notes, all human remains of children discovered by archaeologists are buried alongside men rather than women.[21]

The continued practice of cooperative breeding among Scythian communities should not come as a surprise. If anything, a complete lack of it would have been more suspicious. After all, cooperative breeding is one of, perhaps even *the*, key to humanity's evolutionary success. It's also a habit that makes everybody happier: fathers who spend significant time caring for their children report much greater happiness and life satisfaction than fathers who do not.[22] It is perhaps self-evident that women whose male partners perform care work are also much happier than women whose male partners do not.[23] The archaeological record indicates that Scythian women and men were not as hung up about gender stereotypes as their

Greek counterparts, that there was more slippage and overlap between gender identities. Men were routinely buried with earrings, jewellery, awls, and spindle-whorls, indicating that a man in Scythia could have cared for a child, popped in a pair of earrings, and spun wool to make a warm cloak for their partner without experiencing a deep sense of emasculation.

I can imagine Kheuke, now a grown woman, meeting such a man. His name might be Berossus. A slight man who enjoys boxing and made a living as a goat herd, a trade he learned from his grandfather. He was given a mirror as a child, as most children are, but has lost it on the meadows of the Pontic Alps. He tends to lose things, and the first gift Kheuke will give him is a new mirror she acquired in Thrace. Berossus thinks of it as normal that Kheuke goes out to hunt every day, not least of all because his own mother was a hunter. He thinks consent is the most natural thing in the world, which may be down to one of his role models. Instead of the tale of Achilles, Berossus may have heard the story of Warzameg, arguably the most important hero of the Nart sagas, and how he came to marry his wife Psatina.

I still remember the delight I felt when I first read the Nart sagas, in a translation by John Colarusso, who has also given us the joy of Scythian name meanings, such as 'leader of the council' for Khasa and 'brave warrior' for Otrera. I felt the delight especially deeply because I had just come off a reread of the *Iliad*, which I found deeply painful and frankly infuriating, unable to unsee what Achilles and Agamemnon, Hector and Paris were doing to the women they claimed to love, or own, or care for.

A life of reading the Western canon had normalised the representations of patriarchal oppression and male violence against women – just another fact of life, I thought, and what other way would there even be to tell a story, certainly 'back then'. I had not been prepared for the Nart sagas, passed down through the ages by female and male bards in the Caucasus and today's Georgia. Those bards had known all along about how sexy consent can be. Imagine my surprise when Warzameg refuses to marry the heroine Psatina before she herself has agreed to the match. They have gone through much hardship together to defeat the giant Arkhon Arzokh. After their victory over the giant, Psatina and Warzameg return home together on the horse Zhaqa, the fastest horse in the world, which carries humans into the afterlife when they die, to the land where nothing moves. Psatina's parents are so grateful for the return of their daughter that they free their slaves and offer her hand in marriage to Warzameg.

> They brought back people whom the scaly giant had enslaved, livestock, and everything else that was there. They set the slaves free. They distributed the livestock among themselves. Of the former slaves, those who wanted to go back to their homes did so; those who wanted to remain stayed. They said to Warzameg, 'Now that you have endured so much hardship for Psatina, we think that it is fitting that you take her as your wife.'
>
> 'Indeed, I want her,' he said, 'but what matters is what she herself says.'[24]

In simply not assuming consent, Warzameg seems well ahead of most heroes of Western storytelling.

Teamwork

It will not surprise you to hear that Helen of Troy is not asked for consent when Menelaus wins her in the Greek myth, like some sort cash prize or giant stuffed toy at a fair. Life-changing as the prize certainly was, Helen turns out to be more than a mere stuffed toy. We cannot know what inspired this mythical woman to leave her husband, or whether she was given an Amazon puppet by her mother, who her role models were when she made the leap towards freedom. However, we know that Amazon puppets were given to real girls in Athens, so we can imagine that the historical Neaera may have given one to her daughter Phanos, to remind her that she was strong and independent and deserved to be treated as an equal. It was a lesson that Phanos took to heart. Neaera, Phanos and Atalia knew the consequences of their nos. When they said no, the men and state authorities around them murdered or persecuted them.

Women today still feel that consequence, every day. Six women are murdered every hour of every day worldwide. In the UK, a woman is killed by a man every three days.[25] In six out of seven cases, the killer is a man she knows, and seventy-four per cent of women are killed in their own homes.[26] As women, we are aware how dangerous our homes may be, whether the knowledge is conscious or not. My friend R left in secret, stole away in the dead of night because she too feared violent retribution. This was sensible, as data from the Femicide Census shows that 'separation is a risk factor for intimate-partner femicides',[27] as violent men may choose to kill women rather than lose control over them. The fate of another friend of mine bears testimony to this fact. My dear friend S, one of the most intelligent, capable, and confident people I know, had to leave the country she was born and raised in to escape an abusive and violent male partner. As Margaret Atwood once wrote, men are afraid that women will laugh at them. Women are afraid that men are going to kill them.[28]

Atalia was indeed killed by the Assyrian state, as far as we know. We cannot be sure of the fate of Neaera and Phanos, but Phanos's husband brought charges against them with the aim of stripping them of their Athenian citizenship, forcing them once more into sexual slavery. No record of the end of the court case survives, but historian Eric Berkowitz does not see much hope for them in the misogynist, xenophobic slave society of Classical Athens.[29] We all know how Helen's mythical story ends, and it is not a happy ending: Menelaus uses her escape as a pretext to raise an army and destroy the beautiful city of Troy, murder and enslave the entire population, and bring her back to Sparta, where she secretly prepares and feeds him a narcotic potion in the evening so that she may escape his dominance for a few hours.

It may seem difficult at times to find hope in Greek myth, but it can be found in Scythia, in the Stone Age, even in the earliest periods of human history. In the graves of our foremothers and forefathers, the women who were warriors with and without children, the men who wore jewellery, made warm cloaks, and cared for their children. Think of all the children who grew up with their fathers. In fact, I will raise you one: think of all the children who grew up with happy mothers and happy fathers, who had the chance to grow into happy people themselves, because they did not have to choose between hunting and motherhood, or masculinity and a pair of earrings. They could share care work, and they could inspire us to do the same today. Even better, they could help us to think of these things as normal. No more complimenting fathers for taking their children to the playground, no more shaming mothers for going to work, or any of the other things that mothers are shamed for. Instead: sharing the care work equally, and recognising that this is the key to humanity's success, and that we have done it for ninety-eight per cent of human history, and it is time to end the patriarchal outlier. Instead: being happy. Women and men alike.

Imagine you are leaving your partner. You have to do so in the middle of the night, because you are frightened of their reaction. You have packed your suitcase and hid it in the wardrobe. You have put it off for as long as you could, until you realised that there wasn't a right moment. You just had to go.

Now, it is time. Open the wardrobe, the one in the hallway, not the one in the shared bedroom. Take out the suitcases. Go downstairs. Avoid the step that squeaks, open the front door as silently as possible. Walk out, feel the night air on your face, make your way to the car that you have parked as nearby as possible, unlock it. Flinch at the noise it makes when it unlocks, they all make a noise now. Open the boot, haul the suitcases into the boot, get in, and then drive, drive, drive, into the night, into freedom.

This is the experience of countless women who leave their husbands or boyfriends. Even after they have driven away, they still may not be safe from their former partners: half of women murdered are killed by a current or former lover.[30] The story of Helen speaks to that experience across the ages: Helen was not real, but women like her were. Women who left their husbands because they had the power to say yes to an uncertain future and no to the present they were leaving behind.

Throughout human history, women have always had power. We do not think so, in part, because we tend to begin the telling of history with Greek antiquity, but contemporary researchers are finally pushing for a change in perception, emphasising how damaging, as well as incorrect, it is to begin histories of just about any subject in Ancient Greece, or even in Middle-Eastern antiquity as a whole. Ancient Greece and Rome were chosen as our foundational periods only in the nineteenth century, by men who had an interest in justifying legitimate patriarchal gender relations, colonial conquest and the ethnic cleansing, genocide, and oppression of colonised groups; people who they argued were on a 'lower' rung of 'human development'.[31] *As Carel van Schaik and Kai Michel point out, this perspective on human history ignores ninety-five per cent of our actual history, most of which takes place outside the West and further back than 700 BCE. 'This is fatal particularly for women', they write, 'because the past five thousand years are those years in which power was firmly in the hand of men. It is our limited perspective that makes the patriarchy appear as something normal and natural, and misogyny as a part of the male* conditio humana, *when nothing could be further from the truth.'*[32]

Whether the labour of childrearing was divided equally between women and men cannot be conclusively proven from bones buried in a graveyard, but van Schaik and Michel are convinced that inequality between women and men only developed once agriculture began spreading among human communities. Their research indicates that homo sapiens may have been successful precisely because women and men shared the duties of childrearing, and that prehistoric men may have been as happy to do so as are men today, most of whom report to be keen to spend more time with their children – and to be happier when they do.

There are of course families where the childrearing is not shared between a man and a woman, but between two women, two men, or multiple adults of varying genders. In fact, it is common, and part of humanity's success strategy, that a village raises a child, and many people chip in to different degrees and in different ways to care for and nurture our children. It is time to stop thinking of childrearing as a gendered activity that takes place only in the nuclear family. No child is raised by two persons alone.

This also has personal implications. Some of us may enjoy the idea of being the main carer for our child. It makes us the most important person in their life, and it gives us control over one of the most precious, purposeful processes in life, that of raising a child, guiding them into adulthood. While parents may always be among the most important people in a children's life, usually the most important, it is perhaps time to let go off the idea that it is one's only purpose in life to raise a child, and that no one else is allowed to be a part of that process, or if they are, that one still always knows best. It truly does take a village, and it takes friends and family, neighbours and kind strangers, the state and our communities. It takes non-binary folk, it takes women, and it takes men. This way, we may all be a little happier, and so might our children.

When I think of Kheuke, the young woman who has just met Berossus, I imagine her as a happy woman. He, too, may well have been a happy man, as we will find out in the next chapter. Human history, I promise you, has many secrets to tell us about men, and how they might have lived happier, longer, better lives than some do today.

Meet Berossus.

7. PARTNERSHIP

I had the good fortune of growing up with two supportive brothers. Throughout my childhood, my twin was always on, and indeed by, my side, never failing to make me laugh and to have my back, and so was my older brother. Raised the same way as me, my brothers are both feminists and it has never occurred to them to think that women should be treated any differently than men, or that they could or should do different things from them. Not to make them out as paragons of virtue, but growing up with my brothers did not prepare me for some of the men I would meet out in the world once I started working, studying, and dating. Some of them were like my brothers; others were not.

Initially I was puzzled when I met a man who thought that women were different, or should do different things, or were capable of different things than men, and it took me a few years to understand just how widespread these misogynist attitudes still are. I have mentioned before that men (among them long-term partners) have said to me that women are not capable of having a qualified opinion on misogyny because they are biased on the subject, another (a close family member) that women are biologically not as ambitious as men, another (a much shorter relationship) that women are irrational when on their period and incapable of making decisions. It is disheartening, to say the least, to hear these things from men who consider themselves progressive, and to hear it from men I have been very close with. I have heard similar things from women, who can be equally guilty of internalising misogyny.

I spent a good long while hoping that all this was mere anecdotal evidence, until I discovered a wealth of studies showing that widespread misogyny persists in the West. Mary Ann Sieghart has assembled a dataset of studies on the subject in her book *The Authority Gap*. I will give you a taste here. When sent identical applications for a position of lab manager, female and male science professors at top universities prefer the male applicant. They consider him 'significantly more competent and hireable',[1] and offer him 'a higher starting salary and more career mentoring'.[2] Budding male writers are more likely to receive guidance and representation from agents.[3] Students rate the performance of an online instructor higher when they think that he is a man, and lower when they think she is a woman.[4] Men will perceive a woman as dominating a conversation when she has talked for as little as thirty per cent of it.[5] The data would even apply to this book: men are much less likely to pick up a book written by a woman, whereas women make no such distinction.[6]

It is odd that this type of misogyny persists if you consider how much men and women both profit from gender-equal societies. We have heard of fathers who are much happier for spending time caring for their children instead of spending all their lives at work, but there is so much more. There is a wealth of studies now to show that gender equal societies make men happier, just as much as they improve the lives of women. Men in more gender equal societies sleep better and have more and better sex than men in societies with gender inequality.[7] Women, too, sleep more soundly in countries with greater gender equality. Not only are women and men both happier and healthier in egalitarian relationships, but so are their children.[8] Adolescents report great life satisfaction in gender equal societies, both boy and girls.[9] Men enjoy better health and greater life satisfaction, and if they work flexibly to care for their children and take parental leave, they are much closer to their children and report greater satisfaction with their work-life balance. The sons of those fathers are less likely to become violent and more likely to pass on those positive behaviours to their peers and their own families, and their daughters are much more confident to realise their dreams and ambitions, to go for what they want.[10] As Sieghart explains, men in gender-equal societies in Europe, and in the more gender-equal states of the US, have healthier and more long-lasting marriages, are much less likely to die a violent death or inflict violence on others, and are much more content, as the sociologist Øystein Gullvåg Holter has found.

If you are a man reading this book, I suspect that not all of this will be news to you. As Sieghart points out, men also get bullied by patriarchal men, and as we have seen in previous chapters, women and men have fought together for our immense progress in gender equality. The public has recognised this. According to one survey, forty-two per cent of Britons believe that the promotion of equal rights for women has had a positive impact on today's young men.[11]

Why, then, does the patriarchal ideal of masculinity persist? If men are so much happier in gender equal societies, if the public is aware of this, why do we still see one in six young men today believing that feminism has done more harm than good to society, one out of three young men believing that it will be harder to be a man than a woman in the future, and one in five young men reporting favourable views of toxic masculinity influencers?[12]

This, too, can be related in important ways to the construction of cultural memory. The past, our foundational past, is still remembered as a place of toxic masculine ideals, including the valorisation of violence, and of suffering in silence, as well as stereotypes of men as inevitable perpetrators. Today, many adult men are already living alternative versions of masculinity – healthier, happier versions. But these versions have not been integrated into our cultural memory, into our foundational past.

In this foundational past, women are not always taken seriously. As classicist Mary Beard points out, the *Odyssey* begins with a man telling a woman to shut up.[13] Penelope is silenced by her own son. 'When it comes to silencing women,' writes Beard, 'Western cultures has had thousands of years of practice.' The mechanisms that refuse to take women seriously are just as deeply embedded in our culture.[14] As are the mechanisms that tell men that they are only worth something, that they are 'real men' only if they are dominant, successful, and willing to commit acts of violence. Think of the Greek heroes we have met in the pages of this book: Theseus kidnaps a ten-year-old Helen to make her his child bride, and brutally kills whoever he comes across. Heracles first sleeps with the Amazon Hippolyta only to then slaughter her and all her warriors in their sleep. He then goes on to kill his wife and children in a fit of rage. Odysseus returns home after a ten-year journey and slaughters the female slaves of his household, who have

Partnership

been raped by the male suitors for his wife, who came to his palace during his prolonged absence.

And then there is Achilles, who is remembered as the greatest warrior in the world, the epitome of the hero. And yet, all his achievements come to nothing. Even during the Trojan War, he realises that the war is pointless. He sees that the Trojans have done him no wrong, and would much rather be at home. While he left for the war convinced that it would bring him riches and glory, in its tenth year he realises that all it brings is death.[15]

And indeed, death comes to him, too. Returning to the fighting after the death of his beloved partner Patroclus, Achilles is killed in turn. He loses the love of his life, and then his own. His soul goes to Hades, the Greek underworld. In the *Odyssey*, Homer's sequel to the *Iliad*, the Greek hero Odysseus travels to the underworld where he meets Achilles, who tells him: 'Glorious Odysseus: don't try to reconcile me to my dying. I'd rather serve as another man's labourer, as a poor peasant without land, and be alive on Earth, than be lord of all the lifeless dead.'[16]

Better at peace and alive than a war hero and dead, is what Achilles has learnt after ten years of warfare. Sometimes considered to glorify war and violence, the *Iliad* is in fact the very opposite: a story that tells us what becomes of the men and women ravaged by violence and warfare.[17] It is a story of what toxic masculinity leads to.

Evidence from Scythian communities is useful here for how it paints a different picture of masculinity. The mirrors, earrings and spindle-whorls they were buried with suggest that gender roles were more fluid among semi-nomadic and nomadic communities on the steppes than in Ancient Greece, and that men in these communities may have been able to live lives that revolved around values other than violence.[18] It is not simply that these were objects that we codify as feminine today, but more importantly that we see the same objects in both female and male graves. These objects, these beautiful things that bring so much joy and happiness in everyday life, were there for everyone to enjoy, and men may have cherished beauty and happiness just as much as women did.

I am particularly fascinated by the earrings, perhaps in part because we are seeing an increasing number of younger men wear jewellery today. Global stars such as Harry Styles, Timothée Chalamet, Paul Mescal and most notably Gucci creative director Alessandro Michele have made jewellery for men fashionable again in the twenty-first century.[19] I can only applaud them, assure everyone that this is a happier world, and congratulate the men have finally got to discover the pleasures of an outfit colour-coded to match their rings and earrings. Instead, that is, of having to buy jewellery they like for the women they are with, who might not share their taste.

There is a more personal reason why I am fascinated with jewellery in Scythian burial mounds. That is because I myself, for a long time, chose to live life without beautiful things, fearing that they would be considered too feminine. I have since discovered what happiness they can bring once you embrace them. I did so only in my early thirties, after I had become aware that I was, in fact, a woman, and that there was nothing wrong with being a woman, it was only that other people made you feel that there was (and for a while, I had internalised what they said).

Imagine the Scythian men and their earrings. Warzameg, the hero of the Scythian Nart sagas, may have worn earrings.

Partnership

Maybe his story can be of help to us, the story of how he and Psatina defeat the giant; maybe it could make up part of a collection that also included the story of the Pirate Amazons. We will need Warzameg's story, and many more stories like his, if we are to tell each other a version of history that allows men to fully embrace the happiness that gender equality brings them in the present.

Further evidence for gender fluidity can be found in the case of the gender-crossing priests called Enareës, described by Ancient Greek scholars Herodotus.[20] As priests, shamans, and soothsayers, they are believed to have held positions of great social and political importance among the Scythians.[21] They were accepted and cherished in their communities, setting a precedent for a healthier vision of masculinity in the human past and suggesting a better life for all men: one where they did not need to prove their virility through violence, warfare, or domination.

We can do small things to contribute further to this expanded idea of masculinity. Give flowers to men. Wear earrings, or a necklace, or a bracelet, if you like them, whether you are a man or a woman. If you are a man, and you see a stone you like, do not give it your girlfriend. Wear it yourself. (Buy her something that she actually wants.) We can encourage little boys when they put on nail varnish rather than tell them this is something that girls do. We must make sure that there is space and visibility for non-binary persons, in the professional and the private sphere. We must make room for everyone at the table and ensure that we do everything so that they are part of the conversation.

All of these are things we can do together, as women, men and non-binary people. However, I also believe that one of the most important spurs to retelling the story of our past, our foundational past, will have to come from men. Historians, novelists, playwrights, screenwriters, digital and interactive storytellers, curators, journalists, and archaeologists who identify as male will have to step up to the job, unleash their imagination, and go looking for the stories of men like Warzameg, men like the Scythians, men like their Stone Age forefathers, who are nothing like Odysseus, Achilles, or Theseus. Such men are everywhere in our past, but men are not telling their stories. Instead, they are retelling, over and over again, stories of violent men, of killing men, of dead and unhappy men. Of men who succeed or fail through dominance, through physical strength, men who do not ask a woman's consent, men whose life is all about them rather than the people around them.

Such choices will continue to lend credence to toxic masculinist in the present. Toxic masculinity influencers, some of them criminals, will continue to target those among us who are most vulnerable: young men. They will continue to target our children, the boys my niece will be meeting in primary school, any sons I may one day have.

We have to offer our boys something better than this. Many male storytellers will see their pictures and novels and documentaries funded at a speed that their female and non-binary colleagues could only dream of. So what are the male storytellers doing? Where are the stories about decent men who consider women their equals? Why has no one told the story of Berossus, the man who could have been Kheuke's partner in Ancient Scythia? His love of boxing, his mother the hunter, his grandfather the shepherd, him meeting a woman who he falls for head over heels, and who loves him back? Perhaps they met a boxing competition. Perhaps their courtship was a competition, as it is in so many stories passed down about warrior woman throughout the ages, where women challenge young men to compete with them in horse races, foot races, or duels.[22] When Atalanta met her beloved, she made him race her, agreeing only to marry him if he was able to catch her. I believe this could have happened to Berossus or Kheuke. I think she may have challenged him to a horserace, which he would have lost, then to an archery competition, which he would have lost, before finally challenging him to a boxing match, which she knew he would win. It would make for a great story. We are waiting for it to be told.

I suspect that one of the reasons why we are not seeing these stories as much as we should is that the most famous male storytellers are successful precisely because they tell what are considered 'male' stories: historians talk about warfare, journalists about the economy, novelists about violent young men engaged in crime. A director like Martin Scorsese makes impressive films about the damaging consequences of toxic masculinity, but where are the positive visions? Where are the hopeful pasts? I am looking forward to hearing the stories that say: it is normal for men to be happy, and to like nice things, and to consider women their equal. I would love to watch a film about a young man who lives an unhappy existence, only then to discover that his life changes once he starts taking women seriously. One of the more ambitious projects we have seen in this category to date is Greta Gerwig's 2023 film *Barbie*. Her Ken is a beautiful and clever portrayal of toxic masculinity, and how it drives men to suicide and to violence against women. First, Ken takes over the land of the Barbies. Then, when his coup proves unsuccessful, he threatens to throw himself off the top floor of the

Barbie mansion. Fortunately, Stereotypical Barbie manages to talk him out of it.

I would like for *Barbie*, and for this book, to be seen as an invitation. My invitation would go out to the vast majority of men in the West – those of you who know that life is better when women and men are equals. If you are a young man, look for the stories of men who live happy lives because they know that women are their equals, in the past but also in the present. If you are a storyteller of any kind – perhaps in the arts, media or culture – tell the stories of the men who have lives of their own, and that help us understand that each person has to make a life of their own, women and men alike, and that we cannot use other human beings, no matter their gender, to prop up our self-esteem, or prove something to the world, or to feel loved if we do not love ourselves enough. There is Barbie, and there is Ken. Barbie has told her story. Now, where is Ken?

If you are no longer a young man, then this invitation also goes out to you. If you are an older, established storytelling professional, you may already be well-respected, well-funded – all the more powerful! If you are a researcher, research those men who did believe in gender equality. If you are a director, make films about them. If you are a writer, write about them, whether as a historian or a journalist or a novelist. If you are an actor, look for those parts. And help younger men, women, and non-binary artists who want to tell those stories.

Such as the tale of Berossus. I can imagine him with his baby on his bare chest, the infant fast asleep, while Kheuke is asleep somewhere, exhausted from giving birth. His mirror and hers are sitting beside their beds, to send light signals to each other if they have to: are you awake? The baby is hungry. I can imagine that she is not replying, that she is asleep. So he carries the infant outside when the child begins wailing, so as not to wake her. I can imagine him being very happy, if sleep-deprived, to be holding their precious child and going out to hunt for some goat's milk.

There is always the risk of romanticising the past. This is a romantic episode, perhaps too much so, born of my desires, my expectations, the attitudes that I bring to bear on the past. But there *are* men like Berossus in the world, and there always have been. I am more than happy to leave their stories to you. Make a man up. Tell me what he is like. I cannot wait to hear about him.

I have said this time and again throughout this book, but it bears repeating: our cultural memory is not working, and it is not working for men or for women. Who knows who is let down by it more: the women whose only option seems to be to present as inferior versions of men, or the men whose only option is to act superior to women. Rather than, you know, be happy. It must be stressful surrounding yourself with people you think it is your sole responsibility to take care of, rather than stopping to ask yourself: who am I, and what is my purpose beyond deciding on the fates of other people?

While I was revising this book, I came across a podcast conversation between two men. They were talking about what it means to be a man in the twenty-first century, and how to be a role model to boys and young men who are looking for a mature masculinity to emulate. One of the guests suggested that men need to be needed, and that we should build society around this need.

Much as we need men to step up and take on their fair share of caring work in our society, as so many have already begun to do, there is a problem with building your identity around being needed. The passive voice did important work here: the guest did not have to say that there were other people involved, mainly women, mainly children. People who would have to do the needing in order for men to feel that they were living their best lives. As we have seen, men live happier lives in egalitarian societies, in which they are not 'needed' in the sense of being financially or physically depended on by women and children. Instead, they are free to participate in raising their children, in going to work, in making laws, in writing articles and books and directing films as independent and free subjects alongside other independent and free subjects. It will help, in building such societies, if we tell more of those kinds of stories.

I concluded the previous chapter on a passionate plea to men to tell different stories. If you are a man, particularly of middle age, consider following my invitation, and if you do, consider including some women of your own age in those stories. Your female peers are currently having a much, much harder time than you to make themselves seen and heard.

A few women are lucky. They are visible throughout their lives, shaping the societies they live in. Simone de Beauvoir spent her life working on developing the philosophy of existentialism and fighting for women's empowerment. She remained a visible activist and political figure well into middle and old age, but sadly, de Beauvoir was unusual in remaining part of the public debate for all her life, permitted the limelight perhaps because she was considered an exceptional woman, and to be different from other women. Her experience is not that of most women in the West. They still have a very different experience of aging from that of men. Middle age tends make them invisible, at precisely the time when they have so much to offer to our debates.

As we will see, this is at odds with how women of middle and older age were represented in the artworks of our Stone Age ancestors. Their bodies used to be omnipresent – and I am hopeful that they may be so again. This hope is the subject of the following chapter.

8. SPOTLIGHT

Women today are still having a very different experience of aging than men do: they become effectively invisible to the public eye between the ages of 30 and 60, a period that covers most of their professional lives.[1] In a 2014 TED Talk, Chilean author Isabelle Allende talked about feeling invisible as an older woman in Latin American culture.[2] What she wanted in her life, what she felt she was being denied, was passion, pleasure, fun.

Allende wanted just as much of all of those inspiring emotions as she did when she was younger, but our cultural memory offers no narrative and no visual template for active, passionate women in pursuit of pleasure in the prime of their lives. They only appear in our stories and images as mothers, servants or maiden aunts, safely at home. Male artists throughout the ages have endlessly painted them as such, and so have female artists, because those were the spaces they were allowed to occupy. In addition, women were not allowed to train as painters over long stretches of time.[3] As a consequence, their work was viewed as homely and unthreateningly feminine.[4] Berthe Morisot, who lived and worked in Paris in the late nineteenth century, is one of the artists whose work has been received as such. While it is true that Morisot chooses domestic settings, her work speaks to the existential psychological consequences of being shut away in these spaces. 'Morisot's is an art of dislocation – from the city, from oneself, from one's environment,' writes art critic Catherine McCormack in *Women in the Picture* (2021), 'a dislocation that brings all the muddied ennui and frustrations of women's experience to the surface. But she has not always been recognised in art history as the radical existentialist that she was.'[5]

Muddied ennui and frustration are precisely not what Isabelle Allende is asking for; when your horizons shrink, when you find yourself bound to the house or your immediate neighbourhood, when no one looks at you anymore with interest and curiosity, it would be normal to succumb to such feelings of frustration and, indeed, anger. Anger is the emotion my mother chose to feel when, accompanying me on my field research in Turkey, she was routinely ignored by our guide – a man in middle age. Given that I was researching lives of the women in more egalitarian ancient societies, for her to be ignored rankled all the more.

Women in middle age become invisible, and it is happening to women all around us, even though we may be blind to it: I did not realise that our guide was ignoring my mother and talking only to me, until my mother pointed it out to me. To my embarrassment, I must admit that my first instinct was to defend the guide instead of trusting her testimony and lived experience. I checked myself, however, and joined in her anger. Still, that moment helped me realise how easy it is to turn a blind eye to injustice when it is not directed at yourself, and how important it is to listen to the testimonies of those who experience those injustices.

As we have seen throughout this book, Greek myth is no friend to middle-aged women. The *Odyssey* opens on a young son telling his mother Penelope to go back to her room and not interfere with 'the business of men'. 'There is something faintly ridiculous about this wet-behind-the-ears lad shutting up the savvy, middle-aged Penelope,' writes Mary Beard about the episode, 'but it is a nice demonstration that right where written evidence for Western culture starts, women's voices are not being heard in the public sphere.'[6] Not only are their voices not being heard, the women themselves are not to be seen: the son does not tell his mother merely to be silent, he tells her to 'go back up into your quarters, and take up your own work, the loom and the distaff'.[7]

This episode is so instructive because it is one of the few moments in Greek myth where a middle-aged woman even appears, and has something to say. In another notable example, you may not be surprised to hear that the woman in question is made into a monster rather than a human: Medea.

We have met Medea before. She is the woman from Colchis, who marries Jason, then murders their children when Jason betrays her. In spite of the gruesome act, her part is coveted by actors. One part of this is surely the great challenge of portraying a woman who would commit such a crime, but another part may be more banal: she is one of the few women of middle age in Greek tragedy who has a reasonable number of lines. She is the protagonist of her story, and of this play, for better and for worse. It takes a mother murdering her children for a woman of middle-age to appear centre-stage.

One exception to this rule is Euripides's *The Trojan Women*. The Greek playwright seems to have made it his mission to write about women, and could serve as a role model for male artists today. Instead of writing about the victorious Greek men coming home from the Trojan War, he gives over the play to the women who have lost the war, the women who have been enslaved by the Greeks. Some of them are even of middle age, most notably the Trojan Queen Hecuba. It is a powerful piece of theatre, full of empathy for the vulnerable, the oppressed, the losers of a war that the Greeks celebrated in their most famous epic.

Still, it does not exactly make for a cheerful read, or viewing experience, today. The women in the play are all suffering the worst imaginable fates, from enslavement to rape to murder, and they continue to suffer throughout. They turn on each other and lament their losses, which is understandable, but does not make for an inspiring night out at the theatre.

Middle-aged women who experience pleasure and passion are as rare in Greek myth as they are in films, television, and novels today. There have been some notable exceptions of late, such as *Babygirl* starring Nicole Kidman or *Good Luck to You, Leo Grande* starring Emma Thompson, but the majority of studio executives still seem to hold on to the idea that mainly young women, preferably looking for love, will be of interest to viewers. The writer Deborah Levy describes meetings with studio executives where she pitches a script about a middle-aged mother and writer, and even she thinks of her idea as ridiculous. 'The female character I was describing would be a subversive character, but if he were a male character he would not be subversive.'[8] I remember talking to a producer affiliated with a major US streaming platform at my agency's annual spring party. He was a young man in his twenties, fresh off a philosophy degree where he had spent far too much time thinking about Nietzsche and other rather pessimistic nineteenth-century male thinkers (I told him this when we met, so I do not mind telling you all). He said that female protagonists were now all the rage. I hope that this is true, but he cannot have been referring to women of middle age. Those parts are still far and few between on our screens.

Art is failing to imitate life in this regard. After all, there are countless middle-aged women on television as journalists, moderators, or delivering documentaries. These women, however, pay a heavy price for appearing in public. Mary Beard, a prominent classicist who appears regularly on television, reports that she receives ample online abuse whenever she puts herself into the public sphere, including threats of rape, mutilation, and murder.[9] Women of all ages who show themselves in public receive this kind of abuse,[10] whereas men receive much less of it, unless they are men of colour or working class. When the *Guardian* analysed ten years' worth of comments, they found that the ten writers most strongly targeted by trolls were four white women, four women of colour, and two men of colour.[11] Of course, these women are particularly likely to be of middle age by the time they have reached positions of power and influence.

This paints a depressing picture for women of middle age. Either you accept that you become invisible as you age, or you insist on putting yourself out there, which will make you the target for the worst imaginable threats and abuse. Is there any evidence that there were periods in our past where women of middle age were appreciated, when they were visible?

This time, we will need to travel even further back then the first millennium BCE – all the way to the Stone Age.

The Palaeolithic, Mesolithic, and Neolithic are fascinating periods of human history because we are currently seeing a tremendous, rigorous, far-reaching re-evaluation of the evidence preserved from those times.[12] For decades, our idea of prehistoric times was shaped so fiercely by the prejudices of the men who founded the fields of prehistoric study that we thought human life before the Bronze Age had been uniform, and uniformly boring: people lived in small groups. They inhabited caves. Women stayed in the caves and took care of the children. Maybe they sometimes brushed their hair. Men left the caves in the morning and went out to hunt. They came back in the evening with a dead mammoth. Well done, men.

This picture is not only incorrect, it is also curiously reminiscent of the gender stereotypes experienced by European gentlemen in the nineteenth century.[13] These men may have had a proclivity for digging around in the ground, but they lacked a sense of imagination. They did not imagine that the *social* world in 50,000 BCE could have been significantly different from their own. The only difference they seemed to be willing to entertain was that people had not quite started building railways and water-closets yet. Fortunately, this did not have to worry them, as there was a simple explanation. These groups of humans were just more primitive versions of the Victorian society that these men lived in. It had always been inevitable that Stone Age people would one day build railways, and discover the joys of a water-closet, and that they would invent the script so that men could write about women and people from the past and people of colour as their inferiors, and continue to ignore the women of middle age who lived in their houses, had raised their children, and made sure they had a clean and tidy place to come home to.

While individual archaeologists may have felt differently, this is the narrative that emerged. This narrative of progress is deeply influenced by the Bible and Christian values, indeed the Christian narrative of humans born into sin, progressing into living a life of virtue, and eventually going to heaven to live in eternal bliss.

Needless to stay, this is not at all what happened in human prehistory. Christianity did not even exist then, and nor did any of the other three monotheistic religions that dominate humanity today, Islam and Judaism. Hinduism and Buddhism, too, were a long way away from being invented, and God in the singular had not even been thought of then.

Our Palaeolithic forebearers seem to have spent their time thinking not about God, or religion, or sin, but instead about women. In fact, quite specifically about women of middle age. Women of middle age and their vulvas.

The single most common symbolic artefact we retain from prehistoric times are figurines of women. Eighty to ninety per cent of all depictions of humans or sexual organs from the period depict women or vulvas.[14] These are women with hanging breasts, large bottoms, and clearly visible vulvas. In fact, vulvas are the single most frequent motif in prehistoric art.[15] This period of human history may have been many things, but phallocentric was not one of them.

The prehistoric figurines that have been discovered all over the world are extraordinary works of art and craftsmanship.[16] They have recently undergone an exciting re-evaluation: once believed to represent a fertility goddess such as a Greek Aphrodite or Roman Venus, they are now believed by scholars to be much more likely to represent middle-aged or older women who may have held prestigious positions of political power in prehistoric communities.[17] These were found in living areas and dwellings, more rarely in graves, so it is likely that they were not hidden away but exposed for all to see. Some of them may have been worn as pendants.[18] These figurines were consistently produced over a period of some 25,000 years in places as far apart as the south of France and Siberia, so it is unlikely that they were always used in the same way, or created for the same reasons.[19] As Belinda Crerar, curator at the British Museum, writes in the catalogue of the 2022 exhibition 'Feminine Power', interpretations of these figurines often 'reveal more about the social values and gender prejudices of the authors [...] than those of the cultures that created them.'[20] As most of these figurines have been interpreted by scholars living under the patriarchy, it is perhaps unsurprising that some have suggested that these figurines were created to arouse heterosexual male desire. This streak of interpretations originated in the 1920s and has continued to this day. Crerar describes how, when archaeologists discovered the prehistoric figurine known as the Woman of Hohle Fels in 2008, an article in *Nature* 'noted that the large breasts and prominent genitalia of this figure [...] 'could be seen as bordering on pornographic'".[21] Imagine looking at a wooden sculpture that is 35,000 years old, currently the oldest prehistoric figurine that we know, and then imagine that your imagination stretches no farther than to say, 'reminds me of the porn I watch'.

That is not to say that some of these figurines may not have served erotic desires. Some almost certainly depict pregnant women, and may have been part of fertility rites, although I suspect that there may be a much more banal explanation: some of these figurines could be made quite quickly, especially by a skilled artist, so perhaps they were simply the equivalent of photos of pregnant mothers today, shared full of excitement with family and friends.

Spotlight

Whether such an interpretation holds water or not, I wish to point out that these figurines demonstrate a completely different relationship to female and feminised bodies than is prevalent today. They depict women of all ages, including and most notably women of middle and old age. We live in a world where advertisement and media products endlessly confront us with the air-brushed bodies of thin, young, and still mostly white women, to the degree that any other body shape seems unnatural and unhealthy. These figurines suggest that, in prehistoric times, women, men, and children were most likely continuously exposed to the depiction of the naked bodies of women of middle age.

Whatever happened to women of middle age in prehistoric times, they were most certainly not invisible. In fact, the opposite is true. As soon as they reached middle age, with hanging breasts and large thighs and bums, they must have seen themselves reflected everywhere they went. In their houses, in the homes of their friends, perhaps even in the streets. Ethnographic research indicates that the loss of visibility and prestige for middle-aged women is not universal. Middle age may bring opportunities and authority, as a period where women (begin to) run businesses, become midwives, doctors or ceremonial leaders, or cross into enemy-territory to recover the bodies of the fallen.[22]

I had the pleasure of seeing some of these prehistoric figurines in person when I went to Athens to research this book, as well as a novel that I was writing at the time. A very special collection of them had just been returned from Princeton to Greece. They were on display at the Museum of Cycladic Art on the Neofitou Douka, a busy road bordering Athens' famous Zygmata Square. I had come to the museum through the Ethnikos Kipos, the National Gardens of Greece, a beautiful park designed for the pleasure of the people. My nose was full of the rich scent of pine trees and the fruity aroma of ripe oranges hanging from the boughs of citrus trees stretched across its paths. The museum was cool and modern, and I was already inclined to like whatever I saw that day, but the figurines surpassed even the gardens and the marbled museum. They were made of Parian marble, a type of semi-translucent marble of purest white. This material was also used in the creation of the Niké of Samothrace, the winged sculpture greeting millions of guests every year at the top of main staircase in the Louvre in Paris. It is a work of stunning beauty, and I had the pleasure of seeing it once a week while I lived in Paris as a student, and was allowed to go into the Louvre free of charge. I spent many happy hours there plotting novels set in the distant past, or thinking about what life must have been like in Ancient Babylonia, or admiring the bust of La Poetesse, who may have been Sappho.

In contrast to the grand sculptures I visited in the Louvre, the figurines I saw in the Cycladic Museum in Athens were small, perhaps thirty centimetres tall. They were produced at the very end of the Neolithic period, in the third millennium BCE, on a group of islands called the Cyclades in the Aegean Sea. These islands sit right between the cost of mainland Greece and Asia Minor, and archaeological evidence suggests that they were cosmopolitan hubs of trade and travel.

What struck me about these figurines was this: they looked so normal. The women they portrayed had all kinds of body shapes, just like the women I know. Some of them had large breasts, others were smaller. Some of them had long necks, others almost no neck at all. Noses, when they were depicted, could be large or small. The artist had engraved vulvas into most of these statues, and these women of stone stood in their display cabinets, with their vulvas exposed as if it were nothing – a far cry from the uproar caused by Gustave Courbet's painting of a vulva entitled *L'Origine du monde* in 1866.

I was moved by the display I saw in the museum that day, and even happier to find that the figurines had found their way into the museum shop. A stylised version of their silhouette could be bought as pendants, earrings, or printed on tote bags. Some designers had already taken inspiration from the Stone Age to make women of middle age, and of all sizes and shapes, more visible today.

If we are able, like these designers, to try and revise our cultural memory, if we look further back than Ancient Greece, we find the most exciting depictions of female, feminised, and non-binary bodies that I have ever come across. We can wear them as earrings, as necklaces, as tote bags. We could put them into our homes, on prints, as vases or candles. These acts may seem small, but they should not be underestimated. The private is, after all, political, and we would do well to grow reacquainted with the beauty of the bodies and minds of middle-aged women where we can. If this must start in our homes, then so be it.

However, that can only be the first step. It will be down to the storytellers again, the curators, artists, photographers, directors, historians, archaeologists, to put women in middle-age centre stage. To write the plays that are about them and their desires, write the novels that tell us of their pleasures, find the documents in the archives that help us learn of their goals and ambitions. Put their art on display, and the art that portrays them. There is a hypothesis that I find very convincing that the prehistoric figurines may be self-portraits, or portraits of real women that the artist knew: women creating art of women as they saw them, or as they saw themselves. Women making portraits of their mothers, their friends, their neighbours, their grandmothers. Women as artists, of all ages.[23]

We are seeing some of these stories emerge already. The Old Vic theatre in London, for example, put on a play in its 2024 summer season called *The Constituent*. Its audiences witnessed how a relationship between a female member of parliament and one of her constituents starts out hopeful and then goes sour. I will not give away the ending of the play, but it was refreshing to see a woman over the age of forty, in a position of power, in a central role on stage.

Unfortunately, in spite of her character's centrality, most of the lines in the play went to the male constituent; most of the talking was done by the two men on stage. They had troubles, grievances, lives, a past, and they were not shy to talk about them. While this may be quite an accurate reflection of how much time men spend talking, and how little time is given to women, we learned very little about the woman's life, and nothing about what she wanted, or desired, or liked to do. She was kind, and generous, and caring, and that seemed to be enough.

The Constituent would not have passed the Bechdel test. Where is the play about a female member of parliament whose life does not revolve around her male constituents and her husband? Who is not settled with all the care work (another point frequently made in the play), and is not considered unusual?

These plays are still rare, and we will only have more of them if we push for them. Women, men, and non-binary storytellers can all contribute to this. And so can everyone else. Sometimes, subtle changes to the narrative can be as simple as wearing a pair of earrings. Whether they are worn by a woman, a man, or a person of any other gender. Such actions can also bring a great amount of pleasure. And we can never have enough of that – particularly in old age.

In her 2021 book Real Estate, *the author Deborah Levy reports on her attempts to sell a script to a production company. She wants the protagonist to be a middle-aged woman who does things that a middle-aged man would, but the producers are not convinced. She believes that they feel that this protagonist would not be likeable enough – that a woman making her own way in the world in middle age would so shock audiences that no one would turn up to see the movie.*

There do exist films with middle-aged protagonists, even romantic comedies. In The Idea of You (2024), Anne Hathaway romances a British boyband musician played by Nicholas Galitzine, in a story based on a fanfiction written by a woman. Such developments are wonderful, and it is good to see female fantasies and desires explored on the big and small screen.

And yet, more often than not, women still disappear from the public eye in middle age. If they do appear, they do so as mothers, or 'mums', one of the most uncomfortable collective terms used in British and American broadcasting today. Even in the film about the woman and her boyband lover, the female protagonist is obliged to give up her immense happiness and newfound love because it upsets her teenage daughter. It is cast as a matter of fact that such a sacrifice would be expected of a mother. No one, including her daughter, who considers herself as a feminist, seems to stop and think for a moment that perhaps her mother's happiness might also be important. We are not quite there yet, it seems. Even I know very little about the life of my grandmother in middle age. I know she must have done *amazing things: she went back to work and sold clothes and skiing equipment in a department store in Hamburg, a job that gave her great pleasure and purpose, as well as expert knowledge on all things related to skiing and underwear. I never asked her about this period in her life, but I wish I had. I wish I had stopped to think, when was my grandmother happiest? What did she experience in that department store? What did it feel like to have a paycheck? What did she buy with the money?*

I did not ask. I am a creature of the same cultural memory we all share. A woman still has to be a mother first and foremost, even while selling skis to merchants in Hamburg or touring Europe with a global popstar by day and sleeping with him by night. If they decide that they want things for themselves, women are punished. I often think of the Greek myth of Clytemnestra: she avenges herself on her husband Agamemnon after he kills their daughter Iphigenia, sacrificing her for favourable winds so that he may sail to Troy to make war on the city. While he is away, Clytemnestra takes a lover, rules Mycenae, and eventually kills Agamemnon on his return from the Trojan War. After that, she is killed by her children, who want to avenge their father. Her story is a powerful and important warning that violence begets more violence, but it is also a story about punishing a woman who did not want to let the murder of her daughter go unpunished. That is the cultural memory we are working with.

This remains true for women as they leave middle- and enter into old age. At this period of their lives, they are often portrayed as either grandmothers or unhappy, or, even less flattering, as villains. The image comes to mind of the fairytale witch, an old, mean woman who must be conquered by heroes and heroines. Any measure of independence, or of a will of their own, is transformed into evil and villainous intentions.

This is the legacy of our stories, our myths, fairytales, plays, novels, and legends, but it is not what old age has to be. It can be a period of immense pleasure and freedom. Our foremothers knew this. Time to share in their wisdom.

9. PLEASURE

Female pleasure today is not readily associated with old age. Our foremothers from Scythia and the Stone Age will help us see how misguided this view is, but let us begin with the status quo: pleasure today is frequently linked to young bodies and the domestic sphere. Additionally, it is often thought of from the perspective of the 'male gaze'. This is a term coined by Laura Mulvey in her 1975 essay 'Visual Pleasure and Narrative Cinema'. Applying psychoanalysis to the study of cinema, Mulvey argued that films are produced in such a way as to please men visually: 'Traditionally, the woman displayed has functioned on two levels: as erotic object for the characters within the screen story, and as erotic object for the spectator within the auditorium', she writes. The male gaze projects its fantasy 'onto the female figure which is shaped accordingly'.[1]

Present-day advertising can demonstrate the logic of the male gaze just as well as 1970s cinema. A thin, photoshopped, often white woman in a bathtub, relaxing by candlelight, still serves as a stock image of female relaxation and pleasure in certain spheres of advertising, corporate publishing and marketing. This can have amusing side effects: in 2019, users on social media noticed that advertisers were using images of women in bathtubs with bathtub trays carrying an ever growing number of electronic gadgets, sipping wine and coffee simultaneously, and snacking on cheese platters and salads.[2] Users' comments on this were very funny, but their reaction has a serious undertone: the campaigns they were criticising demonstrate that the stock image of a thin white woman in a bathtub still holds currency in some areas of advertising. Such an image is titillating for the male gaze, as it both hides and reveals a woman's naked body. The woman in the bathtub is an erotic object for the male viewer. For a woman, the image is more complicated. On the one hand, it allows her to imagine herself in a bathtub, resting and relaxing. On the other, it also makes her imagine that she is being looked at while in the bathtub, and to go through all the ways in which her body might be found wanting by the male gaze compared with the model photographed for the advertisement. Relax, but relax only to please the male gaze. Rest, but in a way that stays alert to male desire. In truth, there is no rest and relaxation to be found in these images: there is only the tension of comparing oneself to a fantasy body.

The promise of pleasing the male gaze, of which girls from the earliest age are so painfully aware, is what allows such images to sell products as diverse as mini vacations, e-readers, and razors. These images make a promise to the woman that she will be able to use e-readers, mini-vacations, and razors, both for her own pleasure and that of the men who are watching her. In our public iconography, women are allowed pleasure, but only those pleasures that also please men.

If we trace our prototypical image of female pleasure through art history back to Ancient Greece, it becomes obvious how it has been shaped by and for heterosexual men. In the Louvre, we find an amphora which depicts Amazons dressing for battle on one side, and bathing on the other, entirely nude. Ancient Greek pottery depicting bathing women may have been made specifically for the communal viewing pleasure of wealthy men.[3] These were images they consumed at social gatherings. These vases could be turned to reveal a sequence of events, for example women warriors undressing before the bath. Modern equivalents might be men attending peep shows or strip clubs together. What links the vase in the Louvre to modern-day advertising campaign is the depiction of young women: there are no older women bathing here.

Time and again throughout this book, we have seen that Ancient Greece may not be the ideal starting point for telling the history of women. This includes histories of older women. Older bodies do not appear on the Ancient Greek vases betraying erotic desire,[4] and when older women do appear in the ancient or prehistoric record, they have not been recognised as such.

One particularly intriguing example are the prehistoric figurines that I have already discussed. Consistently created for 25,000 years by communities stretching from the south of France to Siberia, these figurines have many different shapes and sizes, and will have served many different functions. Many of them take the shape of women with hanging breasts, large bellies, and large buttocks. This led (male) scholars to the assumption that the figurines portrayed pregnant women, so young women rather than older women past the menopause.

However, feminist archaeology and prehistory have begun to do away with this interpretation. 'We must challenge the number of portrayals of pregnant women', writes Marylène Patou-Mathis, 'because the morphology of women in the Old Palaeolithic period was surely just as diverse as the morphology of women today.'[5] In other words: women have always had different body shapes, and just because a woman has a large bum, a large belly, or hanging breasts, this does not mean that she is pregnant. (Although some of the figurines may well be portraits, even self-portraits, of pregnant women.)

In fact, as we saw in the previous chapter, it may mean that these are figurines of older women. Older women may have found their bodies celebrated and cherished as they aged, even put on display.[6] The French prehistorian Claudine Cohen suggests that older women in prehistory were revered for their wisdom, as protectors, and as invaluable contributors to the social cohesion of a community.[7] The figurines may have been created by older women, for women, depicting themselves, pregnant daughters or friends, peers in positions of authority, or revered ancestors – for no other purpose than artistic pleasure or communal celebration rather than pleasing the male gaze.

The desire to interpret figurines as young or pregnant women chimes with an apparent desire among some (male) prehistorians and archaeologists to interpret prehistoric drawings and art works as erotica. Prehistoric drawings of figures bending over, figures who may or may not be female, have been interpreted as 'first erotic images' meant to 'invoke the pleasures provided by the female body for the gaze and the other senses'.[8] Never mind that there are countless reasons why people bend over – having sex is not the only one! There is no reason to automatically assume that a figure bending over is bending over for sex, or that that this must necessarily be the depiction of a sexual act. In spite of the lack of evidence, some (male) scholars have insisted that figures bending over are 'ideal women' offered to the desires of men, as Marylène

Patou-Mathis explains.⁹ The assumptions made here are not just that a person bending over is a sexual object but also that all men are heterosexual; that a person who is sexual object must be a woman; and that women are there to please men.

None of these assumptions are particularly likely to be true. These figures may portray women or men or non-binary persons. They might be engaged in sexual acts, including solo sex, or they may be bending over for entirely different reasons. I do not know about you, but I most frequently bend over to pick up my glasses, or my phone, or my in-ear headphones, or any other of the many items that I seem to drop at will. I also frequently pick up toys left lying around by my niece while she plays, or to examine the ground I am walking on when out on a hike on Dartmoor or in the Pennines, to make sure I do not step into rabbit holes or a deep muddy puddle hiding away under the long grass. In the Stone Age, our ancestors spent their days hunting, laying traps, or gathering food. Is it so unlikely that the figures depicted are bending over to track large game, inspect a trap, or collect some tasty blackberries to indulge in the pleasures of food?

Our foremothers may have much to teach us about the pleasures of old age, not all of which are sexual. The vase depicting bathing Amazons takes us back again to women in Scythia, where no such imagery survives in the material record. However, ancient sources speak of other pleasures. One of the Scythian graves I have already mentioned contained the bones of a sixty-year-old warrior woman. At sixty, she was still riding out to hunt and fight, drawing the string of her bow across her chest, feeling the touch of her worn leather finger pad on her chin just before she let the arrow fly. And whyever would she not? Her community would have been foolish not to make the most of her experience and expertise as a hunter and warrior. Pseudo-Plutarch – a name given to a collection of unknown ancient authors whose writing has been falsely attributed to Plutarch in the past – writes about the halinda plant and its juices. When rubbed into the skin, it heats up and relaxes the muscles, not unlike the heat plasters used by runners, athletes, and older women for pain relief today.[10]

All this evidence suggests that our foremothers took pleasure in their bodies and the agency of their bodies, caring for their muscles, sinews, and tendons. Pleasure, to them, may have been bound up with the active use of their bodies well into old age, with the loving touch of their own skin.

In fact, these women may have experienced important freedoms. We also retain period calendars from the Stone Age, indicating that women attempted to track their cycle, perhaps as a means of natural contraception, or as indicators of early pregnancy[11] or the arrival of the menopause. They may have used self-knowledge about themselves and their bodies in order to have control over their sexual lives and their bodies. While some of our prehistoric ancestors may not have lived to see the arrival of the menopause, there would have been many that did, and experience all the physical changes that come with it. As bell hooks details in *Communion* (2002), the women in her family rejoiced in the changes that came over their bodies in later life, as they went through menopause.[12] Her mother and grandmother had grown up at a time when contraception was not widely available, and any sexual encounter, including acts of sexual violence, could result in a pregnancy. These women had spent most their lives caring for others. Only when they lost their fertility did they finally feel free; free to be themselves, free for adventure, free to go where they pleased. Free to run, to cycle, to sail, to say yes to life. bell hooks's book is aptly titled *Lieben lernen* in the German translation, which means 'learning to love', and perfectly describes the process these women went through: they learnt how to love life and how to love themselves.

This process is not new – not just a late phase of life gifted to women by the invention of the birth control pill. As we have seen in a previous chapter, when prehistoric men began coparenting, this proved such a great advantage that men became more caring as a result of evolutionary selection, giving humanity a greater chance at survival. Equally useful may have been the presence of post-menopausal women who participated in the rearing of children: researchers have found that one of the great advantages of our species is that women enter into menopause.[13] As they lose the ability to have children themselves, they may turn to the children of others in the community. Older women adopt roles as teachers and advisors, passing on skills, sharing their experience and expertise, inspiring younger people and leading them. This goes far beyond, and sometimes does not include, any conventional notion of childcare. My nan was an inspiration to me in how to stand up for myself even when I wasn't sitting at her dining table at lunchtime, and women such as Margaret Atwood and Annie Ernaux have been essential to my success as a writer as they continue to achieve artistic greatness while inspiring younger women to become better writers and leading acts of political resistance against the loss of reproductive rights and classism. The support between younger and older women enabled women in early human history to live lives independent of men: women did not depend on men for their or their family's survival, as younger and older women 'won the bread' together.[14] The male breadwinner, and the economic dependence of women on men, is a cultural invention made long after the Stone Age, fundamentally strengthened and institutionalised by the three monotheistic religions of Christianity, Islam, and Judaism. The Christian religion did not start out with patriarchal structures. These were developed later, in the process of founding and institutionalising the Church.[15]

That is not to say that old age is a phase of unmitigated pleasures. As we grow older, our bodies become frailer, and sometimes, so do our minds. But Isabelle Allende speaks eloquently on what she gained in old age: freedom. The freedom from other people's judgements and opinions, from stereotypes and society's expectations. She points out that the Spanish word for retirement is *jubilación:* jubilation, celebration. Freedom is something to celebrate indeed, and so are the minds and bodies of older women, treasurers of pleasure, freedom and adventures in the late stages of life.

The data suggests that this is no small amount of pleasure. In fact, studies indicate that women are at their happiest from the age of fifty-five, and at their unhappiest in their twenties, thirties, and early forties.[16] Goodness me, so much to look forward to! Women over sixty report 'higher levels of overall satisfaction, happiness, and well-being, and lower levels of anxiety, depression, and stress', explains US clinical psychologist and author Mary Pipher, and the older the woman, 'the better her mental health tended to be'.[17] Older women consistently outperform men in their happiness ratings, and census data indicates that that happiest people in the United Kingdom are women between the ages of 65 and 79.[18]

The data shows, then, that older women are living happy and fulfilled lives, which goes against the cultural stereotype of the 'hag', or of older women as annoying, unhappy, lonely, or dangerous witches. That is because our memory is faulty. We do not remember the past as it was. We are used to remembering those periods that suited the patriarchal, misogynist, and colonialist mindsets of nineteenth-century. Older women are happy. We just don't know it.

There is no reason to continue to remember the past in this way. Data shows that many of us hold positive opinions about equality between the genders and aspire to create a gender-equal society.[19] It seems we are ready to remember the Stone Age, the prehistoric period, the Scythian communities where women were warriors in their sixties, where older women made art and served as models, where they are the ones to give us advice, wisdom, leadership, and freedom.

The last time we meet Helen in the *Odyssey*, she is probably thirty or forty years old, back in the palace that she tried so desperately to escape. I like to imagine a version of the story in which she sneaks away again, past child-bearing age, well into her fifties, even her sixties. She would have been wise enough, then, not to worry about bringing her silk nightdress, her pretty mirror. She would have brought a pocket mirror instead and the Amazon puppet, a gift to give to someone else's child; she would have brought her warm overcoat, spun from wool; she would have brought her hairbrush. In my version, she would not have gone with another man. She would have been wise enough to know that she did not need one. She may have dressed as an old man, changing genders like the seer Tiresias, or she may have gone to visit her daughter Hermione, now married herself, before vanishing altogether.

In her 2005 *Penelopiad*, a modern telling of the story of Odysseus's wife Penelope, Margaret Atwood writes about

Helen in the underworld, and finds her to be shallow and cruel. Yet there is no reason to think that this would have been her end. As she grew older, surely Helen would have grown wiser and happier. If we were to go down into the underworld to look for Helen, I do not believe that we would find her. She would be too clever to reveal herself to us, would want none of the fuss, would most certainly not want her husband to find her. Instead, she might play the guide, the shepherdess, the ferryman. She might lead us through the underworld, keep an eye on us, and show us the ghosts of those who give good advice: Achilles, speaking against war. Penelope, warning us against meekness. Atalia from Babylon, speaking eloquently on the value of freedom, of choosing a free life, no matter how brief, no matter the cost. Phanos, telling us to resist when someone wants to take away our rights, and her mother Nearea, saying yes to living life the way we want to. We might meet the women and men from the Stone Age in this underworld we are imagining, whose names we do not retain, and listen to them speak about the joys of acting as a team, of caring for children, of advising the young, of creating beautiful works of art, no matter your age.

    I like to imagine a Helen who grew to an old age, and an old age that suited her. Even as she grew older, as she experienced more aches and pains, she might have come to love her body in a whole new way: not as an object to please men, but as her own body, her own skin, allowing her to experience so many pleasures.

Our cultural conception of old age is woefully inadequate for the lived realities of millions of women growing older in our societies today. Women and men experience pleasure in old age, and retirement should better be thought of as a jubilation, a celebration of entering into a new phase of life, one that is no longer defined by the needs, demands, or opinions of others.

Old age can be a period of immense pleasure. It may be useful to recall the words of Achilles, the quintessential Greek hero, who chose to die young in battle rather than return home to his family with his lover. When Odysseus meets him in the underworld, as we have heard, he tells him that now he would do anything to grow old, that he would give up his fame, the glory won in battle, only to be alive again, to regain the years he lost, all those years he could have lived.

The Greek myths can be wiser than our cultural memory gives them credit for. Achilles can be an inspiration to us in our endeavours to rethink old age as a period of pleasure, a period where pleasure matters most of all, because we know how precious it is – because we know it cannot last. One day, we will die.

10. MOURNING

We live in a society that struggles with death. As British-American biologist and Nobel prize winner Venki Ramakrishnan puts it, the certainty of death is 'so terrifying that we live most of our lives in denial of it'.[1] This is true, but it is not the way it has to be. There are many stories we could be telling each other about death and the afterlife, and so many stories that humans have told each other throughout the centuries. It is not all heaven and hell, salvation or suffering. And when we tell each other a different story about death, we can also find a different way of mourning. Certainly, the way we mourn is shaped by the way we think of death, and for many millennia, the way we have been conceiving of death has been detrimental to women. It has favoured lavish funeral rites for men and the retention of their names, while women have been pushed to margins, their names and lives forgotten.

I will introduce you to a different piece of history – to the funeral rites of Minoan Crete, where grief and death were social rather than private. I also will tell you how some of the Scythian communities thought about death. To me, this is the best story to come out of Scythia yet, and it contains much wisdom for the present.

In order to appreciate the beauty of the Scythian story, we must understand our own traditions first. You may think that we are all equal in death, as the saying goes, but that is unfortunately not the case in the stories we have been telling each other about death and the afterlife in the West for the past two millennia. As Ramakrishnan points out, the fear of death has fundamentally shaped our religious beliefs, and this immediately brings to mind the promise of salvation and Paradise made by the monotheistic religions. If you do this or that, and not this or the other, you will make your way to Paradise, and be with the God who made you.

There is one catch to this statement: entering Paradise is much more difficult if you are a woman. I will speak here of the Christian faith, because it is the belief system that I know best, and because the Christian Church has been one of the strongest force of oppression in the lives of women in the West in the common era, tracing its origins back to the ancients, through Greek myth and the Roman Emperors.[2]

The story I am about to tell you is a tragic story, because the early days of Christianity were filled with courageous and respected women, and Jesus of Nazareth treated them as his equals.[3] However, the founders of the Christian Church made a concerted effort to erase these women from history, arguing stridently that women were inherently sinful.[4] Important men of the Christian faith from the apostle Paul to the Roman Emperor Augustine declared that women were to blame for the fall from Paradise, that women had been created to please men, and that women were passing on the original sin to their daughters, and their daughters after them, and their daughters after them.[5] According to the Book of Genesis and the story of Adam and Eve, women were not equal to men at birth, and

Mourning

they were cast as weak, voluptuous, and easy prey for the devil, who would have no hard time tempting them into sin.[6]

In theory, then, women could find salvation in death, but all this made it much more difficult. The disadvantage for women here has a striking resonance with Ancient Greek beliefs about the afterlife. These beliefs were complex and often contradictory, but the version of them we mostly think of today includes parallels with the Christian concept of heaven and hell. The Greek underworld was called Hades. Here, you would find three different areas: the fields of Elysium for those who had been given the epithet of hero (mostly won through committing acts of violence against others); the Asphodel Meadows, for the average sort of soul; and Tartarus, where those were punished who committed evil deeds in their lives.

As Greek women were excluded from warfare, it would be nigh on impossible for them to go to the fields of Elysium in the afterlife. Most of them, I suppose, would have been found on the Asphodel Meadows. Some stories say that those who cross onto the meadow must drink water from the river Lethe, losing their identities and memories in the process. The stories that the Ancient Greeks told each other about death were prescient: they already knew that the lives of most women from Ancient Greece would never be remembered. Their names would be lost in a metaphorical river Lethe, the same way that women have for millennia lost their names in marriage, lost their sense of self as they looked in the mirror and saw the male gaze staring back at them.

Still, the Syrian writer Publilius Syrus, who came to Rome in the first century BCE, wrote that 'as men, we are all equal in the presence of death'. Publilius had once been a slave, but won his freedom after flourishing as a writer. In 45 BCE, he won a competition against an established Roman mime writer, receiving his prize from general and dictator Julius Caesar. He was a contemporary of the orator Cicero, and his work has been passed down to us in the form of aphorisms which scholars found in his mimes in the century after his death.

As a formerly enslaved man, Publilius must have known that there was no equality in life, but perhaps he wanted to tell a story of death in which the man who had been enslaved could claim equality with his new peers, who had been born free. I certainly do not begrudge him this story.

Yet however empowering for him, his aphorism has been repeated in different guises throughout the centuries in ways that overlook the reality for women. We must all die, but the roles of women and men in mourning were starkly segregated in Ancient Greece, according to its literature.

If we look at the *Iliad*, already considered a foundational cultural text in Ancient Rome, washing and preparing the dead for their final journey is women's work. However, the performance of public funeral rites falls once again to the men. Homer describes a number of burials in great detail in his *Iliad*, and many of them include public games held by men, where men compete against each other to win prizes that included enslaved women. The death of a man in battle had consequences for the women he had enslaved.

The *Iliad* is aware of this in its portrayal of Briseis, a woman whom Achilles has enslaved. She receives kindness from Achilles's lover Patroclus, and when he dies, she mourns his death with many tears and lamentations. Storytellers have taken this to mean that she was in love with Patroclus, or that there was some form of ménage-à-trois going on between Patroclus, Briseis, and Achilles, but Briseis may also be worried for her life, now that the only person to show her kindness has gone. After the death of Achilles, she is enslaved again by his son.

We do not learn of the circumstances of Briseis's death in the *Iliad*, or the death of any of the other women. It is men who receive glamorous burials in this epic, although both men and women die in the war.

The Greeks were aware that there were alternatives. They even talked about them in their stories. In Quintus of Smyrna's *Posthomerica* – created approximately three hundred years after Homer's *Iliad* to narrate the events that follow the death of Hector in the Trojan War – the Amazon warrior woman Penthesilea receives the same honours as the Greek heroes after she is killed by Achilles in the Trojan War.[7] She has come to Troy not to win glory, but to fight at the side of her longstanding ally Priam,[8] the king of Troy, coming to his aid at his most desperate hour, when his son, heir, and most formidable warrior, Hector, has been killed. Her death is mourned by Trojans and Greeks alike, and she is given a funeral fit for a queen:

> Strongly moved by pity for noble Penthesileia
> And even by admiration, the royal sons of Atreus
> Gave her to the Trojans to carry with her armor
> Back to the city of famous Ilos, when they heard
> The message sent by Priam. He desired, he said,
> To lay the valianthearted maiden with her armor
> And horse inside the great tomb of rich Laomedon.
> He had a funeral pyre outside the city heaped
> Both high and broad. On top he had them place
>   the maiden
> With all the possessions it was fitting to burn

> On the pyre of a wealthy queen who had fallen in battle.
> So she was consumed by the fire god's mighty force,
> Destroying flames. Then, standing on every side, the people
> Hastened to quench the pyre with fragrant wine.
> Gathering up the bones, they drenched them in perfumed oil
> And laid them in an empty casket. Over the bones
> They packed the abundant fat of a heifer, the best
> Of all the herds that grazed on Ida's hills.
> The Trojans wailed as for a daughter dearly loved,
> And grieving they buried her beside their stately walls,
> Close to a jutting tower with the bones of Laomedon,
> To honor the god of war and Penthesileia herself.[9]

We do not know if women were present at her funeral, but we must hope so. As Quintus of Smyrna tells us, she inspired the Trojan women to take up arms, led by a Trojan woman called Hippodamia. It is difficult to imagine that Hippodamia and her recruits would not have attended the funeral of the woman who had so inspired them. Let us imagine that they did.

The story of Penthesilea shows that even in Greek myth, we find traces of a different story to be told about death, about mourning. Her historical counterparts were then and today believed to be the Scythian warrior women who enjoyed much greater gender equality than their Greek counterparts. This equality extended to their burials.

Mourning

In archaeology, the Scythians are best known for their rich burials[10] and extensive burial rites, which Herodotus described with accuracy in his *Histories*, including rich golden burial gifts and multi-day processions displaying the dead body.[11] In terms of pomp, they are no less impressive than their Greek counterparts, perhaps even more so. Some of these burials certainly took place in deeply patriarchal contexts, but others may not have, and women and men alike were buried with impressive treasures, such as the Pazyryk 'Ice Princess' who was buried with six horses 2,500 years ago in today's Republic of Altai.[12]

These horses are significant when it comes to Scythian beliefs of the afterlife. According to some archaeologists, there were multiple horses in a single grave because the road to the afterlife was long, and the dead would have to change horses to reach their goal.[13] According to the Nart sagas collected by John Colarusso, it is the horse Zhaqa that takes the dead to the afterlife. We met Zhaqa before, when Psatina and Warzameg escaped death on its back. Zhaqa, in the sagas, is the fastest horse in the world, and its name translates to Grave Mound.[14]

Zhaqa may take Psatina and Warzameg from the world of the dead to the world of the living, but for the rest of us, the journey can only be attempted in reverse. Zhaqa takes us to the land of death. There is no hell here, no heaven, no meadow of lost names, faces, and stories. Instead, we come to a different land. It is the land where nothing moves.

This belief in death as the land where nothing moves made a deep impression on me, from the first time I read about it in the Nart sagas. Colarusso describes it in his translation as 'a land where nothing stirs, not even a bird in the sky'.[15] When I travelled to the Pontic Alps south of the Black Sea to prepare for a novel I was about to write, where some Scythian communities would have lived, I realised how apt his translation was, and that the Scythians had been describing a place that they knew. The lands in the Pontic Alps are so still, to this very day. I was alone, and I felt as if I was the last living being on Earth, in a land where nothing moved.

It was a frightening sensation. In spite of the landscape stretching far and wide around me, the stillness gave me a sense of claustrophobia. All of my ambitions suddenly seemed pointless: writing a book, going out into the field, making any plans for the future or thinking about the past. It all collapsed in face of the overwhelming stillness. For a brief moment, I experienced what some Scythians associated with death.

The land where nothing moves is not a paradise in the Nart sagas. It is the realm of death, the kingdom of a monstrous giant or serpent. As far as we are aware, there are no alternatives. There is no heaven to go to, no hell. No salvation, no suffering. We must all go to the land where nothing moves. Zhaqa will take us there.

Experiencing this moment made me wonder what they may have thought of as the essence of life, as the opposite of death. The answer that I found most convincing was: movement. Being able to say no to one thing, and yes to another. To go, or ride, or cycle, or sail, or row a boat until you reached the life you wanted to say yes to. This story seems to make sense for nomadic and semi-nomadic communities whose lives depended on moving, on crossing territories and borders, on riding horses for thousands of miles. It made sense for them to fear stillness. And it also made sense to me, who dressed her grandmother in her favourite cap and coat, lifted her into her wheelchair, and went out into the fields with her to visit the horses.

Mourning

I believe the belief in the land where nothing moves can make sense to us just as much as it made sense to people in Scythia, because it also contains a warning: not to let anyone take that freedom to move from you. Not to let anyone keep you in the house, or in a relationship you do not want, or living a life that is not your own.

The tale of the land where nothing moves warns us to say no to all those who would restrict our freedom: where we go, when and why, be it up a career ladder or across borders. The story warns us to fight for our freedom of movement, and to put it to good use.

Empowering as I found this, it also made me wonder: what are we saying yes to, then? As enamoured as I am with the story of the land where nothing moves, as much as I think that it speaks particularly to women in the twenty-first century, it is not a cheerful version of the afterlife. Nor is it the story we are telling ourselves about the afterlife in the West today. With many of us no longer belonging to organised religion, or often not practicing our faith if we do, visions of a Christian afterlife in Heaven have been replaced with a denial of death.

Many of us do not like to think about death. I certainly do not. After all, who likes to dwell on the fact that there may be nothing, nothing at all, waiting for us at the end of our lives, on the other side of existence? However, it is worth thinking about the many stories we have been telling about death in the past. Let us turn once more to the women and men of Minoan Crete, who experienced a change in burial customs in the third millennium BCE, just as their civilisation was beginning to flourish.[16] It is an important, and perhaps an instructive change.

We do not know at present what the Minoans believed about the afterlife throughout their long history. However, their funeral rites seem to have been more akin to communal feast, where families, friends and communities came together to celebrate with and beside the dead, and to eat a meal in their honour. These rites seem less about preparing the dead for the afterlife, for example by providing them with funeral goods or embalming their bodies (the metaphysical dimension), than about the social dimension of a funeral.[17] During these ceremonies, it was important to regenerate life, to look to the future, and to reallocate the roles and resources of the dead among the living, as the archaeologist Giorgos Vavouranakis suggests.[18]

This shift in focus draws attention away from the individual towards their social circle: those who a dead woman helped, mentored, loved, respected, or cherished, for example. What will the living do with what the dead have left for them, how will they step up to their new roles? It is about continuing, rather than about the end. A gaze directed not at the past but towards the future.

As we think of the deaths of the ones we love, or in fact of our own deaths, this is a gaze we may adopt, a question we might ask of ourselves: what will we do, specifically with the memories of the women we have loved? How will we honour those who have loved, mentored, and inspired us? And what would we like for those who have loved us to take away from our lives, and make part of their own?

When my grandmother passed away, she had been battling dementia for a long time, but she had also experienced many pleasures in old age. As her ashes were put into the ground, I experienced a curious sensation. A shift seemed to be taking place in the generations of my family. Both my grandmothers had now passed. This had made my mother and her sister the oldest generation of women in the family, and it had turned me into the middle generation, the only girl born to, and still surviving in, our family on my mother's side. My cousin Maria had died of a life-threatening disease many years earlier.

Walking away from the graveyard on the day of my grandmother's funeral, I realised that this, more than anything else, had helped me understand that I was a grown woman. It was not the jewellery, or the nail polish, or a professional career I had always wanted. It was the realisation that my mother would grow old, and that she, too, would leave us eventually, that her memories would be lost, and that my mother and grandmother, my aunts and our ancestors, had given me so much: a sense of dignity, a strong will, the desire for and pleasures of freedom. It was my time now to pass these things on, however I chose to do it.

So I looked into the past. I looked at what my mother and grandmother had given me, and wondered what I wanted to do with it. I looked at what our foremothers had given us, I looked at the way they had been forgotten. I looked at Greek myth, the story of Helen, and the lives led by women in Classical Athens, the women who are said to make up our foundational past. I realised that we may look at our past in a different way, that we do not have to begin our histories in Ancient Greece. We could think of ourselves as descendants of women like the mythical Amazon warrior Penthesilea, Kheuke the Scythian warrior and hunter, or the rulers of Minoan Crete, if not in body, then in spirit. As Kheuke may still have ridden out onto the steppes in old age, still bringing her mirror with her, still sending signals to Berossus, to their child, to her friends, so my grandmother came out into the fields of flowers and horses in her wheelchair, still bringing her favourite cap, her favourite blanket. When I blink, in that short moment when my eyes are closed, I can see them together: my nan in her wheelchair in a field, with her black lambswool cap, turned towards a tall brown horse, and Penthesilea, holding the horse by the reins. Perhaps this is Zhaqa. Perhaps Penthesilea has come to take my grandmother to the afterlife.

Women such as Penthesilea have been dead for thousands of years. My nan died three years ago. If we look closely enough, we can find the traces of both their lives in the material, archaeological, and literary record, in our memories and the memories of those around us: these are our personal, communicative, and cultural memories.

What we have done in this book is recover some of these memories, so that we can finally remember our foremothers, whether they died a few years or a few millennia ago – how they lived, how they died, and what we can learn from the today as we turn towards the future. Death, they teach us, is nothing to fear. Death is the reason we have to step up when we must, to look to the future, and to make sure we live a life worth living. A life of pleasure.

None of the stories we tell each other about death and the afterlife can tell us where we actually go when we die, but I don't believe that that is what they are for. These stories are all about life. They want to tell us how to live our lives, what to cherish in life, and how to move on when we have lost someone we have loved. Humans have been telling each other such stories for as long as we can remember. Some of them are more useful to us than tales of heaven and hell, particularly to women. Some women have periods, and those who do will know that life is both cyclical and linear. We must die one day, but we do not live as a lone individual, without connection to those who came before us, without a role to play in the lives of those who follow after us. I realised during the funeral of my grandmother that I was part of a long line of women, stretching far, far back into the past, perhaps as far as Kheuke, an old woman with her hands on the reins of a horse, the fastest horse in the world, still riding out to hunt, alone after the death of her husband Berossus.

We can all of us can go looking for the treasures of the past. We can recall memories, we can make new ones, and we can pass them on. Death comes for all of us. Forgetting does not.

CONCLUSION – AFTERLIFE

Five thousand years ago, there was something curious going on in the Cycladic islands. The Cycladic islands sit in the Aegean Sea between Greece and Turkey. They include Mykonos, Naxos, Andros, Keros and many more isles. This is a region of movement, islands that connect one continent to the other, in the same way that the United Kingdom connects mainland Europe with the United States and Ireland today. The Cycladics are where you land when you are travelling by sea between Asia Minor and Greece. This is where you stop, this is where you move on from. These islands are places of passage, as so many islands are.

Five thousand years ago, the Trojan War had not even been thought of. Homer was another 4,300 years away. Wilusa was already there, a city on the Hellespont, but no one had thought to call it Troy, not yet. No one would, for a good long while. This was a period when cities began to emerge, when humans travelled more and farther across the Aegean Sea, when ideas and stories and news travelled as quickly as olive oil or wine or marble.[1]

In this period, countless figurines were made on the Cycladic islands. They bear a great resemblance to the Stone Age figurines we have encountered before, but there is such a great diversity of shapes found on these isles, and the craft of creating them has been so far perfected, that archaeologists consider these Cycladic figurines as masterpieces of pre-historic art.[2] Many of them are made from marble, and most of them portray women, as far as we can tell.

When I first saw one of these figurines, I had not been looking for them. Two years after the death of my grandmother, one year after the birth of my niece, I found myself on a research trip in Athens. I had planned to look into the depiction of Amazons in Greek art and architecture, and to walk some of the paths that a woman such as Penthesilea may have gone along, to see the places where she might have travelled. This was research for the novel I was writing at the time, and I had been on trips such as this one before, for example to Turkey, to see Troy and the Black Sea and the steppes she may have ridden across.

I was very busy with this research, which was often quite tiring. It demanded that I put my body in remote and uncomfortable places, usually when it was very hot or very cold, no matter whether it was raining or the sun was out. I was not looking to come across another story, a different period of the past that did not feature Amazons. I went to the Museum of Cycladic Art only to make sure that I did not miss a trace of the Amazons, the depictions of Scythian warrior women I had come to Greece to find.

What I found instead were those figurines. Most notably, ten figurines dating from the Neolithic to the Early Cycladic period (5300 to 2400 BCE) which were depictions of the female body and had spent most of their modern lives outside of Greece at the Metropolitan Museum of Art in New York. The year

Conclusion — Afterlife

I went to Athens, they had come back for an exhibition called 'Homecoming'.

I had not planned to fall in love with them, but I did. I recognised these figurines as precious works of art. The masterful craftsmanship impressed me just as much as their different shapes and expressions, some of them sceptical, some of them cheeky. Then there was their smooth material, the marble in white, ochre, and green. I appreciated them as the work of a fellow artist, living five thousand years before me.

But I also appreciated them as a woman. Their shapes, different as they were, were so much like the bodies of the women I knew, including myself. I felt so seen by these figurines that I thought of them as mirrors rather than artworks, despite the many years that lay between their creation and my visit to Athens on a hot summer day in early June. As I looked at them, I felt as if I was looking at myself, but without the demands of the male gaze I had internalised from a young age. There was no room for that gaze. These were women as I knew them. This was me. I did not feel as if the figurines were judging me, that they wanted either to be emulated or to repulse. I felt that they simply existed, and I existed among them.

All my life, I had lived among pictures of women, on posters and on screens, that were almost painfully thin and obviously photoshopped. My response to these was compounded by growing up in the 1990s and 2000s, when directors wanted us to believe that Renée Zellweger as Bridget Jones was fat, and pop stars such as Britney Spears and Christina Aguilera were constantly judged on their weight and looks.

Standing in the exhibition space of the Museum of Cycladic Art, surrounded by those ten figurines, I remember that I felt, for the first time, that my body was normal. That it was natural. That it did not have to look different from the way it already looked. Much as I do not agree with the terms 'normal' and 'natural', as I have outlined in the introduction to this book, experiencing the feelings that I associate with those terms in that moment was transformative. Never before had I felt so at peace with my body as I did in that room. I felt as if I belonged there. That is the better way of putting this: not to feel normal, but to feel as if you belong.

There was a third element that bewitched me that day in Athens: the devotion, care, and honour shown to these figurines. In this room, women were important, and not just exceptional women. People of the Neolithic and Early Cycladic period did not depict queens, or goddesses, or priestesses, women who had been particularly clever or particularly beautiful. That these women simply existed was enough to make them matter.

We retain no written records from this period, so we do not know what these figurines were used for, but we can still look at them and imagine. Standing in the blissfully cool exhibition space of the Museum of Cycladic Arts, I wondered if the omnipresence of these figurines on the Cycladic Islands might have meant there was a place on those isles for women just as they were. That women were not made to feel ashamed of their bodies, that they were not silenced in public debate, that they were free to come and go as they pleased. I imagined that they would have been proud to speak out, proud of the way they looked. Then I imagined them as not even needing to be proud; imagined that this was the way things had always been for them. It would have seemed normal to them to live that life, to have a history, a present, and a future.

Conclusion — Afterlife

That is what I would like for us to have, as women: a history of our own. A memory that makes us feel that we belong.

Memory serves to make the status quo appear inevitable: it grounds the present in the past and gives us the sense that we know the shape of the future. In terms of personal memory, it allows us to sustain a stable sense of ourselves. In spite of the immense change we undergo as we move through life, memory helps us to link the person we were at five with the teenager we become at thirteen and the adult who gets up every day to go to work and the pensioner who takes up piano lessons, starts learning Spanish, or cares for their garden. Personal memory allows us to think of ourselves as one and the same person as we move through the different stages of life.

In a similar way, collective memory allows us to feel that we belong to a stable group, even if that group, in reality, is always changing, always gaining and losing new members, always changing its idea of itself, always changing who is out and who is in, what the rules of belonging are.

Cultural memory allows us to believe that this group has been and will be stable through time. Think of the mythical figure of King Arthur, a supposed descendant of the survivors of the Trojan War and legendary king of early Medieval Britain. He is known as the king who was and shall be, the once and future king. With this epithet, he epitomises the power and pretension of cultural memory: to create continuity in a world that is always changing, where nothing is certain but death. In cultural memory, humans get a taste of immortality, not for themselves, but for the community they belong to. King Arthur was king, and he will be king again. The king is dead, long live the king. In cultural memory, times becomes cyclical rather than linear.

Cultural memory is powerful because of this impression of immortality; it has the power to make temporary things such as nations and gender stereotypes appear everlasting, and elevates them to become part of an assumed natural order of the world. It turns human constructions into things that pretend to be natural laws, and it turns them into the sun that we gravitate around. Cultural memory can even be dangerous. The Nazis revered a figure not unlike King Arthur, who was called Frederick Barbarossa. A historical ruler of the Holy Roman Empire from 1155 to 1190, Barbarossa was said to sleep in the Kyffhäuser mountains and would come to Germany's rescue in its hour of need. The story is ridiculous – just imagine a medieval king come out of a thousand-year-old grave in the 1940s, brandishing an iron sword, trying to rescue a soldier in the trenches of Belgium, France, or Poland. And yet, the Nazis made it a part of their narrative of the thousand-year Reich ruled by violent men that they were going to build.

In the end, their Reich lasted seventeen years. Nothing lasts forever. Similarly, cultural memory is a construction, an invention, the sum of all the stories we keep retelling each other, over and over. It is up to us to tell the stories that are going to be useful for us, that are going to take us towards the future we want.

In terms of the stories we have been telling each other about women from the past, we have seen that our cultural memory is not doing women any favours at the moment. There are too many stories we do not retell even when we could: the story of the Pirate Amazons, the legend of Penthesilea, of the night that Helen flees from her home in Sparta to go to Troy. There are too many histories we ignore: the powerful women of Minoan Crete, the Scythian warrior women, the female army of Dahomey. There are too many storytellers, male and female, who do not tell the stories of the joy and happiness we experience in a more egalitarian society, every hour of every day, and how much greater it would be still if we became a truly gender-equal society.

Instead, we still focus on the same stories, retelling them over and over, always reaching back into antiquity and looking no farther than Classical Athens. This is not merely an oversight, a blind spot, a trivial convenience that we indulge in. In repeating the same stories, the same memories, the same histories, we do ourselves harm. We have created a memory of the past that makes gender equality appear unnatural. We have constructed a history for women that always forces us to relive the trauma of violence, oppression, and confinement.

Traumatic History

Women's history as we tell it today is a traumatic history. Like a patient suffering from post-traumatic stress disorder, we remember the same scenes over and over, reliving and replaying the brutality of oppression. We pride ourselves on retelling the scenes from our own point of view, on giving a voice to the victim, but we are still caught in the reliving, the replaying of it, we are still the victim of history instead of its creator. We make violence and oppression a part of who we are as women and tell ourselves a story where only very few, exceptional, outstanding women may break out of the cycle of violence and incarceration to shape the world and move freely through the life they want. We make ourselves prisoners of history, consoling ourselves with the tales of great escapes that we imagine will never be able to execute ourselves.

In *Unclaimed Experience* (1996), US literary scholar Cathy Caruth outlines how trauma theory may usefully be applied to literary studies to outline a new model of history. In her book, she writes about how literature explores trauma, and the workings of traumatic memory, illuminating the way the mind incarcerates itself in the replaying of the traumatic memory.[3] She explains the workings of trauma in a clear and useful way. There are two components to the experience of trauma – on the one hand, the horrific nature of the event, so terrible that the memory of it cannot be controlled or contained, and on the other hand the shock of survival.[4] The mind is so surprised that it is still alive, Caruth writes, that it cannot account for its own survival in the face of the violence it has experienced. The traumatic memory is replayed out of the shock of survival, of having made it, having come through it, when others did not.

Our cultural memory of women, our women's history, is founded on this shock. We look back at the past in shock, unable to believe that women survived the oppression they experienced, that we are still here. Overcome by this shock, we retell the traumatic circumstances of oppression over and over, as if to assure us that we truly are alive, that we truly did come out of it, that women still exist.

This may be a reasonable psychological reaction to learning about the horrors experienced by women throughout history, but it is going to keep us in an endless cycle of shock and trauma, where we continue to feed our disbelief at our survival and, as a consequence, our disbelief in a better, more egalitarian way of organising our lives in the present or the future.

Unlike a trauma patient, we as a society have a choice in the matter: we can choose different memories, look to different histories. It is time to do away with the assumption that history begins and ends with Ancient Greece. That is one of the central premises that produces the mental incarceration of women's history. It makes us come to expect oppression as an unfortunate fact of life, like sudden rainfall when you have just put up the washing out to dry, or black ice on the way to work, or the soles coming off your boots during a very wet hike on Dartmoor.

The memory of a wet day on Dartmoor may not be particularly traumatic, but the memory of two thousand years of oppression is. Since Caruth lay the foundations for trauma studies in the 1990s, they have frequently intersected with memory studies, because memory studies in its modern form grew out of the trauma of the Holocaust and its scholars are primarily interested in the memory of acts of collective violence. In fact, the focus on traumatic historical events is so intense that memory scholars have been calling for a rejigging of their field's perspective – for a prioritisation of memories of joy, happiness, pride, and positive attachment, to avoid a study of cultural and collective memory that contributes to a 'collective state of depression', as Dutch memory scholar Ann Rigney argues, where we begin to believe as a society that 'grievance is the core of identity' and the past a mere source of endless grievances.[5]

This trauma cannot be overcome through its endless repetition. We are going to have to change the memory. Our cultural memory. We are going to have to look for other stories that help us snap out of the state of traumatic shock and disbelief at our own survival and appreciate the past for what it is: a place where women have always been, at different times and in different places, free.

A New Story

Remembering Women set out to rewrite women's traumatic history and turn it into a story of hope, even of joy. What has come together in this book is a memory, a story, a history of times and places where women were free. It is the fabulation of a small community on the coast of the Black Sea sometime in the first millennium BCE. Imagine that here, a thousand or so women, men and children have come together to form a summer settlement on the river Thermodon in today's Turkey. They spend the summer in the lush wetlands of the river, where there are plenty of nuts and berries to be gathered, where they lay traps for small animals, where there is plenty of fresh water. Some of them plant a temporary garden, nurtured by the waters of the river. They know that the neighbouring Greeks call them Scythians, but they think of themselves as different groups of people who come together in the summer to live in the same place. Some of them have been coming for years. Others are new to the summer settlement on the banks of the Thermodon.

Among the newcomers are Kheuke and Berossus with their three daughters. They have come down from the Pontic Alps to spend the summer in the river delta. They have arrived in late spring and settled into a routine. Rising at dawn, Kheuke rides out to the hunt, taking her eldest daughter with her, while Berossus stays with the younger two and works the summer garden they are cultivating, watching over their goats and supporting his daughters on their quest around the settlement in search for berries. Once Kheuke returns, Berossus goes to join the boxing by the riverbank, taking his second daughter with him, while the other two go for a ride with their mother. The game is shared among the members of the hunting parties and

Conclusion — Afterlife

prepared by those who have stayed in the delta. Kheuke rubs halinda oil into her aching muscles and cleans herself up in time for the meeting of the council, where they discuss whether to put up more solid, lasting structures at Thermodon, settling the delta all year round.

They will decide against it. Khasa, who leads the council — it is a title rather than a name that is adopted by the woman who sits at the head of the council — organises the vote. She believes that the river is too powerful to settle permanently on its banks. And that some people might get bored, spending all year at its bank, especially during the winters, when there is no protection from the strong winds coming in from the sea. Better to be in mountains when the storms hit.

After the boxing and the riding, everyone has a meal, then Berossus and Kheuke put the children to bed. They ask their daughters which goodnight story they would like to hear. Their eldest loves the story of Penthesilea, the mythical warrior woman who fights Greek heroes, all of whom fall in love with her in their last moments, when she has beaten them in battle and takes off her helmet to make them swoon. She is getting to the age where she would very much like to make a boy or girl swoon.

On that mild summer evening, however, it is the youngest daughter's turn to pick the goodnight story. She loves one of the stories told in this community, a popular goodnight tale among those children who have gathered here for many summers.

In the light of the setting sun, Kheuke and Berossus tell the story to their three daughters: Amazon warrior women rise up against the men who have enslaved them on a ship on the Black Sea. They vanquish their captors, but are cast adrift, not knowing how to operate the sails. Through a stroke of luck and good fortune, they come ashore on the southern coast of the Black Sea, in the fertile delta of the river Thermodon. Here, they come across a herd of fine horses. Stealing the horses brings them into the sights of the men who own them. That is how they meet the Scythians.

Kheuke und Berossus act out the parts with great gusto. Their daughters are still small, so they skip the part of the story that is all about sex, but they will think about it later, when the children are asleep, their youngest clutching her new signal mirror to her chest, a gift given to her by her father that day. In this ideal of a memory, Kheuke and Berossus end the day by making love to each other.

This fabulation is of course an idyll, but that does not mean that no day like this ever took place in the past. Countless days like this take place in the present, the world over: ordinary days, happy days, days where everything goes right. Why should the past have been any different? Who would argue that happy days are an invention of the modern world, and gender equality a conceit of the twentieth century?

Fabulation can be useful in identifying the questions we want to ask of the past: not, who fought this and that battle and which side won, but, for example, what did a happy day look like at that time and in that place? What made people happy, how were they content, how did they live together and respect each other? Archaeological objects found in the ground may not be able to answer those questions definitively, but they allow us to wonder, and to keep looking. Take the Cycladic figurines that depict women of all shapes and sizes. They can prompt us to be curious about their creators, to imagine the women making these self-portraits or portraits of their loved ones, pregnant friends or sisters-in-law, women surrounded by other women. They may have heard the hymns of the Old Babylonian writer

Conclusion — Afterlife

Enheduanna, the first named author in human history. They may have travelled to see the frescoes of women in council, women wielding power, on Minoan Crete. Maybe they brought back a jar, painted with an octopus, as a souvenir. Was that a journey these artists undertook, like Goethe travelled to Italy and Byron to the Rhine? Had they ever been to Babylon, and seen the Tower of Babel, and what had they made of that busy and bustling city?

These questions matter. They allow us to tell a different story about the past. That is what we need to do for the generations coming after us. We owe it to them, not to our foremothers.

Imagine a city where most statues were statues of women; where squares and streets were named after them; where women were encouraged to go out after dark, to have a good time, to make these streets and squares their own.

The aim of this book has been to create such a city. It is a city of the past, and it is a city of our imagination. In this city, women matter. They have always mattered, and they have always retained their names, always lived in freedom, always gone wherever it is that they have wanted to go. They take risks, they reap rewards, they have children or they don't, they have a partner or stay single, have solo sex or sleep with others. These women hold power and they use it. This is a new vision of our past — one in which women have always been people.

Throughout this book, I have combined material objects or literary evidence with acts of imagination. We have imagined a mythical woman like Helen leaving her husband, and imagined a historical Scythian woman by the name of Kheuke asleep after the birth of her child. I have remembered pushing my grandmother in her wheelchair to the fields with the wildflowers, and I imagined her meeting Penthesilea, an old woman holding a cherished signal mirror in one hand

and in the other the reins of Zhaqa, the horse that carries us to the land where nothing moves. We have fabulated a world where women and men never stop moving, where they always say yes to a dance, where they are seen and valued, no matter their age. We have remembered Helen's name, and imagined for her not just a life but a new afterlife. A life where she made choices about who and where she wanted to be, where she snuck away from her husband in the dead of night, taking only her mirror, only her Amazon puppet, so that she would not wake him. Just like my friend R, who spent months planning her escape, who put money aside in secret, who hid her suitcase at the back of the wardrobe.

Through these women, we have imagined a cultural memory that is truly as wild and deep as the sea. In this sea, there is room for all of us: for my grandmother, for my niece, for Helen of Troy, you, for me, for my friend R, for my mother, my aunt, her daughter, for the unnamed warrior women buried in graveyards all around the Black Sea.

Together, we have engaged in object fabulation, a technique we must employ if we wish to tell the lives of those who have left behind no or very few written records.[6] Not everything we imagined took place. Helen was not a real woman. Nor was Penthesilea. But in imagining their lives, in recovering and remembering the traces left by their historical counterparts, we have given ourselves permission to think about what we want our lives to be like in the present. What is useful in our collective memory? Which memories do we want to take forward, which do we no longer need, which treasures must we add to our commemorations?

Because that is what cultural memory is: it is a thing we use, a story we tell each other. We can make choices about which parts of our past we would do well to remember, and which parts we can put aside for the moment. Memories are not mirrors of what happened, whether they are personal or collective. We create them. We put the past back together, we use what we recall and what we make up, what we have been told and what we believe in. We put all these different treasures on display, in museums, in stories, in history, and from these treasures decide what is valuable in the present.

Our new stories will function as scripts for the present. They will help us when we think about how to be better men, how to enable women, how to care for our children.[7] I have reaped the benefits of the progress we have already made as a society and grown up in a position of relative privilege, a position that men take for granted: unlike my aunt and my grandmother, I did not have to ask a man's permission to go to work or open a bank account. Unlike my mother, I did not have to realise that I would never be promoted, no matter how well I did. I was taught how to speak, and how to make myself heard, in a noisy family with confident brothers. Coming from that place, I set out to write this book in the hope that it would do some good in the world. I would be very pleased if it gave you the courage to stand up for your right to move freely through this world, and for the right of everyone else to move as freely as you. I would be very pleased if it gave you pleasure, no matter your age. And I will be very happy if you keep an eye out for women like Helen, Penthesilea, my friend R, my niece, the figurines found on the Cycladic isles, and for Zhaqa, the fastest horse in the world. Women have always had a history of their own: from Neolithic artists to bull leapers on Minoan Crete and warrior women in Scythia. Together, we have begun to remember it.

ACKNOWLEDGEMENTS

I would like to thank the British School at Athens for sheltering a novelist and scholar of literature and memory. I am almost certain that some of the archaeologists and classicists in Athens did not know what to make of me, so their warm welcome meant all the more.

I would also like to thank the School of Arts, Languages and Cultures at the University of Manchester, who enabled me to travel to Athens.

Thank you, as always, to my agent Thérèse Coen, who Coen, who loved this project from the start. I would also like to thank Una McKeown at Susanna Lea Associates for her useful feedback and thoughtful comments.

A heartfelt thank you to Connor Stait and everyone at Icon Books who decided that this book needed to be out in the world. Writers are nothing without editors, publishers, and copyeditors, publicists and sales teams.

I would like to thank Dr Roxanne Douglas and Dr Nat Reeve for reading an early draft of this book and sharing their thoughts with me in the most generous and inspiring fashion. Their ideas have enriched this book beyond measure; needless to say, I take responsibility for all the flaws that remain.

I would like to thank my colleagues and students at the University of Exeter, many of whom encouraged and inspired me to pursue this work.

I would like to thank my colleague Dr Connie Skibinski for meeting me halfway across the world in Athens to research Amazons and Scythian warrior woman together. It has been wonderful to have a partner-in-crime in this project. I would also like to thank my mother for accompanying me and providing invaluable support on my research trip to Turkey.

Finally, I would like to thank my family: my parents, my brothers, my sister-in-law, my niece, my grandmothers and grandfathers, my aunts and uncles, my cousins. It takes a village to raise a child, and it certainly takes a village to raise a writer. You have all been there for me over the years, each of you in different and important ways. I could not do this without you.

I also thank my dear friend Anne Küpperbusch, who is a heritage professional and was kind enough to ask about how this book was going, without fail, every time we spoke.

BIBLIOGRAPHY

Alexander, Caroline (2010): *The War That Killed Achilles. The True Story of Homer's Iliad and the Trojan War.* London: Penguin.

Allende, Isabelle (2014): 'How to live passionately – no matter your age'. *Ted Talks.* Available online at https://www.ted.com/talks/isabel_allende_how_to_live_passionately_no_matter_your_age?subtitle=en, last accessed on 29 September 2024.

D'Angour, Armand (2019): *Socrates in Love. The Making of a Philosopher.* London: Bloomsbury.

Armitage, Simon (2008): *Sir Gawain and the Green Knight.* London: Faber.

Audette, Andre P (2019): 'Gender Equality Supports Happiness and Well-Being'. *The Gender Policy Report.* Available online at https://genderpolicyreport.umn.edu/gender-equality-supports-happiness/#:~:text=We%20broke%20our%20results%20out,slightly%20more%20so%20for%20women., last accessed on 26 November 2024.

Assmann, Aleida (2008): 'Canon and Archive'. In: Astrid Erll und Ansgar Nünning (eds): *Cultural Memory Studies. An*

International and Interdisciplinary Handbook. Berlin: Walter de Gruyter, pp. 97–108.

Assmann, Jan (2008): 'Communicative and Cultural Memory'. In: Astrid Erll und Ansgar Nünning (eds): *Cultural Memory Studies,* pp. 109-188.

Atwood, Margaret (1982): *Second Words. Selected Critical Prose (1960-1982)*. Toronto: Anansi Press. Quoted in *Oxford Essential Quotations*, 6th Edition, 2018. Available online at https://www.oxfordreference.com/display/10.1093/acref/9780191866692.001.0001/q-oro-ed6-00000530, last accessed on 30 September 2024.

Barkova, Ljudmila (2007): 'Die Fürstengräber der Pazyryk-Kultur'. In: Menghin, Wilfried, Parzinger Hermann, Nagler, Anatoli et al. (eds): *Im Zeichen des Goldenen Greifen. Königsgräber der Skythen*. München: Prestel, p. 127.

Barker, Pat (2018): The Silence of the Girls. London: Picador.

Barron, Danielle (2024): 'Want to live longer? Avoid fast food, remember to floss – and don't expect to enjoy those extra years'. *Irish Independent*. Available online at https://www.independent.ie/life/health-wellbeing/want-to-live-longer-avoid-fast-food-remember-to-floss-and-dont-expect-to-enjoy-those-extra-years/a667880508.html, last accessed on 30 September 2024.

Bates, Laura (2022): *Fix the System, Not the*. London: Simon & Schuster.

Beard, Mary (2018): *Women & Power*. London: Profile Books.

de Beauvoir, Simone (2015 [1949]): *Extracts from The Second Sex*. Annotated and introduced by Martine Reid. London: Vintage.

Bentley, Gillian et al. (1993): 'The Fertility of Agricultural and Non-Agricultural Traditional Societies'. *Population Studies* 47, pp. 269–281.

Bibliography

Berger, John (1972): *Ways of Seeing*. London: Penguin Books.

Berkowitz, Eric (2013): *Sex and Punishment. 4000 Years of Judging Desire*. London: The Westbourne Press.

Bojs, Karin (2024): *Mütter Europas*. München: C. H. Beck.

Borowski, Susanne (2022): *Penthesilea und ihre Schwestern. Amazonenepisoden als Bauform des Heldenepos*. Amsterdam: Brill.

Broom, Douglas (2020): 'As the UK publishes its first census of women killed by men, here's a global look at the problem'. *World Economic Forum*. Available online at https://www.weforum.org/agenda/2020/11/violence-against-women-femicide-census/, last accessed on 27 September 2024.

Brown, Judith K (1982): 'Cross-Cultural Perspectives on Middle-Aged Women'. *Current Anthropoloy* 23 (2). Available online at https://www.jstor.org/stable/274235, last accessed on 30 September 2024.

Buchwald, Emilie, Pamela Fletcher, and Martha Roth (eds, 2005 [1993]): *Transforming a Rape Culture*, Minneapolis: Milkweed Editions.

Burns, Judith (2018): 'Hate mail and firebombs: How women won the vote'. *BBC Education*. Available online at https://www.bbc.co.uk/news/education-42840160, last accessed on 27 September 2024.

Caruth, Cathy (1996): *Unclaimed Experience. Trauma, Narrative, and History*. Baltimore: John Hopkins University Press.

Charlton-Robb, Kate; Draper, Tara; Caron, Valerie (2019): 'How three scientists navigated the personal and career implications of a name change with marriage'. *The Conversation*. Available online at https://theconversation.com/how-three-scientists-navigated-the-personal-and-career-implications-of-a-name-change-with-marriage-114918, last accessed on 27 September 2024.

Cline, Eric H. (2013): *The Trojan War: A Very Short Introduction*. Oxford: Oxford University Press.

Cohen, Richard (2022): *Making History: The Storytellers Who Shaped the Past*. London: Weidenfeld and Nicholson.

Cohen, Richard A. (1986): *Face to Face with Emmanuel Levinas*. Albany: State University of New York Press, p. 22.

Colarusso, John (2015a): 'Preface'. In: Colarusso, John (ed.): *The Nart Sagas*. Princeton: Princeton University Press, pp. xix–xxiv.

Colarusso, John (2015b): *The Nart Sagas*. Princeton: Princeton University Press.

Coole, Maria (2021): 'Why is rape still so prevalent in 2021?'. *Marie Claire*. Available online at https://www.marieclaire.co.uk/reports/rape-cases-and-the-shockingly-low-conviction-rate-683839, checked on 27 September 2024.

Crerar, Belinda (2022): *Feminine Power. The Divine to the Demonic*. London: The British Museum.

The Crown Prosecution Service (2021): 'Rape and Sexual Offences – Annex A: Tackling Rape Myths and Stereotypes'. Available at https://www.cps.gov.uk/legal-guidance/rape-and-sexual-offences-annex-tackling-rape-myths-and-stereotypes, last accessed on 13 November 2024.

Cunliffe, Barry (2019): *The Scythians: Nomad Warriors of the Steppe*. Oxford: Oxford University Press.

Demand, Nancy H (1994): *Birth, Death, and Motherhood in Classical Greece. Ancient Society and History*. Baltimore: Johns Hopkins University Press.

Díez, Marcos García (2022): 'Üppige Schönheit. Venus der Steinzeit'. *National Geographic History* 5, pp. 90–103.

The Editors (2024): 'Editorial. The Guardian view on the Booker prize shortlist: a cause for celebration'. *Guardian*. Available online at https://www.theguardian.com/commentisfree/2024/sep/20/the-guardian-view-on-the-booker-prize-shortlist-a-cause-for-celebration, last accessed on 27 September 2024.

The Editors of the Encyclopedia Britannica: 'Publilius Syrus'. Available online at https://www.britannica.com/biography/Publilius-Syrus, last accessed on 30 September 2024.

Ellis, S., Franks, D.W., Nielsen, M.L.K. et al (2024): 'The Evolution of Menopause in Toothed Whales'. *Nature* 627, pp. 579–585. Available online at https://www.nature.com/articles/s41586-024-07159-9#:~:text=Just%20as%20in%20humans%2C%20menopause%20in%20toothed%20whales%20evolved%20by,in%20general%2C%20including%20in%20humans, last accessed on 30 September 2024.

Erll, Astrid (2018): 'Homer: A Relational Mnemohistory'. *Memory Studies* 11 (3), pp. 274–286.

Facts and figures: Women's leadership and political participation.' Available online at https://www.unwomen.org/en/what-we-do/leadership-and-political-participation/facts-and-figures#_edn, last accessed on 24/06/2024.

Flood, Alison (2015): 'Books about women less likely to win prizes, study finds'. *Guardian*. Available online at https://www.theguardian.com/books/2015/jun/01/books-about-women-less-likely-to-win-prizes-study-finds, last accessed on 27 September 2024.

Forst, Rainer (2017): *Normativity and Power*. Oxford: Oxford University Press.

Forst, Rainer (2015): *Normativität und Macht*. Berlin: Suhrkamp.

Fry, Stephen (2018): *Heroes. Mortals and Monsters, Quests and Adventures*. Penguin Random House: London.

Gambelin, Anne-Marie (2018): 'Fatherhood has a huge impact on your happiness, studies say'. *Motherly*. Available online at https://www.mother.ly/parenting/fatherhood-has-a-huge-impact-on-your-happiness-studies-say/, last accessed on 27 September 2024.

Gecsoyler, Sammy (2024): 'English councils call for national men's health strategy'. *Guardian*. Available online at https://www.theguardian.com/society/article/2024/aug/24/english-councils-call-for-national-mens-health-strategy, last accessed on 30 September 2024.

Godden, Salena (2024): *With Love, Grief and Fury*. Edinburgh: Canongate.

Gottschall, Jonathan (2008): *The Rape of Troy*. Cambridge: Cambridge University Press.

Graeber, David; Wengrow, David (2021): *The Dawn of Everything. A New History of Humanity*. London: Allen Lane.

Greenblatt, Stephen (2017): *The Rise and Fall of Adam and Eve. The Story That Created Us*, p. 63.

Groot, Jerome de (2010): *The Historical Novel*. London: Routledge.

Hartman, Saidiya (2008): 'Venus in Two Acts'. *Small Axe* 12 (2), pp.1–14.

Haynes, Natalie (2020): *Pandora's Jar. Women in Greek Myths*. London: Picador.

Haynes, Natalie (2018): 'Phryne'. *Natalie Haynes Stands Up for the Classics, Season 4*. BBC Radio 4.

Haynes, Natalie (2014): 'Aspasia'. *Natalie Haynes Stands Up for the Classics, Season 1*. BBC Radio 4.

Henin, RA (1970): 'Nomadic Fertility as Compared with that of Rain Cultivators in the Sudan'. *Egypt Population Famine Planning Review* 3(2), pp. 81–91.

Hirsch, Annabelle (2022): *Die Dinge. Eine Geschichte der Frauen in 100 Objekten*. Zürich: Kein & Aber. Published in English in 2023 as *A History of Women in 101 Objects. A Walk Through Female History*. Edinburgh: Canongate.

Homer (2004 [8th century BCE]): *The Odyssey*. Translated by AS Kline. Available online at https://www.poetryintranslation.com/PITBR/Greek/Odhome.php, last accessed on 26 November 2024.

hooks, bel (2022): *lieben lernen. Alles über Verbundenheit*. Hamburg: Harper Collins. Translation into German from the 2002 original: *The Female Search for Love*. New York: William Morrow

Jordan, A.M. (2016): 'Her Mirror, His Sword: Unbinding Binary Gender and Sex Assumptions in Iron Age British Mortuary Traditions'. *Journal of Archaeological Method and Theory* 23, pp. 870–899.

Jubber, Nicholas (2022): *The Fairy-Tellers. A Journey into the Secret History of Fairy Tales*. London: John Murray.

Koutsopetrou-Møller, Sotiria Rita (2021): 'Rape Culture in Classical Athens?' *Clara* 7, pp. 1–32. Available online at https://journals.uio.no/CLARA/article/download/8833/271/29516, last accessed on 27 September 2024.

Lee, Mireille M (2017): 'The Gendered Economics of Greek Bronze Mirrors'. *Arethusa* 50 (2), pp. 143–168.

Levy, Deborah (2021): *Real Estate*. London: Penguin.

Lipscomb, Suzannah; Carr, Helen (2021). *What is History, Now?* London: Weidenfeld and Nicholson.

Lipscomb, Suzannah (2021): 'How Can We Recover the Lost Lives of Women?' In Lipscomb, Suzannah; Carr, Helen (2021). *What is History, Now?* London: Weidenfeld and Nicholson, pp. 143–156.

Liptak, Adam (2022). 'In 6-to-3 Ruling, Supreme Court Ends Nearly 50 Years of Abortion Rights'. *New York Times.* Available online at https://www.nytimes.com/2022/06/24/us/roe-wade-overturned-supreme-court.html, last accessed on 26 November 2024

de Looze, M.E., Huijts, T., Stevens, G.W.J.M. et al (2018): 'The Happiest Kids on Earth. Gender Equality and Adolescent Life Satisfaction in Europe and North America'. *J Youth Adolescence* 47, pp. 1073–1085.

Marlowe, Christopher (2008 [1592]): *Doctor Faustus.* Edited by Roma Gill and Ros King. London: Methuen.

Marsh, Sarah (2017): 'Girls as young as seven in UK boxed in by gender stereotyping'. *Guardian.* Available online at https://www.theguardian.com/world/2017/sep/21/girls-seven-uk-boxed-in-by-gender-stereotyping-equality, last accessed on 27 September 2024.

Maume, D. J., Hewitt, B., & Ruppanner, L. (2018): 'Gender equality and restless sleep among partnered Europeans'. *Journal of Marriage and Family,* 80 (4), pp. 1040–1058.

Matos, Gregory (2022): 'What's Behind the Rise of Lonely, Single Men?'. *Psychology Today.* Available online at https://www.psychologytoday.com/us/blog/the-state-our-unions/202208/whats-behind-the-rise-lonely-single-men, last accessed on 27 September 2024.

Mayor, Adrienne (2021a): '"Especially in the Use of Weapons": Plato and the Amazons'. *Antigone Journal.* Available online at https://antigonejournal.com/2021/03/plato-and-the-amazons/, last accessed on 27 September 2024.

Mayor, Adrienne (2021b): 'Amazons'. *Oxford Classical Dictionary*. Oxford: Oxford University Press. Available online at https://oxfordre.com/classics/display/10.1093/acrefore/9780199381135.001.0001/acrefore-9780199381135-e-342, last accessed on 9 July 2024.

Mayor, Adrienne (2015): 'Foreword'. In: Colarusso, John (ed.): *The Nart Sagas. op. cit*, pp. xiii-xviii.

Mayor, Adrienne (2014): *The Amazons. Lives and Legends of Warrior Women Across the Ancient World*. Princeton: Princeton University Press.

Mayor, Adrienne; Colarusso, John; Saunders, David (2014): 'Making Sense of Nonsense Inscriptions Associated with Amazons and Scythians on Athenian Vases'. *Hesperia: The Journal of the American School of Classical Studies at Athens* 83 (3), pp. 447–493.

McCormack, Catherine (2021): *Women in the Picture: Women, Art and the Power of Looking*. London: Icon Books.

Molodin, Vjačeslav; Polos'mak, Natal'ja (2007): 'Die Denkmäler auf dem Ukok-Plateau'. In: Menghin, Wilfried, Parzinger Hermann, Nagler, Anatoli et al. (eds): *Im Zeichen des Goldenen Greifen. Königsgräber der Skythen*. München: Prestel, pp. 142–143.

Morgan Stanley Research (2019): 'Rise of the SHEconomy'. Available online at https://www.morganstanley.com/ideas/womens-impact-on-the-economy, last accessed on 27 September 2024.

Mulvey, Laura (1975): 'Visual Pleasure and Narrative Cinema'. *Screen* 16 (3) pp. 6–18/

Muschett, Michelle; Vaeza, Maria-Noel (2024): 'There is no democracy without gender equality'. *United Nations Development*

Programme. Available online at https://www.undp.org/blog/there-no-democracy-without-gender-equality, last accessed on 27 September 2024.

Museum of Cycladic Arts (2022): *Homecoming. Cycladic Treasures On Their Return Journey*. Athens, Greece.

Nuwer, Rachel (2016): 'The Enduring Enigma of Female Sexual Desire'. *BBC Future*. Available online at https://www.bbc.com/future/article/20160630-the-enduring-enigma-of-female-desire, last accessed on 27 September 2024.

O'Callaghan, Clarrie; Ingala Smith, Karen (2021): *Femicide Census 2021*. Available online at https://www.femicidecensus.org/wp-content/uploads/2024/07/2021-Femicide-Census-Report.pdf, last accessed on 27 September 2024.

O'Callaghan, Clarrie; Ingala Smith, Karen (2022): 'Femicide Census: there's a disturbing reason for the falling number of murders'. *Guardian*. Available online at https://www.theguardian.com/society/2022/feb/27/femicide-census-theres-a-disturbing-reason-for-the-falling-number-of-murders, last accessed on 27 September 2024.

Oksanen, Sofie (2024): *Putins Krieg Gegen die Frauen*. Köln: Kiepenheuer & Witsch.

Olick, Jeffrey; Vinitzky-Seroussi, Vered; Levy, Daniel (eds) (2011): *The Collective Memory Reader*. Oxford: Oxford University Press.

Papada, Evie; Lindberg, Staffan (2022): 'Does Democracy Promote Gender Equality?' Policy Brief, *V-Dem Institute*. Available online at https://www.v-dem.net/media/publications/pb_37_aAwHJrz.pdf, last accessed on 27 September 2024.

Paquette, Danielle (2021): 'They were the world's only all-female army. Their descendants are fighting to recapture their humanity'. *Washington Post*. Available online at https://

www.washingtonpost.com/world/2021/08/26/amazons-dahomey-benin/, last accessed on 27 September 2024.

Parzinger, Hermann (2007): 'Die Reiternomaden der Eurasischen Steppe während der Skythenzeit'. In: Menghin, Wilfried, Parzinger Hermann, Nagler, Anatoli et al. (eds): *Im Zeichen des Goldenen Greifen. Königsgräber der Skythen.* München: Prestel, p. 31.

Patou-Mathis, Marylène (2021): 'Weibliche Unsichtbarkeit'. Berlin: Hanser. Translated from the 2020 original *L'homme préhistorique est aussi une femme !*, Paris: Allary Editions.

Pennington, RL (1996): 'Causes of Early Human Population Growth'. *American Journal of Physiological Anthropology* 99 (2), pp. 259–274.

PEW Research (2021): 'A record number of women are serving in the 117th Congress.' Available online at https://www.pewresearch.org/fact-tank/2021/01/15/a-record-number-of-women-are-serving-in-the-117th-congress/, last accessed on 19/02/2025.

Pipher, Mary (2019): 'Want to Be Happy? Live Like a Woman Over 50'. *Literary Hub.* Available online at https://lithub.com/want-to-be-happy-live-like-an-woman-over-50/#:~:text=Contrary%20to%20cultural%20stereotypes%2C%20many,for%20life%20as%20they%20age, last accessed on 30 September 2024.

Plato (1967–1968 [428–347 BCE]): *Laws. Plato in Twelve Volumes.* Cambridge, Massachusetts, Harvard University Press. Translated by R.G. Bury. Cambridge. Available online at http://www.perseus.tufts.edu/hopper/text?doc=Perseus%3Atext%3A1999.01.0166%3Abook%3D7%3Asection%3D794c, last accessed on 27 September 2024.

Quintus of Smyrna (2004 [third century BCE]): *The Trojan Epic. Posthomerica.* Translated by Alan James. Baltimore: John Hopkins University Press.

Ramakrishnan, Venkatraman (2024): *Why We Die. The New Science of Aging and Longevity.* London: Hodder.

Rape Crisis England and Wales (2024): 'Myths vs facts'. Available online at https://rapecrisis.org.uk/get-informed/about-sexual-violence/myths-vs-realities/, last accessed on 13ᵗ November 2024.

Rape Crisis England (undated): 'Rape and sexual assault statistics'. Available online at https://rapecrisis.org.uk/get-informed/statistics-sexual-violence/, last accessed on 26 November 2024.

Rigney, Ann (2018): 'Remembering Hope: Transnational Activism Beyond the Traumatic'. *Memory Studies*, 11 (3), pp. 368–380.

Rousseau, Jean-Jacques (1762): *Emile*. Project History: Liberté, Egalité, Fraternité. Exploring the French Revolution. Available online at https://revolution.chnm.org/d/470/#:~:text=To%20please%20them%2C%20to%20be,taught%20them%20from%20their%20infancy., last accessed on 27 September 2024.

Saini, Angela (2023): *The Patriarchs. How Men Came to Rule.* London: 4th Estate.

Samadder, Rhik (2024): '"I suspect I'd look like a five-year-old cosplaying as Mr T": can I pull off the new men's jewellery?'. Available online at https://www.theguardian.com/fashion/2024/apr/06/i-suspect-id-look-like-a-five-year-old-cosplaying-as-mr-t-can-i-pull-off-mens-jewellery, last accessed on 27 September 2024.

Sappho (*c*. 600 BCE): *The Poems of Sappho.* Translated by Edwin Marion Cox in 1924. Accessible online at https://

en.wikisource.org/wiki/The_Poems_of_Sappho, last accessed on 13 November 2024. For readers interested in a modern translation, I recommend Sappho (2015): *Come Close*. Penguin: London. Translated by Aaron Poochigian.

Savage, Maddy (2020): 'Why do women still change their names?' *BBC Worklife*. Available online at https://www.bbc.com/worklife/article/20200921-why-do-women-still-change-their-names, last accessed on 27 September 2024.

van Schaik, Carel; Michel, Kai (2020): *Die Wahrheit über Eva. Die Erfindung der Ungleichheit von Frauen und Männern.* Hamburg: Rowohlt.

van Schaik, Carel; Michel, Kai (2016): *Das Tagebuch der Menschheit. Was die Bibel über unsere Evolution verrät*. Hamburg: Rowohlt, p. 477. Published in English in 2016 as *The Good Book of Human Nature: An Evolutionary Reading of the Bible* by Basic Books in New York.

Schweizerische Eidgenossenschaft (2023): 'Wahlen 2023. Frauenstimmrecht in der Schweiz'. *Swiss Federal Government*. Available online at https://www.ch.ch/de/wahlen2023/geschichte-der-wahlen/frauenstimmrecht/#kantone-und-gemeinden-folgen-dem-beispiel-des-bundes, last accessed on 27 September 2024.

Seedat, Soraya; Rondon, Marta (2021): 'Women's Wellbeing and the Burden of Unpaid Work'. *BMJ 347*.

Sieghart, Mary Ann (2021): *The Authority Gap. Why Women Are Still Taken Less Seriously Than Men, And What We Can Do About It*. London: Doubleday.

Simpson, Alison (2017): 'Over a third of adults would blame a woman for being raped if she was drunk or wore short skirts'. *We Are The City*, available online at https://wearethecity.com/over-a-third-of-adults-would-blame-a-woman-for-being-raped-if-she-was-drunk-or-wore-short-skirts/, last accessed on 26 November 2024.

Soffer, O., Adovasio, J. M.; Hyland, D. C. (2000): 'The "Venus" Figurines Textiles, Basketry, Gender, and Status in the Upper Paleolithic'. In: *Current Anthropology* 41 (4), pp. 511–537.

Solnit, Rebecca (2019): *Whose Story Is This?* London: Granta.

Stewart, Andrew (1995): 'Imag(in)Ing the Other: Amazons and Ethnicity in Fifth-Century Athens', *Poetics Today*, 16 (4), pp. 571–597.

de la Torre Laso J., Rodríguez-Díaz J.M. (2022): 'The relationship between attribution of blame and the perception of resistance in relation to victims of sexual violence'. *Frontline Psychology*, 25 (13).

UK Government (2022): 'UK Sustainable Development Goals: Indicator 5.5.1'. Available at https://sdgdata.gov.uk/5-5-1/, last accessed on 19/02/2025.

UK Parliament (not dated): 'Women get the vote'. Available online at https://www.parliament.uk/about/living-heritage/transformingsociety/electionsvoting/womenvote/overview/thevote/, last accessed on 27 September 2024.

United Nations Women (2022): 'Facts and figures: Women's leadership and political participation.' Available online at https://www.unwomen.org/en/what-we-do/leadership-and-political-participation/facts-and-figures#_edn9, last accessed on 24/06/2024.

de Visé, Daneil (2023): 'Most young men are single. Most young women are not'. *The Hill*. Available online at https://thehill.com/blogs/blog-briefing-room/3868557-most-young-men-are-single-most-young-women-are-not/, last accessed on 27 September 2024.

Weidmann, R., Chopik, W. J., Ackerman, R. A et al. (2023): 'Age and gender differences in narcissism: A comprehensive study across eight measures and over 250,000 participants'."*Journal of Personality and Social Psychology*, 124 (6), pp. 1277–1298.

Women in Sport (2023): 'Girls as young as five years old don't feel that they belong in sport'. Press release. Available online at https://womeninsport.org/news/girls-as-young-as-five-years-old-dont-feel-that-they-belong-in-sport/, last accessed on 26 November 2024.

Zhou, Muzhi; Kan, Man Yee (2023): 'The Gendered Impacts of Partnership and Parenthood on Paid Work and Unpaid Work Time in Great Britain, 1992–2019'. *Population and Development Review* 49 (4), pp. 829–857.

ENDNOTES

Introduction
1. De Beauvoir, Simone (2015 [1949]) *Extracts from The Second Sex*. Annotated and Introduced by Martine Reid. London: Vintage, p. 10.
2. *Ibid.*, p. 11.
3. See, for instance, van Schaik, Carel; Michel, Kai (2020): *Die Wahrheit über Eva. Die Erfindung der Ungleichheit von Frauen und Männern*. Hamburg: Rowohlt, p. 48, p. 381, p. 442, p. 497.
4. *Ibid.*, p. 48, p. 442, p. 497.
5. See Haynes, Natalie (2020): *Pandora's Jar. Women in Greek Myths*. London: Picador, p. 8.
6. *Ibid.*
7. When enquiring into 'what is generally believed', it is always useful to take a look at the appropriate Wikipedia entry. As of 2 May 2022, the online lexicon describes 'Western culture' in the first paragraph of its English entry as 'most strongly influenced by Greek philosophy, Roman law, and Christian culture'. A host of scholarship corroborates this assessment, consistently understating the importance of influences from the Near, Far and Middle East and

the Americas as well as the hybrid nature of all cultures. This emphasis on the Bible and the Classics in studies on 'Western culture' continues to paint a picture of the past in which only white men were able to act, travel, write, lead, and innovate. What we call 'Western culture' or 'Western civilisation' today should perhaps more accurately be referred to as 'white patriarchal culture', or even 'white patriarchal nationalism', a tradition, historiography and collective memory invented and created with the foundation of the modern European nation-states around 1800.

8. See van Schaik, Carel & Michel, Kai (2016): *Das Tagebuch der Menschheit. Was die Bibel über unsere Evolution verrät.* Hamburg: Rowohlt, p. 477. Published in English in 2016 as *The Good Book of Human Nature: An Evolutionary Reading of the Bible* by Basic Books in New York.
9. See Erll, Astrid (2018), 'Homer: A Relational Mnemohistory'. *Memory Studies* 11 (3), pp. 274–286, p. 277.
10. See Schaik, C. & Michel (2020), p. 60.
11. See Forst, Rainer (2015): *Normativität und Macht.* Berlin: Suhrkamp, p. 21.
12. Adrienne Mayor surveys the archaeological and literary evidence for the existence of warrior women in the ancient world in her 2014 book *The Amazons: Lives and Legends of Warrior Women Across the Ancient World.* Princeton: Princeton University Press.
13. Assmann, Jan (2008): 'Communicative and Cultural Memory'. In: Astrid Erll und Ansgar Nünning (eds): *Cultural Memory Studies. An International and Interdisciplinary Handbook.* Berlin: Walter de Gruyter, p. 109.
14. See Erll, A. (2018), p. 276.

15. Armitage, Simon: *Sir Gawain and the Green Knight*, London: Faber, p. 7, p 12.
16. Cline, Eric H. (2013): *The Trojan War: A Very Short Introduction.* Oxford: OUP, p. 27, p. 56.
17. Assmann, Jan (2008), p. 114.
18. Forst, Rainer (2017): *Normativity and Power.* Oxford: Oxford University Press, p.12._
19. Forst, Rainer (2015), pp. 21–23.
20. Liptak, Adam (2022). In '6-to-3 Ruling, Supreme Court Ends Nearly 50 Years of Abortion Rights.' *The New York Times*. Available online at https://www.nytimes.com/2022/06/24/us/roe-wade-overturned-supreme-court.html, last accessed on 26 November 2024.
21. Assmann, Aleida (2008): 'Canon and Archive'. In: Astrid Erll und Ansgar Nünning (eds): *Cultural Memory Studies. An International and Interdisciplinary Handbook.* Berlin: Walter de Gruyter, pp. 97–108, p. 103.
22. Simpson, Alison (2017): 'Over a third of adults would blame a woman for being raped if she was drunk or wore short skirts'. *We Are The City,* available online at https://wearethecity.com/over-a-third-of-adults-would-blame-a-woman-for-being-raped-if-she-was-drunk-or-wore-short-skirts/, last accessed on 26 November 2024. Based on a 2017 report by the Fawcett Society, available online at Sounds-Familiar-January-2017.pdf, last accessed on 26 November 2024. A more recent study confirmed that the behaviour of the victim still influences the degree of blame assigned to them: de la Torre Laso J, Rodríguez-Díaz JM (2022): 'The relationship between attribution of blame and the perception of resistance in relation to victims of sexual violence'. *Frontline Psychology*, 25 (13).

23. Rape Crisis England and Wales (2024) 'Myths vs facts'. Available online at https://rapecrisis.org.uk/get-informed/about-sexual-violence/myths-vs-realities/, last accessed on 13 November 2024. The Crown Prosecution Service has published comprehensive guidelines on how to tackle rape myths and stereotypes, which is available at https://www.cps.gov.uk/legal-guidance/rape-and-sexual-offences-annex-tackling-rape-myths-and-stereotypes, last accessed on 13 November 2024.
24. *Ibid.*
25. Coole, Maria (2021): 'Why is rape still so prevalent in 2021?'. *Marie Claire.* Available online at https://www.marieclaire.co.uk/reports/rape-cases-and-the-shockingly-low-conviction-rate-683839, last accessed on 27 September 2024.
26. Paquette, Danielle (2021): 'They were the world's only all-female army. Their descendants are fighting to recapture their humanity'. *Washington Post.* Available online at https://www.washingtonpost.com/world/2021/08/26/amazons-dahomey-benin/, last accessed on 27 September 2024.
27. Mayor, Adrienne (2014).
28. *Ibid.* For an accessible and engaging summary of key findings, see Rothaman, Joshua (2014): 'The Real Amazons'. *New Yorker.* Available at https://www.newyorker.com/books/joshua-rothman/real-amazons, last accessed on 27 September 2024.
29. Mayor, Adrienne (2014).
30. Lipscomb, Suzannah (2021): 'How Can We Recover the Lost Lives of Women?' In Lipscomb, Suzannah; Carr, Helen (2021). *What is History, Now?* London: Weidenfeld and Nicholson, pp. 143–156.

31. Mayor, Adrienne (2021a): '"Especially in the Use of Weapons": Plato and the Amazons'. *Antigone Journal*. Available online at https://antigonejournal.com/2021/03/plato-and-the-amazons/, last accessed on 27 September 2024.

Chapter 1

1. Savage, Maddy (2020): 'Why do women still change their names?' *BBC Worklife*. Available online at https://www.bbc.com/worklife/article/20200921-why-do-women-still-change-their-names, last accessed on 27 September 2024.
2. Criado Perez, Caroline (2019): *Invisible Women*: Exposing Data Bias in a World Designed for Men. London: Chatto & Windus.
3. Charlton-Robb, Kate; Draper, Tara; Caron, Valerie (2019): 'How three scientists navigated the personal and career implications of a name change with marriage'. *The Conversation*. Available online at https://theconversation.com/how-three-scientists-navigated-the-personal-and-career-implications-of-a-name-change-with-marriage-114918, last accessed on 27 September 2024.
4. See van Schaik; Michel (2020), p. 293.
5. *Ibid*.
6. *Ibid*., p. 308.
7. Sappho (*c*. 600 BCE): Fragments 30–31. From *The Poems of Sappho*. Translated by Edwin Marion Cox in 1924. Available online at https://en.wikisource.org/wiki/The_Poems_of_Sappho, last accessed on 13 November 2024.
8. *Ibid*., Fragment 3.
9. Koutsopetrou-Møller, Sotiria Rita (2021): 'Rape Culture in Classical Athens?' *Clara* 7, p. 4, pp. 9–10. Available online at https://journals.uio.no/CLARA/article/down-

load/8833/271/29516, last accessed on 27 September 2024.
10. Haynes, Natalie (2020), p. 139.
11. Flood, Alison (2015): 'Books about women less likely to win prizes, study finds'. *Guardian*. Available online at https://www.theguardian.com/books/2015/jun/01/books-about-women-less-likely-to-win-prizes-study-finds, last accessed on 27 September 2024. This study is from a decade ago, and the 2024 Booker Prize shortlist was cause for celebration, with five out of six nominated writers identifying as female, with three out of the five books focusing on a female protagonist. According to a study by Nicola Griffith, the Pulitzer Prize was at no point between 2000 and 2015 given to a woman writing about women (Sieghart, Mary Ann (2021): *The Authority Gap. Why Women Are Still Taken Less Seriously Than Men, And What We Can Do About It*. London: Doubleday, p. 149). Additionally, only 18 women have won the Booker Prize since its inception in 1969. For a celebration and summary of the key facts, see The Editors (2024): 'Editorial. The Guardian view on the Booker prize shortlist: a cause for celebration'. *Guardian*. Available online at https://www.theguardian.com/commentisfree/2024/sep/20/the-guardian-view-on-the-booker-prize-shortlist-a-cause-for-celebration, last accessed on 27 September 2024.
12. Haynes, Natalie (2014): 'Aspasia'. *Natalie Haynes Stands Up for the Classics, Season 1*. BBC Radio 4.
13. D'Angour, Armand (2019): *Socrates in Love. The Making of a Philosopher*. London: Bloomsbury.
14. Natalie Haynes (2014), BBC Radio 4.
15. Natalie Haynes (2018): 'Phryne'. *Natalie Haynes Stands Up for the Classics, Season 4*. BBC Radio 4.

16. See Lipscomb, Suzannah; Carr, Helen (2021). *What is History, Now?* London: Weidenfeld and Nicholson. Suzannah Lipscomb's contribution to the volume, 'How Can We Recover the Lost Lives of Women?' is especially enlightening, recounting the challenges encountered by historians wishing to tell the stories of historical women and suggesting some solutions.
17. Paquette, Danielle (2021): 'They were the world's only all-female army. Their descendants are fighting to recapture their humanity'. *Washington Post*. Available online at https://www.washingtonpost.com/world/2021/08/26/amazons-dahomey-benin/, last accessed on 27th September 2024.
18. According to Leonard Wantchekon, professor for International Affairs at Princeton University, cited in Paquette, Danielle (2021).
19. Colarusso, John (2015b): *The Nart Sagas*. Princeton: Princeton University Press.
20. Mayor, Adrienne (2015): 'Foreword', p. xv. In: Colarusso, John (ed.): *The Nart Sagas*. Princeton: Princeton University Press, pp. xiii-xviii.
21. *Ibid.* See also Colarusso, John (2015a): Preface to: Colarusso, John (ed.): *The Nart Sagas*. Princeton: Princeton University Press, p. xxi.
22. A recent archaeological discovery suggests that perhaps the Scythians may have been in possession of an alphabet after all: Mayor, Adrienne (2015): Foreword toColarusso, John (ed.): *The Nart Sagas*. Princeton: Princeton University Press, p. xv.
23. Mayor, Adrienne; Colarusso, John; Saunders, David (2014): 'Making Sense of Nonsense Inscriptions Associated with Amazons and Scythians on Athenian Vases',

p. 450. *Hesperia: The Journal of the American School of Classical Studies at Athens* 83 (3), pp. 447–493.

Chapter 2

1. Marsh, Sarah (2017): 'Girls as young as seven in UK boxed in by gender stereotyping'. *Guardian.* Available online at https://www.theguardian.com/world/2017/sep/21/girls-seven-uk-boxed-in-by-gender-stereotyping-equality, last accessed on 27 September 2024.
2. *Ibid.*
3. Lee, Mireille M (2017): 'The Gendered Economics of Greek Bronze Mirrors'. *Arethusa* 50 (2), pp. 143–168.
4. Weidmann, R., Chopik, W. J., Ackerman, R. A et al. (2023): 'Age and gender differences in narcissism: A comprehensive study across eight measures and over 250,000 participants'. *Journal of Personality and Social Psychology*, 124 (6), pp. 1277–1298.
5. Stephen Fry (2018) writes beautifully, and with a wonderful sense of humour, about Perseus's exploits in his marvellous book *Heroes*. Unfortunately, even Fry's wonderful wit cannot take away from the fact that Perseus murders a rape victim, amidst many other episodes of bloodshed.
6. Mulvey, Laura (1975): 'Visual Pleasure and Narrative Cinema'. *Screen* 16 (3), pp. 6–18.
7. Haynes, Natalie (2020), Chapter 1: Pandora. Ebook edition.
8. Jubber, Nicholas (2022): *The Fairy-Tellers. A Journey into the Secret History of Fairy Tales.* London: John Murray.
9. Berger, John (1972): *Ways of Seeing.* London: Penguin Books, Chapter 3. Ebook edition.
10. This is an ongoing discussion: Jordan, A.M. (2016) 'Her Mirror, His Sword: Unbinding Binary Gender and

Sex Assumptions in Iron Age British Mortuary Traditions'. *Journal of Archaeological Method and Theory* 23, pp. 870–899.
11. Patou-Mathis, Marylène (2021): 'Weibliche Unsichtbarkeit'. Berlin: Hanser, p. 81. Translated from the 2020 original *L'homme préhistorique est aussi une femme !*, Paris: Allary Editions.
12. Skogstrand, Lisbeth (2023): 'A Safe Space for Women Archaeologists? The Impact of K.A.N. on Norwegian Archaeology'. In: López Varela, S.L. (eds) *Women in Archaeology. Women in Engineering and Science.* Cham: Springer.
13. Patou-Mathis, Marylène (2021), pp. 81–82.
14. Mayor, Adrienne (2014), p. 159.
15. *Ibid.*, p. 65.
16. Plato (1967–1968 [428–347 BCE]): *Laws. Plato in Twelve Volumes.* Cambridge, Massachusetts, Harvard University Press. Translated by R.G. Bury. Cambridge. Available online at http://www.perseus.tufts.edu/hopper/text?doc=Perseus%3Atext%3A1999.01.0166%3Abook%3D7%3Asection%3D794c, last accessed on 27 September 2024.
17. Hirsch, Annabelle (2022): *Die Dinge. Eine Geschichte der Frauen in 100 Objekten.* Zürich: Kein & Aber, p. 61. Published in English in 2023 as *A History of Women in 101 Objects. A Walk through Female History.* Edinburgh: Canongate.
18. *Ibid.*, pp. 61–63.
19. Cohen, Richard A. (1986): *Face to Face with Emmanuel Levinas.* Albany: State University of New York Press, p. 22.

Chapter 3

1. Women in Sport (2023): 'Girls as young as five years old don't feel that they belong in sport'. Press release. Available online at https://womeninsport.org/news/girls-as-young-as-five-years-old-dont-feel-that-they-belong-in-sport/, last accessed on 26 November 2024. The press release cites surveys conducted between 2021 and 2023.
2. Insure4Sport (2023): 'UK Attitudes Towards Women in Sport 2023'. Report. Available online at https://www.insure4sport.co.uk/blog/uk-attitudes-towards-women-in-sport/, last accessed on 26 November 2024.
3. Bresaola, Riccardo (2024): 'Explainer: How have attitudes changed towards women's sports?' *Sportcal*. Available online at https://www.sportcal.com/features/explainer-how-have-attitudes-changed-towards-womens-sports/?cf-view, last accessed on 26 November.
4. Mayor, Adrienne (2021b): 'Amazons'. *Oxford Classical Dictionary*. Oxford: Oxford University Press. Available online at https://oxfordre.com/classics/display/10.1093/acrefore/9780199381135.001.0001/acrefore-9780199381135-e-342, last accessed on 9 July 2024, p. 3; Mayor, Adrienne (2014), p. 134; Stewart, Andrew (1995): 'Imag(in)Ing the Other: Amazons and Ethnicity in Fifth-Century Athens', p.572, *Poetics Today* 16 (4), pp. 571–597.
5. Borowski, Susanne (2022): *Penthesilea und ihre Schwestern. Amazonenepisoden als Bauform des Heldenepos*. Amsterdam: Brill, p. 151.
6. Mayor, Adrienne (2014), p. 118, pp. 134–136.
7. *Ibid.*, p. 125
8. Quintus of Smyrna (2004 [third century BCE]): *The Trojan Epic. Posthomerica*. Translated by Alan James. Baltimore: John Hopkins University Press, pp. 19–20.

9. Mayor, Adrienne (2014), pp. 250-253; Fry, Stephen (2018), pp. 88–93.
10. Herodotus (2013 [490-430 BCE]): *The Histories*. Translated by Tom Holland. Penguin: London, p. 600.
11. Ibid 4.110.
12. Ibid.
13. Ibid.
14. Ibid 4.114.
15. Ibid.
16. Ibid.
17. Ibid. 4.117.
18. A quick glance at the children's books section in the British Museum shop reveals that these stories are contained in Usborne *Greek Myths* (Age 10+), the Usborne *Greek Myth for Little Children* (Age 3+), as well as the Usborne *Illustrated Stories from the Greek Myths* (Age 7+).
19. Hirsch, Annabelle (2022), pp. 28–31.
20. Mayor, Adrienne (2014), p. 63.
21. Demand, Nancy H. (1994): *Birth, Death, and Motherhood in Classical Greece. ancient Society and History*. Baltimore: Johns Hopkins University Press, pp. 10–11.
22. *Ibid*.
23. Mayor, Adrienne (2014), p. 131.
24. *Ibid.*, p. 159.
25. Sedentary lifestyles among humans have been associated with higher fertility rates in earlier studies: Pennington, RL (1996): 'Causes of Early Human Population Growth'. *American Journal of Physiological Anthropology* 99 (2), pp. 259–274; Henin, RA (1970): 'Nomadic Fertility as Compared with that of Rain Cultivators in the Sudan'. *Egypt Population Famine Planning Review* 3 (2), pp. 81–91. Bentley, Gillian et al. (1993): 'The Fertility of

Agricultural and Non-Agricultural Traditional Societies'. *Population Studies* 47, pp. 269–281.
26. Demand, Nancy H (1994), p. 20–21.
27. Summarised by Mayor, Adrienne (2014), pp. 131–132.
28. Eric Cline has published a comprehensive and engaging account of the current state of research on the decline of the Mediterranean civilisations in *1177: The Year Civilization Collapsed* (2015, Princeton University Press), followed by *After 1177: The Survival of Civilizations* (2024, Princeton University Press). The former title was adapted into a graphic novel: *1177 B. C.: A Graphic History of the Year Civilization Collapsed* (Princeton University Press, 2024). Considering that we now have graphic novel adaptations of textbooks on Bronze Age systemic collapse, I can only assume that the graphic novel adaptation of *The Pirate Amazons* is around the corner.
29. *Ibid.*, p. 19.
30. Bates, Laura (2022): *Fix the System, Not the Women*. London: Simon & Schuster, p. 126.
31. *Ibid.*, p. 133.
32. Graeber, David; Wengrow, David (2021): *The Dawn of Everything. A New History of Humanity*. London: Allen Lane, p. 435.

Chapter 4
1. Marlowe, Christopher (2008 [1592]): *Doctor Faustus*. Edited by Roma Gill and Ros King. London: Methuen, pp. 86–87.
2. *Ibid.*, p. 87
3. *Ibid.*

4. Sexual desire is difficult to measure, but a 2016 study indicates that there is no difference between men and women in terms of how much they desire sex: Nuwer, Rachel (2016): 'The enduring enigma of female sexual desire'. *BBC Future*. Available online at https://www.bbc.com/future/article/20160630-the-enduring-enigma-of-female-desire, last accessed on 27 September 2024.
5. Bates, Laura (2020): *Men Who Hate Women*. London: Simon & Schuster.
6. *Ibid.*, ebook, chapter 1.
7. *Ibid.*
8. Jennigs, Rebecca (2018): "Incels Categorize Women by Personal Style and Attractiveness". *Vox*. Available online at https://www.vox.com/2018/4/28/17290256/incel-chad-stacy-becky, last accessed on 13 January 2025.
9. At the time of writing, Russia's offensive war against Ukraine is ongoing, and rape is used as a weapon in this war as it has been used in all others. Estonian author Sofie Oksanen gives an account of Vladimir Putin's war against women in Oksanen, Sofie (2024): *Putins Krieg Gegen die Frauen*. Köln: Kiepenheuer & Witsch.
10. Gottschall, Jonathan (2008): *The Rape of Troy*. Cambridge: Cambridge University Press, p.3.
11. Solnit, Rebecca (2019), p. 93.
12. Koutsopetrou-Møller, Sotiria Rita (2021), p. 4.
13. One example are the otherwise delightfully entertaining retellings of Greek myth by Stephen Fry, e. g.Fry, Stephen (2018), pp. 333–335.
14. Buchwald, Emilie, Pamela Fletcher, and Martha Roth (eds, 2005 [1993]): *Transforming a Rape Culture*, Minneapolis: Milkweed Editions.

15. Barker, Pat (2018): *The Silence of the Girls.* London: Picador, p. 297.
16. Philip Roth quoted in Barker, Pat (2018), p. i.
17. Herodotus 4:113
18. Strabo (c. 7 BCE): The Geography, Book XI, Ch 8.
19. Summarised by Mayor, Adrienne (2014), p. 131–132. Mayor includes a full chapter on the sex lives of warrior women in *The Amazons: Lives and Legends of Warrior Women Across the Ancient World.*
20. Mayor, Adrienne (2014), p. 136.
21. van Schaik, Carel; Michel, Kai (2020), p. 91, pp. 94–95.
22. Lipscomb, Suzannah (2021), p. 187.
23. *Ibid.*

Chapter 5

1. Papada, Evie; Lindberg, Staffan (2022): 'Does Democracy Promote Gender Equality?' Policy Brief, *V-Dem Institute.* Available online at https://www.v-dem.net/media/publications/pb_37_aAwHJrz.pdf, last accessed on 27 September 2024, pp. 1-2.
2. Muschett, Michelle; Vaeza, Maria-Noel (2024): 'There is no democracy without gender equality'. *United Nations Development Programme.* Available online at https://www.undp.org/blog/there-no-democracy-without-gender-equality, last accessed on 27 September 2024.
3. Schweizerische Eidgenossenschaft (2023): 'Wahlen 2023. Frauenstimmrecht in der Schweiz'. *Swiss Federal Government.* Available online at https://www.ch.ch/de/wahlen2023/geschichte-der-wahlen/frauenstimmrecht/#kantone-und-gemeinden-folgen-dem-beispiel-des-bundes, last accessed on 27ᵗSeptember 2024.
4. UK Parliament (not dated): 'Women get the vote'. Available online at https://www.parliament.uk/about/living-herit-

age/transformingsociety/electionsvoting/womenvote/overview/thevote/, last accessed on 27th September 2024.
5. Burns, Judith (2018): 'Hate mail and firebombs: How women won the vote'. *BBC Education.* Available online at https://www.bbc.co.uk/news/education-42840160, last accessed on 27 September 2024. Hirsch, Annabelle (2022), p. 245.
6. UK Parliament (not dated).
7. PEW Research (2021): 'A record number of women are serving in the 117th Congress.' Available online at https://www.pewresearch.org/fact-tank/2021/01/15/a-record-number-of-women-are-serving-in-the-117th-congress/, last accessed on 19/02/2025.
8. United Nations Women (2022): 'Facts and figures: Women's leadership and political participation.' Available online at https://www.unwomen.org/en/what-we-do/leadership-and-political-participation/facts-and-figures#_edn, last accessed on 24/06/2024.
9. UK Government (2022): 'UK Sustainable Development Goals: Indicator 5.5.1'. Available at https://sdgdata.gov.uk/5-5-1/, last accessed on 19/02/2025.
10. United Nations Women (2022): 'Facts and figures: Women's leadership and political participation.' Available online at https://www.unwomen.org/en/what-we-do/leadership-and-political-participation/facts-and-figures#_edn9, last accessed on 24/06/2024.
11. Bates, Laura (2022), p. 115.
12. *Ibid.*
13. Patou-Mathis, Marylène (2021), pp. 72–73.
14. Rousseau, Jean-Jacques (1762): *Emile.* Project History: Liberté, Egalité, Fraternité. Exploring the French Revolution. Available online at https://revolution.chnm.org/d

/470/#:~:text=To%20please%20them%2C%20to%20be,taught%20them%20from%20their%20infancy., last accessed on 27 September 2024.
15. Saini, Angela (2023): *The Patriarchs. How Men Came to Rule*. London: 4th Estate, pp. 128–129.
16. Mayor, Adrienne; Colarusso, John; Saunders, David (2014), p. 450.
17. Graeber and Wengrow (2021) discuss the intriguing evidence for communal and egalitarian decision-making in the pre-historic record throughout their study.
18. In a report to the United Nations Development Programme (UNDP), Fiona Flintan gives a nuanced portrayal of contemporary decision making practices in pastoral societies and provides a range of sources on how such communities were more egalitarian prior to colonisation. Flintan, Fiona (2008): Women's Empowerment in Pastoral Societies. Report to the United Nations Development Programme, p. 1. Schaik and Michel (2020) also discuss the evidence of women as decisionmakers in the past, p. 222-223.
19. Mayor, Adrienne (2014), p. 163.
20. *Ibid.*
21. Saini, Angela (2023), p. 46.
22. Saini, Angela (2023), pp. 31–32.
23. Graeber, David; Wengrow, David (2021), p. 438 – Graeber and Wengrow hypothesis that Minoan Crete may have been ruled by a theocracy of female priests.
24. *Ibid.*, pp. 435-436.
25. *Ibid.*, p. 435.
26. Graeber, David; Wengrow, David (2021), p. 438 – Graeber and Wengrow hypothesis that Minoan Crete may have been ruled by a theocracy of female priests.

27. A term suggested by actress Emma Watson in a 2019 interview with British Vogue.
28. Morgan Stanley Research (2019): 'Rise of the SHEconomy'. Available online at https://www.morganstanley.com/ideas/womens-impact-on-the-economy, last accessed on 27 September 2024.
29. *Ibid.*
30. de Visé, Daneil (2023): 'Most young men are single. Most young women are not'. *The Hill.* Available online at https://thehill.com/blogs/blog-briefing-room/3868557-most-young-men-are-single-most-young-women-are-not/, last accessed on 27 September 2024.
31. Matos, Gregory (2022): 'What's Behind the Rise of Lonely, Single Men'. *Psychology Today.* Available online at https://www.psychologytoday.com/us/blog/the-state-our-unions/202208/whats-behind-the-rise-lonely-single-men, last accessed on 27 September 2024.
32. *Ibid.*
33. Solnit, Rebecca (2019), pp. 143–144.
34. Graeber, David; Wengrow, David (2021), p. 426.

Chapter 6

1. Berkowitz, Eric (2013): *Sex and Punishment. 4000 Years of Judging Desire.* London: The Westbourne Press, p. 38.
2. *Ibid.*, pp. 91–92.
3. Members of the incel community routinely refer to women as 'whores', especially those who will not sleep with them (which, according to incels, is every woman): Jennings, Rebecca (2018): 'Incels Categorize Women by Personal Style and Attractivenes'. *Vox.* Available online at https://www.vox.com/2018/4/28/17290256/incel-chad-stacy-becky, last accessed on 27 September 2024.

4. Seedat, Soraya; Rondon, Marta (2021): 'Women's Wellbeing and the Burden of Unpaid Work'. *BMJ* 347.
5. van Schaik, Carel; Michel, Kai (2021), p. 93.
6. *Ibid.*
7. Patou-Mathis, Marylène (2021), p. 113.
8. *Ibid.*, p. 114.
9. Pathou-Mathis, Marylène (2021), p. 105.
10. *Ibid.*
11. *Ibid.*, p. 116.
12. *Ibid*, p. 129.
13. *Ibid.*, p. 127.
14. *Ibid*, pp. 10–13.
15. Mayor, Adrienne (2014), p. 64.
16. Zhou, Muzhi; Kan, Man Yee (2023): 'The Gendered Impacts of Partnership and Parenthood on Paid Work and Unpaid Work Time in Great Britain, 1992-2019'. *Population and Development Review* 49 (4), pp. 829–857.
17. Mayor, Adrienne (2014), p. 69.
18. *Ibid.* p. 70.
19. *Ibid.*
20. *Ibid.* p. 159.
21. *Ibid.*
22. Gambelin, Anne-Marie (2018): 'Fatherhood has a huge impact on your happiness, studies say'. *Motherly*. Available online at https://www.mother.ly/parenting/fatherhood-has-a-huge-impact-on-your-happiness-studies-say/, last accessed on 27 September 2024.
23. Sieghart, Mary Ann (2021), p. 74.
24. Colarusso, John (2015b): *The Nart Sagas*. Princeton: Princeton University Press, p. 31.

25. Broom, Douglas (2020): ;As the UK publishes its first census of women killed by men, here's a global look at the problem'. *World Economic Forum.* Available online at https://www.weforum.org/agenda/2020/11/violence-against-women-femicide-census/, last accessed on 27 September 2024.
26. O'Callaghan, Clarrie; Ingala Smith, Karen (2021): *Femicide Census 2021.* Available online at https://www.femicidecensus.org/wp-content/uploads/2024/07/2021-Femicide-Census-Report.pdf, last accessed on 27 September 2024. Rape Crisis England (undated): 'Rape and sexual assault statistics'. Available online at https://rapecrisis.org.uk/get-informed/statistics-sexual-violence/, last accessed on 26th November 2024.
27. O'Callaghan, Clarrie; Ingala Smith, Karen (2022): 'Femicide Census: there's a disturbing reason for the falling number of murders;. *Guardian.* Available online at https://www.theguardian.com/society/2022/feb/27/femicide-census-theres-a-disturbing-reason-for-the-falling-number-of-murders, last accessed on 27 September 2024.
28. This is how the quote is paraphrased, even though her actual formulation is slightly more complicated. The full quotation runs: '"Why do men feel threatened by women?" I asked a male friend of mine…"They're afraid women will laugh at them," he said…Then I asked some women students…"Why do women feel threatened by men?" "They're afraid of being killed," they said." It can be found in Atwood, Margaret (1982): *Second Words. Selected Critical Prose (1960–1982).* Toronto: Anansi Press. Quoted in *Oxford Essential Quotations*, 6th Edition, 2018. Accessible online at

https://www.oxfordreference.com/display/10.1093/acref/9780191866692.001.0001/q-oro-ed6-00000530, last accessed on 30 September 2024.
29. Berkowitz, Eric (2013), p. 92.
30. Rape Crisis England and Wales (undated).
31. van Schaik, Carel; Michel, Kai (2021), p. 27.
32. *Ibid.*

Chapter 7
1. Sieghart, Mary Ann (2021), p. 23.
2. *Ibid.*, p. 24.
3. *Ibid.*, pp. 22–23.
4. *Ibid.* 24.
5. *Ibid.*
6. *Ibid*, p. 5.
7. *Ibid.*, p. 73, see also Maume, D. J., Hewitt, B., & Ruppanner, L. (2018): 'Gender equality and restless sleep among partnered Europeans'. *Journal of Marriage and Family*, 80 (4), pp. 1040–1058.
8. Audette, Andre P (2019): 'Gender Equality Supports Happiness and Well-Being'. *The Gender Policy Report*. Available online at https://genderpolicyreport.umn.edu/gender-equality-supports-happiness/#:~:text=We%20broke%20our%20results%20out,slightly%20more%20so%20for%20women., last accessed on 26 November 2024.
9. de Looze, M.E., Huijts, T., Stevens, G.W.J.M. et al (2018): 'The Happiest Kids on Earth. Gender Equality and Adolescent Life Satisfaction in Europe and North America'. *J Youth Adolescence* 47, pp. 1073–1085.
10. Sieghart, Mary Ann (2021), p. 75.

11. Duffy, Bobby; Campbell, Rosie; Skinner, Gideon (2024): 'Emerging tensions? How younger generations are dividing on masculinity and gender equality'. King's Policy Institute. Available online at https://www.kcl.ac.uk/policy-institute/assets/emerging-tensions.pdf, last accessed on 27 September 2024.
12. *Ibid..*
13. Beard, Mary (2018): *Women & Power.* London: Profile Books, p. 4
14. *Ibid.,* p. xiii
15. Homer (2004 [8th century BCE]): *The Iliad.* Book IX, 307-429; see also Alexander, Caroline (2010): *The War That Killed Achilles. The True Story of Homer's Iliad and the Trojan War.* London: Penguin, p. 194, pp. 213–214.
16. Homer (2004 [8th century BCE]): *The Odyssey.* Translated by AS Kline. Available online at https://www.poetryintranslation.com/PITBR/Greek/Odhome.php, last accessed on 26 November 2024.
17. Alexander, Caroline (2010), p. 220–221.
18. Mayor, Adrienne (2014), pp. 138–140.
19. Samadder, Rhik (2024): '"I suspect I'd look like a five-year-old cosplaying as Mr T": can I pull off the new men's jewellery?'. Available online at https://www.theguardian.com/fashion/2024/apr/06/i-suspect-id-look-like-a-five-year-old-cosplaying-as-mr-t-can-i-pull-off-mens-jewellery, last accessed on 27 September 2024.
20. Herodotus 1:105; Cunliffe, Barry (2019): *The Scythians: Nomad Warriors of the Steppe.* Oxford: Oxford University Press, pp. 265–290.
21. *Ibid.*
22. Mayor, Adrienne (2014), pp. 357–429.

Chapter 8
1. Sieghart, Mary Ann (2021), pp. 179–182.
2. Allende, Isabelle (2014): 'How to live passionately—no matter your age'. *Ted Talks.* Available online at https://www.ted.com/talks/isabel_allende_how_to_live_passionately_no_matter_your_age?subtitle=en, last accessed on 29 September 2024.
3. McCormack, Catherine (2021): *Women in the Picture: Women, Art and the Power of Looking.* London: Icon Books, pp. 76–77.
4. *Ibid.,* p. 78
5. *Ibid.*
6. Beard, Mary (2018), p. 4.
7. *Ibid.*
8. Levy, Deborah (2021): *Real Estate.* Penguin: London, p. 80.
9. *Ibid.,* p. 37.
10. Sieghart, Mary Ann (2021), pp. 109–111.
11. *Ibid.,* p. 266.
12. David Graeber's and David Wengrow's *The Dawn of Everything: A New History of Humanity,* Marylène Patou-Mathis's *L'homme préhistorique est aussi une femme,* Carel van Schaik's and Kai Michel's *Die Wahrheit über Eva* are just three examples of books published during the past decade that significantly re-evaluate material evidence from prehistory to produce a much more nuanced and interesting picture of what life may have been like for humanity before 5,000 BCE.
13. Patou-Mathis, pp. 76–80.
14. *Ibid.,* p. 84.
15. Patou-Mathis, pp. 84–85.

16. These figurines have been commonly referred to as 'venus figurines', but in line with Marylène Patou-Mathis, I do not use the term myself, as I believe it is a misnomer and creates serious misunderstandings about what these figurines look like and what their purpose may have been, as they bear no resemblance to depictions of the Roman goddess Venus from later periods of human history.
17. Graeber, David; Wengrow, David (2021). Patou-Mathis, Marylène (2021). Schaik, Carel van; Michel, Kai (2020), p. 219-223. Soffer, O., Adovasio, J.M. & Hyland, D.C. (2000): 'The "Venus" Figurines Textiles, Basketry, Gender, and Status in the Upper Paleolithic'. In: *Current Anthropology* 41 (4).
18. Patou-Mathis, Marylène (2021), p. 87.
19. Díez, Marcos García (2022): 'Üppige Schönheit. Venus der Steinzeit"' p. 92. *National Geographic History* 5, pp. 90–103.
20. Crerar, Belinda (2022): *Feminine Power. The Divine to the Demonic*, p. 18. London: The British Museum.
21. *Ibid.*, p. 19.
22. Brown, Judith K (1982): 'Cross-Cultural Perspectives on Middle-Aged Women'. *Current Anthropoloy* 23 (2). Available online at https://www.jstor.org/stable/274235, last accessed on 30 September 2024.
23. Patou-Mathis, Marylène (2021), p. 92.

Chapter 9
1. Mulvey, Laura (1975): 'Visual Pleasure and Narrative Cinema', p. 11. *Screen* 16 (3), pp. 6–18.
2. Gordon, Amie (2019): "Twitter mocks bathtub tray ads". *Daily Mail*. Accessible online at https://www.dailymail.co.uk/news/

article-6850501/Twitter-mocks-bathtub-tray-ads-showing-women-relaxing.html, last accessed on 18th January 2025.
3. *Ibid.*, p. 118.
4. Johns, Catherine (2000): *Sex Or Symbol? Erotic Images of Greece and Rome*, London: Taylor & Francis, p. 31.
5. *Ibid.*, p. 102.
6. *Ibid.*, p. 91–92.
7. Quoted in Schaik, Carel van; Michel, Kai (2020), p. 222.
8. Patou-Mathis, Marylène (2021), p. 95.
9. *Ibid.*, p. 95.
10. Mayor, Adrienne (2014), p. 161.
11. Patou-Mathis, Marylène (2021), p. 101.
12. hooks, bel (2022): *lieben lernen. Alles über Verbundenheit.* Hamburg: Harper Collins, pp. 25–26. Translation into German from the original: *The Female Search for Love.* New York: William Morrow.
13. We share the menopause with only one more species, the toothed whale, as well as our subsequent prolonged life span. Ellis, S., Franks, D.W., Nielsen, M.L.K. et al (2024): 'The Evolution of Menopause in Toothed Whales'. *Nature* 627, pp. 579–585. Available online at https://www.nature.com/articles/s41586-024-07159-9#:~:text=Just%20as%20in%20humans%2C%20menopause%20in%20toothed%20whales%20evolved%20by,in%20general%2C%20including%20in%20humans, last accessed on 30 September 2024.
14. *Ibid.*, p. 171.
15. *Ibid.*, p. 424.
16. Pipher, Mary (2019): 'Want to Be Happy? Live Like a Woman Over 50'. *Literary Hub.* Available online at https://lithub.com/want-to-be-happy-live-like-an-woman-

over-50/#:~:text=Contrary%20to%20cultural%20stereotypes%2C%20many,for%20life%20as%20they%20age, last accessed on 30 September 2024.
17. *Ibid.*
18. *Ibid.*
19. Duffy, Bobby; Campbell, Rosie; Skinner, Gideon (2024).

Chapter 10
1. Ramakrishnan, Venkatraman (2024): *Why We Die. The New Science of Aging and Longevity*. London: Hodder. Quoted in Barron, Danielle (2024): 'Want to live longer? Avoid fast food, remember to floss – and don't expect to enjoy those extra years'. *Irish Independent*. Available online at https://www.independent.ie/life/health-wellbeing/want-to-live-longer-avoid-fast-food-remember-to-floss-and-dont-expect-to-enjoy-those-extra-years/a667880508.html, last accessed on 30 September 2024.
2. Schaik, Carel van; Michel, Kai (2021), p. 423.
3. *Ibid.*, p. 428.
4. *Ibid.*, p. 450
5. *Ibid.*, pp. 47–49
6. *Ibid.*, p. 484.
7. Quintus of Smyrna (2004 [third century BCE), pp. 21–24.
8. Mayor, Adrienne (2014), pp. 289–291.
9. Quintus of Smyrna (2004 [third century BCE]): *The Trojan Epic. Posthomerica*, p. 23, translated by Alan James. Baltimore: The John Hopkins University press.
10. Parzinger, Hermann (2007), p. 30.
11. *Ibid.*, pp. 31–32.
12. Molodin, Vjačeslav; Polos'mak, Natal'ja (2007): 'Die Denkmäler auf dem Ukok-Plateau', pp. 142–143. In Menghin,

Wilfried, Parzinger Hermann, Nagler, Anatoli et al. (eds): *Im Zeichen des Goldenen Greifen. Königsgräber der Skythen*. München: Prestel.
13. Barkova, Ljudmila (2007): 'Die Fürstengräber der Pazyryk-Kultur', p. 127. In *Ibid*. P. 7.
14. Colarusso, John (2015b), p. 33.
15. *Ibid.*, p. 32.
16. Vavouranakis, Giorgos (2014): 'Funerary Pithoi in Bronze Age Crete: Their Introduction and Significance at the Threshold of Minoan Palatial Society'. *American Journal of Archaeology*, 118 (2), pp. 197–222.
17. *Ibid.*, p. 215.
18. *Ibid.*, p. 216.

Conclusion

1. Museum of Cycladic Arts (2022): *Homecoming. Cycladic Treasures On Their Return Journey*. Athens, Greece, p. 30.
2. *Ibid.*, p. 34.
3. Caruth, Cathy (1996): *Unclaimed Experience. Trauma, Narrative, and History*. Baltimore: John Hopkins University Press.
4. *Ibid.*, p. 58.
5. Rigney, Ann (2018): 'Remembering Hope: Transnational Activism Beyond the Traumatic', p. 369. *Memory Studies*, 11 (3), pp. 368–380.
6. The concept of object fabulation is deeply indebted to Saidiya Hartman's concept of critical fabulation. Cf. Hartman, Saidiya (2008): 'Venus in Two Acts'. *Small Axe* 12 (2), pp.1–14.
7. Lorde, Audre (2017), p. 1.

INDEX

Achilles xix, 20, 50, 70, 75–6, 78–9, 84, 115, 129, 166, 172–3
Adam and Eve xxvii
Adichie, Chimamanda Ngozi xiii
adolescence 58–9, 61–2, 67, 70–1
Aeneid 50
Aeschylus 7
Agamemnon 60, 75, 76, 79, 84, 108, 115, 154
Aguilera, Christina 185
Allende, Isabelle 139, 140, 164
Altai, Republic of 175
Amazons ix–x, xix–xx, xxxiv, 12, 14–15, 56–7, 93–4
    Pirate 50–5, 63, 73, 80, 101, 131, 188, 193–4
    puppets 56, 61, 63, 105, 117, 196
Amazons: Lives and Legends of Warrior Women Across the Ancient World, The (Mayor) 16
Ameinias 28
Anactoria 6–7

Andromache 4
Antigone (Sophocles) 4
Antiope 94
Aphrodite 4, 27, 145
Aphrodite of Knidos 11
Apollo 76
Aragorn 74
archaeology xix, xxi, xxxiii, 15, 31, 32–5, 56, 61–2, 95–6, 112–15, 146, 175, 184
Ariadne 63
Aristophanes 4, 100
Aristotle 4
Arkhon Arzokh 116
Arthur, King xxiii, 187–8
Arwen 74
Asanta 94
Aspasia 5, 10–11, 17
Assmann, Aleida xx–xxi, xxv
Assmann, Jan xx–xxi, xxiv
Assyria, Ancient 106
Asterix (video game) 47
Atalanta 49, 73, 133
Atalia 106, 117, 118, 166
Athene/Athena 4, 30, 31

Athens 100, 106, 108, 117, 147, 184
   Classical xviii, xxxiv, 3, 14, 17, 21, 49, 56–7, 59, 61–2, 77, 77, 86–7, 91, 92, 100, 109, 118, 189
Atthis 5–6
Atwood, Margaret 118, 163, 165–6
Augustus, Emperor xvii, 170
Austen, Jane 8
Authority Gap, The (Sieghart) 126

Babygirl 142
Babylon 9, 148, 166, 194–5
Barbarossa, Frederick 188
Barbie doll 63
Barbie (2023) (Gerwig) 133–4
Barker, Pat 78
Bates, Laura 64, 75, 89
   Fix the System, Not the Women (2022) 64
   Men Who Hate Women (2020) 75
Beard, Mary 128, 141, 143
Beast 41
Beauty and the Beast 9, 40–1
Bechdel test 150
Belle 41
Belle et la Bête, La see *Beauty and the Beast*
Berber culture 30
Berger, John 32
Berkowitz, Eric 118
Berossus 115, 123, 132–3, 134–5, 192–4
Bible xvii–xviii, 145, 170
bicycles 65
birth control 162, 163
Boudicca xxx

breastfeeding 90
breasts 11, 145, 148, 159
Briseis, Queen 75, 78, 84, 172–3
British Museum xxiii, 54, 146
Bronze Age 95, 113
brushes 105, 165
bull-leaping 61–3
   Bull-Leaping Fresco 61, 62
burials xxxiii, 8, 26, 33, 35, 38, 56, 58, 60, 65, 113–15, 118, 122, 129–30, 172, 173, 175, 177, 178
Butler, Judith xiii
Byrd, Stephania 7
Byron 195

Caesar, Julius 87, 172
Calydonian/ Caledonian boar 49
Caruth, Cathy 190
Casanova 74
Cassandra 76
Chalamet, Timothée 130
childbirth 58, 62, 63, 134
childcare xxix, 64, 81, 108, 110–15, 118–19, 121–3
China, People's Republic of xxiii
Cinderella 109
Circassian 15, 93
Clytemnestra 154
Cohen, Claudine 160
Colarusso, John 15–16, 93, 115, 175
Colette 8
Communion (2002) (hooks) 162
competitiveness 48, 57–8, 59, 62
Conkey, Margaret 33
consent xxiii, xxvi, xxix, 70, 74, 83–4, 90, 102, 115, 116–17
Constituent, The 150
Courbet, Gustave 149
COVID-19 pandemic 89–90

Index

Crerar, Belinda 146
Criado Perez, Caroline 12
Cyclades 148, 183, 186

D'Angour, Armand 10–11
Dahomey 12, 188
Dawn of Everything, The (2021) (Graeber and Wengrow) 95–6
de Beauvoir, Simone xi, xvi, 138
death 16, 58, 127, 129, 169–80, 181
democracy 85–7, 92, 94, 103
Disney 40, 54
Doctor Faustus (Marlowe) 69
dolls 63
Dommasnes, Liv Helga 33
Donkey Kong Country 47

earrings 38, 115, 130, 149
Echo 28, 76
Egypt, Ancient xxi, 95
Eleonore/Eleanor of Aquitaine 39–40, 41
Eliot, George 8
Elizabeth I xxx
Enareës 131
Enheduana 9, 195
Enlightenment xxvii, 87, 91–2
Equal Franchise Act (1928) 89
Erasmus of Rotterdam xvii
Ernaux, Annie 163
Ethnikos Kipos (National Gardens of Greece) 148
Euripides 4, 7, 108, 142
Euthymides 93
Evans, Sir Arthur 34, 61, 95
Evil Queen 32

fairytales xi, 9, 23, 31, 40, 109–10, 155
Faustus 70

femicide 117
Femicide Census 117
'Feminine Power' (2022) (British Museum) 146
fencing 47–8, 57, 61
figurines 145–9, 159–60, 183–6, 194
First World War xxii, xxviii, 56, 88
Fix the System, Not the Women (2022) (Bates) 64
Flensborg Fjord 36
Forst, Rainer xxiv
'Fragment Thirty-Six' (H. D.) 7
France 39–40, 112
freedom of movement 101–2, 177
Freeman, Margaret 34

Galitzine, Nicholas 153
Gender Data Gap 12
Gender Pay Gap 2, 12
Georgia xxxiii, 108, 116
Germany xiv, xxii, 1, 9, 22, 188
Gero, Joan 33
Gerwig, Greta 133
Ghana 95
Gladiator (Scott) 54
Goethe 195
Good Luck to You, Leo Grande 142
Gottschall, Jonathan 75
Gouges, Olympe de xxvii
Graeber, David and David Wengrow 95–6, 101
Greece, Ancient ix, xvii–xix, xxiii, xxxii–xxxv, 2, 3–7, 10, 14–15, 21, 26–31, 38, 41, 45, 49–51, 55–9, 62–3, 70, 77, 86–7, 93–4, 107–9, 115, 131, 158–9, 171–4
Greek Mycenae 60
Grimm, Wilhelm and Jacob 9, 31
Guardian 143
Gullvag Holter, Oystein 127

H. D. 7
Hades 171
halinda plant 162, 193
Hansel and Gretel 109
Hassenpflug, Marie 9, 31
Hathaway, Anne 153
Haudenosaunee 94, 101, 103
Hector 115, 173
Hecuba 4, 142
Helen(a) of Troy ix–x, xix, xxx, xxxiv, xxxv, 4, 6, 19, 20, 27, 28, 29, 31, 69–70, 73–4, 75–6, 87, 105–7, 117, 118, 128, 165–6, 188, 195, 196
Hera 4, 28
Heracles/Hercules 51, 54, 63, 94, 108, 128
Heraklion Archaeological Museum 62
Hercules *see* Heracles
Hermione 165
Herodotus 51–6, 58, 59, 62, 65, 80, 93, 131, 175
Hesiod xvii
Hippodamia 174
Hippolyte 'Hippolyta' 14, 50, 93, 128
Hirsch, Annabelle 39
Histories (Herodotus) 51–6, 94, 175
History of Women in 101 Objects, A (Hirsch) 39
Hittite Empire xxiii, 60
'Homecoming' (Museum of Cycladic Art) 185
Homer xxii–xxiii, 3, 75, 172, 173
hooks, bell xiii, 162–3
House of Commons 89
Human Stain, The (1999) (Roth) 79
hunter-gatherer societies 3, 93, 111

Idea of You, The (2024) 153
Iliad (Homer) xxii–xxiii, 75–6, 79, 94, 115, 129, 172–3
Immerwahr, Henry Rudolph 93
incel culture 74, 76
incest 110
influencers 132
Iphigenia 154
Iron Man 74

Jason 108–9, 141
Jason and the Argonauts 54
jewellery 115, 130–1, 179
Jones, Bridget 185

K. A. N. (Kvinner i Arkeologi i Norge or Women in Archaeology in Norway) 33
Kazakhstan 114
Kehlmann, Daniel 109
Ken 133–4
Khasa 16, 87, 92–3, 101, 193
Kheuke 16, 19, 37–8, 59, 81–2, 93, 115, 123, 132–3, 134–5, 192–4, 195
Kidman, Nicole 142
Kinney, Brian 25
Knossos, Crete 61
Kyffhäuser mountains 188

L'Origine du monde (Courbet) 149
La Poetesse 148
Lagarde, Christine xxix
Lancelot 39–40
Lascaux caves 112
Leia, Princess xxx
Lesbos 5
Lévinas, Emmanuel 42
Levy, Deborah 142, 153
lions 49

Lipscomb, Suzannah xxxiv, 83
Little Red Riding Hood 9
lockdown 89–90
Lord of the Rings, The xi, 74
Louvre 148, 159
Lysistrata (Aristophanes) 4, 100

male gaze 26, 29–30, 157–8, 185
Marinn, Sana 89
Marlowe, Christopher xxxv, 27, 69, 76
marriage 58–9, 98–100, 102, 108, 115, 116–17
masculinity, toxic 128, 129, 132, 133
masturbation *see* solo sex
Matos, Gregory 99
Mayor, Adrienne xix, 15–16, 35, 94, 114
McCormack, Catherine 140
Medea 108–9, 141–2
Medusa 29, 42
memory xv–xxxii, 2, 4–5, 7, 11–12, 17–18, 21–2, 26, 31–2, 34, 35, 41, 48, 54–6, 57, 62–3, 67–8, 69–70, 74, 77–81, 83, 88, 90, 108, 128, 137, 139, 149, 154, 165, 187–91
   types of xxi–xxii
Men Who Hate Women (2020) (Bates) 75
Menelaus 60, 70, 75, 107, 117, 118
Menke, Katherine 34
menopause 162–3
Merkel, Angela xxix, 89
Mescal, Paul 130
Metropolitan Museum of Art, New York 26, 184
Michel, Kai 111, 122

Michele, Alessandro 130
Middle Ages 41, 87
Middle-East, Ancient 2, 113
Midsummer Night's Dream, A 14
Mill, John Stuart xxvii
Minoan Crete 60–3, 87, 95–6, 103, 177–8, 188, 195
Minotaur 63
mirrors xxxiii, 23, 25–45, 105, 115, 129, 165, 185
   signal mirror 35–8, 52, 81, 195
Morisot, Berthe 139–40
mourning 172
Mulvey, Laura 30, 157
murder 32, 110, 117
Museum of Cycladic Art 147–8, 184–6
Mycenae 154
myth xvi–xviii, xxii, xxvi, xxviii, xxx, xxxiv, 13, 17, 30, 53, 57, 70, 76–7, 81, 107, 109
   Greek xi, xvii, xix, xxv, 13, 14, 27–30, 49–50, 52, 63, 73, 76–8, 93–4, 107–8, 110, 118, 141–2, 154
   Scythian *see* Nart Sagas

narcissism 28
Narcissus 23, 27–9
Nart sagas 13, 84, 94, 115–16, 130, 175–6
Narts 13
Natalie Haynes Stands Up for the Classics 5
Nature 146
Nazis xxi, 188
Neaera 106, 117, 118, 166
Neanderthals 112
Neolithic 3, 111, 113, 144, 148, 184

New York 107
Nietzsche 143
Niké of Samothrace 148
Nintendo SNES 47
Nolan, Christopher 54
nudity 32, 50, 56, 96, 147, 158

Odysseus 52, 54, 128, 129, 165
Odyssey (Homer) 128, 129, 141, 165
Old Vic theatre, London 150
Orithyia 50, 94
Ovid 27

Palaeolithic 110–112, 144–5, 158–9
Pandora xvii, xxvii
Pankhurst, Emmeline 88
Paradise 170
Paris 70, 73, 105–6, 115
Paris, France 107, 148
Patou-Mathis, Marylene 33, 112, 159–60
Patroclus 129, 172
Paulus/Paul xvii, 170
Pazyryk 'Ice Princess' 175
Peloponnesian War 4
Penelope 128, 141, 165–6
Penelopiad (Atwood) 165–6
Penthesilea, Queen of the Amazons ix–x, xix, xxx, xxxiv–xxxv, 19, 20, 50, 59, 81–2, 87, 93, 173–4, 184, 188, 193, 195
Pericles 10
period calendars 162
Perseus 29, 42, 63
Phanos 106, 117, 118, 166
Phryne 5, 11, 17
Phrynion 106
Pipher, Mary 164

Plato xxxv, 4, 10, 38, 45
poets xxiii, xxv, xxxi, 5–7, 17, 148
Pontic Alps 19, 115, 175–6, 192
porn industry 110
Posthomerica (Quintus) 173
Potts, Pepper 74
Power Rangers 47
pregnancy 146, 159–60, 162
Priam 173
'Problem with Sex is Capitalism, The' 75
Prometheus xvii
Psatina 84, 115–16, 131
Pseudo-Plutarch 162
psychoanalysis 157
Publilius Syrus 171–2
puppets *see* Amazons, puppets
Pythagoras 4

Queer as Folk 25
Quintus of Smyrna 50, 173, 174

R (author's friend) 106–7, 117, 196
rabbits 81
Ramakrishnan, Venki 169–70
rape xxvi–xxix, 28, 29, 31, 51, 65, 75, 76–9, 83–4, 100, 107, 129, 142, 143
Real Estate (Levy) 153
religion 145, 164, 170, 177
Renaissance 41, 87, 91–2
Representation of the People Act (1918) 88
Revolution, French 87, 91
Robb, Kate 2
Rome, Ancient xvii–xviii, 43, 50, 87, 121, 171–2
Room of One's Own, A (Woolf) 8
Roth, Philip 79
Rousseau, Jean-Jacques 91–2

S (author's friend) 117
Saini, Angela 92, 94, 95
Sappho 5–6, 17, 148
Saunders, David 15–16
Sauromatians 53, 80, 93
Scorsese, Martin 133
Scott, Ridley 54
Scythia, Ancient ix–x, xix–xx, xxxi, xxxii–xxxv, 12–20, 21–2, 34–5, 37, 41–2, 45, 56, 58–60, 62, 75, 80–2, 87, 92–4, 103, 113–15, 118, 129–32, 165, 175–7, 188, 192–4, 195
  women's names 16–17
Second Sex, The (de Beauvoir) xi, xiii, xvi
Second World War xxi–xxii, 21–2, 97
Secret of Mana 47
sex 10–11, 52–3, 59, 67, 69–82, 83–4, 101–2, 110, 160–2; slave 75–6, 78–9, 118
sexual pleasure, female 70–4, 76, 77, 80–2, 157; male 74, 76
Shakespeare, William xxxv, 8, 10, 14
Sieghart, Mary Ann 126–7
Silence of the Girls, The (2018) (Barker) 78
slavery 51–2, 75–6, 78–9, 83, 87, 110, 116, 118, 172
Slimani, Leila xiii
Snow White 32, 40–1, 109
Snow White and the Seven Dwarves 9, 31–2
Snow White and the Seven Dwarves (1937 film) 32
social media 23, 37, 42
Socrates 4, 10
Socrates in Love (D'Angour) 11

Solnit, Rebecca 67, 75–6, 100
solo sex 70–1, 74, 83, 161
Sophocles 4, 7
Sparta 12, 49, 73, 100, 105, 108, 118
Spears, Britney 185
Spector, Janet 33
sport 48, 57, 61
stepmothers 109–10
step-parents 109–10
stepsisters 110
Stereotypical Barbie 134
Stokowski, Margarete xiii
Stone Age 111–13, 118, 132, 144–5, 149, 166
stories x, xv, xvii–xviii, xx, xxiv–xxv, xxx, xxxiii–xxxiv, 9–10, 13–14, 21, 40, 48, 50–1, 54–6, 78–9, 81, 83–4, 100, 108–10, 132–5, 138, 150, 169–71, 177, 181, 188–9, 193, 197
Strabo 59, 80
Styles, Harry 130
suffragettes 88

taboos 69, 70, 72, 74, 110
Taylor, Justin 25
theatre 7–8
Thermodon 51, 93, 192
Theseus 54, 63, 73, 94, 108, 128
Thompson, Emma 142
Thrace 81, 93, 115
Tiresias 165
Touareg 93
trauma 110, 189–92
Trojan War ix, xix, xxii–xxiii, xxv, 6, 52, 60, 75, 78, 107, 129, 142, 154, 173–4
Trojan Women (Euripides) 4, 142
Troy ix, 20, 70, 93, 105, 107, 118, 154, 173–4, 183, 184

'Troy: myth and reality' (British Museum) xxiii
Tsai Ing-wen xxix, 89
Turkey xxiii, 140, 184, 192

Ukraine 114
Unclaimed Experience (1996) (Caruth) 190
United Nations 86, 89
United States xxv, 87, 89, 94

van Schaik, Karel/Carel 111, 122
vase painting 14–17, 21, 50, 81, 93, 158–9
Vavouranakis, Giorgos 178
Venus 145
video games 47, 71
Viehmann, Dorothea 9
Villeneuve, Gabrielle-Suzanne Barbot de 9
Virgil 50
'Visual Pleasure and Narrative Cinema' (1975) (Mulvey) 157
voting rights 85–90
vulvas 145, 149

Warzameg 84, 115–16, 130–1
Ways of Seeing (1972) (Berger) 32
Wengrow, David *see* Graeber
What Is History, Now? (Lipscomb) xxxiv
Wild, Henriette Dorothea 'Dortchen' 9
Wittenberg 70
Wolfson of Redegar, Lord 90
Wolley, Sir Leonard 34
Wollstonecraft, Mary xxvii
Woman of Hohle Fels 146
Women in Sport 48
Women in the Picture (2021) (McCormack) 140
women's rights xxvii–xxix
Wonder Woman xxx
Woolf, Virginia 8–9
writers xxiv, xxv, 8–9, 126, 132, 134, 142–3, 163, 171–2, 194

Zellweger, Renée 185
Zeus 4, 28, 52, 73
Zhaqa 116, 175, 176, 195